VOICING the VOICELESS

Literary Representation of the Gendered Subalterns

VOICING the VOICELESS

Literary Representation of the Gendered Subalterns

Editors

Arvind Nawale
Itishri Sarangi
AV Koshy
Sukanya Saha

AUTHORSPRESS

Worldwide Circulation through Authorspress Global Network
First Published in 2022
by
Authorspress
Q-2A Hauz Khas Enclave, New Delhi-110 016 (India)
Phone: (0) 9818049852
E-mail: authorspressgroup@gmail.com
Website: www.authorspressbooks.com

Voicing The Voiceless:
Literary Representation of the Gendered Subalterns
ISBN 978-93-5529-240-7

Printed in India at Thomson Press (India) Limited

Foreword

> "I Raise My Voice – not so that i can shout, but so that those without a voice can be heard...we cannot all succeed when half of us are held back."
>
> Malala Yousafzai

It is rightly said by Yousafzai that today when half of the population is considered 'subaltern' by the other half, no civilisation in the world can truly progress towards a better today and tomorrow. Innumerable discourses exist in the fields of gender studies, literature, sociology, etc. but very few representations are witnessed from this half of the society titled as 'subalterned'.

Collectively, as a global society, efforts should be made to nullify the patriarchal mindsets, which subjugate the existence of women and other marginalised communities. I believe, the trope 'Voicing the Voiceless' in 21st century refers to uprooting age-old dichotomies and take affirmative action such that 'voiceless' voice themselves. Presently, when I look back at my journey; from being an avid reader, learning Kathak classical dance, enrolling into N.C.C. Navy, conducting research with the concept of 'new-womanhood' to becoming a lecturer, tutor, author, mother and today being the only woman vice-chancellor in universities across Gujarat, undertaking projects for inclusive education, 'reaching the unreached' and witnessing effective outcomes; this journey has only made me more aware and more sensible towards a myriad roles that each individual performs with such uniqueness and ingenuity that we all have the right to voice our own selves, voice that uplifts, voice that inspire, and finally voice that creates better tomorrow for the coming generations.

This book, *Voicing the Voiceless: Literary Representation of the Gendered Subalterns,* is the literary representation bringing forth subaltern experiences from the perspectives of psychoanalysis, gendered identity, diaspora; touching upon various genres of literary works, cinema, media, industry, discussing works of authors ranging from R. K. Narayan to Preeti Shenoy. Each chapter in this book provides a newer dimension to subalterned identities, which makes the reader question, "Can any human-being ever be a subaltern?" because each human being has the right to be the author of his/her, own life. It is time that society decolonises itself from the colonisation of patriarchy and oppressive attitudes.

I appreciate and congratulate Dr. Arvind M. Nawale, Associate Professor and Head, Department of English, Shivaji Mahavidyalaya, Latur, Maharashtra for bringing out this scholarly book, a worthy compilation of different perspectives on the concern of 'Gendered Subaltern'. I humbly acknowledge the valuable contribution of Prof. Itishri Sarangi, Dr. Koshy A.V., and Dr. Sukanya Saha in shaping this book. This collection of scholarly articles shall not only be worth reading but also will be shaping the thought process of readers, students, researchers, academicians, and stakeholders.

I am assured that *Voicing the Voiceless': Literary Representations of Gendered Subalterns* shall open new directions and provide new ethos. My best wishes to this endeavour on its journey forward!

Prof. Dr. Ami Upadhyay
Vice Chancellor,
Dr. Babasaheb Ambedkar Open University,
Ahmedabad, Gujrat

Preface

Women are often kept voiceless and even when given a voice, unable to voice out many things due to gender discrimination. They are looked at and considered as the 'other,' and as a result, they suffer from marginalisation, becoming 'subaltern' only on basis of their 'gender'. Even the women belonging to affluent backgrounds have to suffer from 'subalternity' due to their female gender. Sometimes this can happen to men too and it definitely does to all in the gender spectrum of 'LGBTQIA+' away from the given categories by patriarchal institutions. The supremacy of male gender over the other 'Gendered Subalterns' (Women and LGBTQIA+), is evident in almost all societies and the fact serves as the core in women's literature.

The recent past gives abounding glimpses of recognition of the power of women and even LGBTQIA+'. However, despite exemplary contributions in all walks of life, they have often been relegated with ease to the footnotes of history. Over the years they have been systematically deleted from history, their stories discarded, distorted and identities replaced. History is witness as to how women have been instrumental in carving the course of events, fighting for her rights and the forms of human culture. Our ignorance of these women is greatly compounded by the exclusion of information on societies which acknowledge a female's power in public life, diplomacy, religion, medicine, the arts as well as the backbone of the family structure and inheritance. Both prejudice and male chauvinism are mixed up in these deliberate silences and gaps. Woman is empowered by nature to give life yet society is tacitly unwilling to recognise her worth and give her due credit. Women's power on the other hand is unfailing and inevitable. Freedom for women has been a constant struggle between the rigid and routine arrangement against the male-female dichotomy. Male chauvinism is one of the oldest fixtures on the earth. Women ought to act or react in order to continue to exist, to escape, or transform their circumstances where they face obstacles.

The 18th-century British proto-feminist Mary Wollstonecraft's *A Vindication of the Rights of Woman: with Strictures on Political and Moral Subjects* (1792), Virginia Woolf's essays 'A Room of One's Own' (1929) and 'Killing the Angel in the House' (1931), Simone-de Beauvoir's *Second Sex* (1949), Gayatri Spivak's 'Can the subaltern speak?' (1985) and Edward Said's *Orientalism* (1988) are ground-breaking works which still resonates in feminism and human rights and give a proper and philosophical vent to treat 'gendered subalterns' with equality and dignity.

In theory and literary criticism with the arrival of critics like Luce Irigaray (born 1930), Katherine Murray "Kate" Millett (1934-2017), Hélène Cixous. (born1937), Germaine Greer (born 1939). Elaine Showalter (born 1941), Julia Kristeva (born 1941). Gloria Jean Watkins 'bell hooks' (1952-2021), Kimberlé Crenshaw (born 1959) and many others, the voiceless became voiced that cannot be ignored. Soon the world of women writing heralded a sea-change worldwide with writers like Jane Austen, Emily Bronte, Charlotte Bronte, Anne Bronte, George Eliot and Elizabeth Barrett Browning and in India this found its echo in the writings of people like Sarojini Naidu, Toru Dutt, Krupabai Sathianadhan, Ashapurna Devi and so on. India was not left out due to social activists/ feminists/ writers like Savitribai Phule (1831-1897), Tarabai Shinde (1850-1910), Pandita Ramabai Sarasvati (1858-1922), Ismat Chughtai (1915-1991), Mahasweta Devi (1926-2016), Kamala (Surayya) Das (1934-2009) and so on. There are also others stalwarts in the fields of activism and creative writing like Shashi Deshpande, Kamala Markandeya, Arundhati Roy, Bama, Janu, Anita Desai, Romila Thapar and so many others. These activists/ feminists/writers gave voice to the voiceless with an unmistakable intensity and clarity.

However, 'Gendered Subalterns' is a concern and not a concept. It is not mandated to just embark on protest marches with candles, posters, or placards in hands, yelling slogans to utter ideologies. The need is to wake the intellectual reading public who would in turn carry the torch to light up the dark crevices of society from where oozes the venom of discrimination and unfair practices against 'gendered subalterns'.

The chapters in this book convey the heterogeneousness and disagreement within feminism with approachable lucidness. The analysis of key terms equips readers with a critical understanding of the vocabulary of feminist debates that will be invaluable to research. In this compilation of scholarly papers, one would come across a wide range of issues, women and LGBTQIA+ confront while reeling under rigid constraints of patriarchy and how these issues are highlighted in literature. The author, Megha Soni, for instance, writes that Mahasweta Devi addresses "the struggle of the women to overcome the oppression and violence brought by high-cast landlords, moneylenders and corrupt government officials." According to Dr. Sharad Chavan, "the novels of Shashi Deshpande represent the declining condition and complex experiences of her women characters." Maharudra Kapse points out, "Ishiguro's female characters demonstrate highly complex behaviours in the novels." C. Leela and Dr. M. Premavathy remark that, "in India, girls are supposed to be the alien's wealth and sent off to some stranger's house." Dr. Atul Acharya's paper, "talks about the various splits that Taslima Nasrin is confronted with, and how she shows resistance in overpowering them." R. Devendiran and Dr. B. Kathiresan focus on "the condition of transgender community in Indian society and also brings out the struggles and discriminations faced by the transgender individuals in employment and housing and also in their daily life as reflected in Ajay Pandey's *An Unexpected Gift* and the many other papers deal with rest issues that are too many to be mentioned here. The contributed papers overview and focus on the pattern of feminism and issues of the rest gendered subalterns bringing them to life with extent of actions and activism for newcomers, adding new perspectives to the students and researchers of literature.

This volume of scholarly papers cover writers like Anita Desai, Safia Elhillo, Atiq Rahimi, Manju Kapur, Aurobindo, Sujata Bhatt, Bharati Mukherjee, Meena Alexander, Mulk Raj Anand, Charlotte Bronte, Ruth Prawer Jhabvala, R. K. Narayan, Tendulkar, Preeti Shenoy, Salma (a Tamil writer), Mahasweta Devi, Kazuo Ishiguro, Shashi Deshpande, Taslima Nasrin and so on and themes as wide as transgenders and gender theory, projection of women in male writings, the treatment of women as well as women in the travels of Hollywood and Indian cinema are critically explored. The readers will find this an excellent reference book on all things related to 'gendered subalterns' and all the interdisciplinary fields allied to it. The topics covered in this edited volume could become the basis for additional research and analysis, giving many possibilities for students and researchers to identify one that interest them for further research.

The present book *Voicing the Voiceless: Literary Representation of the Gendered Subalterns* is an attempt to rediscover history of gendered subalterns which include women and LGBTQIA+ and renovate all the dimensions that reflect their experiences and achievements in proper perspective and adequately compensate for the distorted and forgotten past of their world which has been neglected by the standard textbooks and mass media. The book further challenges the binary system and the construction of difference in literary works drawing from empirical research. It could be deduced from the analyses of literary texts that women have been putting in serious efforts in bringing radical changes in the conventional patriarchal incline. The transformations may take longer, yet the efforts in voicing the yearning for their emancipation is loud and clear.

We wish to express our gratitude to Mr. Sudarshan Kcherry, Managing Director of Authors Press for taking up the initiative to publish this book and for executing it meticulously. We also thank our esteemed contributors from different states of the country for contributing their scholarly papers and helping us accomplish this project promptly. We must acknowledge our special gratitude to Prof. Dr. Ami Upadhyay, renowned author, scholar, feminist, critic and Vice Chancellor of Dr. Babasaheb Ambedkar Open University, Ahmedabad, Gujrat for writing the Foreword to this book. Thanks are also due to our University and institutional authorities for their inspiration. We wish all the readers a meaningful reading experience. Read and spread the word to get the most out of it. Thanks.

Dr. Arvind Nawale
Dr. Itishri Sarangi
Dr. AV Koshy
Dr. Sukanya Saha

Contents

CHAPTER 1

The Inner Suppression, Violence and Survival Strife of Women Trio in Anita Desai's *Fire on the Mountain*

Arvind M. Nawale

Abstract

Men have treated women as servants from the dawn of humanity, and patriarchal measures have been used to muffle their voices. Nanda, Ila, and Raka are the female trio who thread the events of Anita Desai's *Fire on the Mountain* together and their willingness to face the world with dignity and determination reflects the contemporary situation of women in Indian society. Their internal monologue and cognitive processes allude to patriarchal society's pitiful treatment of Indian women in general. Anita Desai realistically depicted the suffering of Indian women in this novel, including the challenges, trials, conventional restraints, male violence, isolation, alienation, professional discrimination, and bondage in the name of marriage, all of which are still prevalent in our society. This paper aims to investigate the inner violence and oppression of these three women – Nanda, Ila, and Raka who represent the tensions and subjugation of female society in the post-independence era, as well as their struggle to establish themselves as individualistic constructs on the search for identity.

Keywords: Anita Desai, Fire on the Mountain, Inner Suppression. Violence, Survival Strife, Women Issues

Introduction

Since time immemorial, men treat women as servants and utilise patriarchal methods to silence their voices, despite the fact that females contribute equally, and sometimes more substantially, to the growth of a nation. Even in postcolonial Indian society women are considered as simply "things" and "others". Anita Desai, a key writer in twentieth-century Indo-English fiction has supported the concept of feminism that tackles women's fight with patriarchal oppression through her fictional writings.

Anita Desai, a leading Indian woman writer, "who holds a peculiar stature among the contemporary Indian women novelists" (Emara 197) is noted for her insightful portrayal of female characters in her novels and short tales. Her novel, *Fire on the Mountain* is one of important contributions to the literature. It caught the critics' eye as soon as it was published in 1977 and won the 'Sahitya Academy Award' in 1978. Desai herself considers this novel as her most satisfying work. She says, "the work in which I have come closest, to what I set to do, and I don't think I very often do, is *Fire on the Mountain*" (Jain 9).

The novel is split into three parts. Part I – "Nanda Kaul at Carignano," is about her lonely life in the enormous Carignano estate. Part II – "Raka Comes to Carignano" illustrates initial disliking as well as later reconciliation between Nanda Kaul and her great granddaughter Raka, and Part III – "Ila Das Leaves Carignano," depicts Nanda Kaul's reunion with Ila Das, a childhood friend and Ila Das' horrific rape and death. In novel, Desai features three women: Nanda Kaul who becomes an outsider in retaliation for a life spent in devotion to others, Raka, great granddaughter of Nanda Kaul who is a born loner who shuns human company and third Ila Das who was raised as a refined lady but was later abandoned in the real world due to the selfishness of the men in her family and brutality of the society. This paper attempts to explore the inner violence and suppression of these women trio – Nanda, Ila, and Raka, which symbolises the tension and subjection of female society in the post-independence era, as well as their fight to prove themselves as individualistic constructs with a quest for identity.

The Inner Suppression, Violence and Survival Strife of Women Trio

The female trio Nanda, Ila, and Raka weave the events of *Fire on the Mountain* together, and their willingness to confront the world with dignity and determination mirrors the current state of women in Indian society. Their internal monologue and cognitive processes refer to the pathetic position that patriarchal society impose on Indian women in general. The novel, as observed by Maha Abdel Moneim Emara:

> represents a discourse on violence that centers on the lives of the three women who are victims, either physically or mentally, of the patriarchal system. Nanda Kaul, a widowed great-grandmother, is a victim of her role

> as a dutiful wife to an unfaithful husband and as a mother to many children. Raka, her exclusive, withdrawn great-grandchild, is the victim of an abusive father. Ila Das, Nanda's childhood friend, unmarried, and the victim of her selfish brothers and her own reformist idealism. (198).

M. Rameshwor Singh too, rightly calls this novel as "the oppressed women's discourse" (888).

The novel opens with a morning in Carignano, the house in Kasauli where Nanda Kaul has retired to. Nanda is unique in her elegant isolation, cutting herself off from almost anyone and anything. When we meet Nanda first, we see her husband has died and she is living a secluded life in the Kasauli hills. She appears to have outlived her usefulness, having completed all of her responsibilities as a wife and mother. All of her sons and daughters have families of their own and she is left to live alone here in Kasauli. As a result, she is forced to live in seclusion and longing for completely cut off from the outside world.

Nanda Kaul is introduced as a woman who "suffered a life-time of unhappiness caused by a loveless marriage" (Chahal 1955) and who has purposefully preferred to live in Carignano, which is unaffected by the outside world. Here, she creates "a space of her own and embraces a life of solitude, privacy and confinement," and loves this place "for its barrenness and isolation, its steep heights, scary ravines and slopes and becomes one with this desolate landscape" (Emara 198). Even the postman's entrance is considered an intrusion into her carefully guarded privacy and is frowned upon because he would be instrumental to connect her to the outside world. "It was the place, and the time of life. .. She wanted no one and nothing else" (Desai 3). When she got information through letter that her great granddaughter Raka is coming to stay with her, she sees her arrival as "an unwanted disruption of her peaceful retirement" (Emara 199) and reacted strangely thinking it will disturb her isolation. She sees this world free of the duties and various roles she had assumed. She desires utter isolation in this forest as a means of dealing with the experiences of her previous life that she is unable to convey, as well as a means of attempting to forget them. But it is a desolate world, and she is compelled to live in it, which is little more than a skeleton.

She yearns for some relaxation after spending her childhood in an affluent home and her adult life as the wife of the vice-chancellor of Punjab University, effectively maintaining the household with several children, ayahs, staff, guests and so on. Though her life as the Vice-wife Chancellor's was busy and full of social events, it was actually aimless and uninspiring for her as her husband treats her "as some decorative yet useful mechanical appliance needed for the efficient running of his household" (Dubbe 117). There have been far too many visitors coming and going, leaving her very little privacy. "Can I not be left with nothing?" (18).

For the rest of the world, Nanda Kaul is the 'queen,' the dignified wife of Punjab University's vice-chancellor. However, only she knows how she is the 'betrayed,' because her husband had been having an affair with another woman, a mathematics teacher, Miss David for years. This affair of her husband with Miss David, which lasted his entire life, has devastated her, returning her to her own existential abyss. She just sees her husband going away from her, and she feels as though she is as far away from him as love is from their marriage. Hence, in her husband's house, she didn't feel like she belonged truly there. She had taken on a variety of responsibilities and successfully performed them. She wants to avoid the responsibilities and obligations that have been imposed upon her. As a result, she yearned for a break from these roles. Finally, her husband's death frees her to hunt for it, which she does in Carignano. Krishnaswamy rightly pointed out, "She treasures her freedom, her privacy, glad her responsibilities towards her family are over, glad she needs nobody and nobody now needs her" (260).

In the second part of the novel, Raka arrives in Carignano. Both Raka and Nanda Kaul try to avoid one other at first. Raka doesn't say much and seems to be lost in her own thoughts. Her strange behaviour could be attributed to the fact that she hails from a dysfunctional household. Raka is the child of an ill-matched couple: a subservient mother who is afraid to take risks in her life and a diplomat father who drinks and verbally and physically harasses her mother. Raka is a witness to these events, which may have influenced her isolation from society and morbid obsession with sights of destruction and fire. She is unaffected by societal customs, thus she is not as meek as Indian girls are expected to be. She has been rejected, and as a result of her frustration, she develops hate against others. Her "troubled familial experiences have turned her into a scary, hallucinating and agitated child (Emara 200). Desai described it vividly:

> Somewhere behind them, behind it all, was her father home from a party, stumbling and crashing through the curtains of night, his mouth opening to let out a flood of rotten stench, beating at her mother with hammers and fists of abuse – harsh, filthy abuse that made Raka cower under her bedclothes and wet the mattress in fright, feeling the stream of urine warm and weakening between her legs like a stream of blood, and her mother lay down on the floor and shut her eyes and wept. Under her feet, in the dark, Raka felt that flat, wet jelly of her mother's being squelching and quivering, so that she didn't know where to put her feet and wept as she tried to get free of it. Ahead of her no longer on the ground but at some distance now, her mother was crying. Then it was the jackal crying. (78-79)

Even Raka does not find affection from her great grandmother since she has grown hermetic to any human contact as a result of her own familial problems. This made Raka blatantly independent, reserved, stoic, stubborn and uninterested in the realm of play and fantasy that children enjoy. Raka, by being wild, mute, and engulfed in her own world and grief, reflects her parents' failing marriage. She has completely distinct definitions for what we call a house, which is to say a building, because she feels never at home there. She is traumatised in this society to which she does not belong. She is developed as a result of parental trauma, mental abuse, physical torture and a dysfunctional family connection. The ornamentation and goodness do not fill her imagination or offer her with any consolation and became whimsical, abnormal and carefree. "I don't care, I don't care, I don't care for anything" (80).

Her act of lighting a fire in the forest and announcing it with elation to Nanda Kaul, "Look Nani, I have set the forest on fire" (159) enables her restless soul to reach out and accept Nanda Kaul's bond of relationship. But it was too late as her great grandmother was no more as a result of the trauma of learning of Ila Das' death. It seems, she begins her search for purpose in life with a symbolic act of purification and destruction by setting the mountainside on fire, which may lead to self-realisation. Yet, "the independent aspect could also be seen in character like Raka who despite all bondages could set herself free and live a life of her own choice. Her setting the entire forest on fire is a way of retaliating to the old set norms which can be seen as an example of challenging the colonial outlook" (Bhowmick 260).

Ila Das, Nanda's long-time friend is introduced in the third section of the novel. Ila travels to Carignano to see Nanda. When her father was alive, she had seen better days. However, following his death, the family fortune was divided among Ila's three drunken brothers, leaving nothing for Ila, her sister or their mother. The most pathetic of the women trios present in *Fire on the Mountain*, is Ila Das. Physically, her appearance which is plain doesn't allow her to secure a marriage. In addition, she is cursed with a 'hideous voice' (21). She is unattractive, and of unpleasant disposition with her repulsive voice and ludicrous gestures. It got described in her a very first appearance in the novel:

> ...with her uneven, rushing step, in her ancient white court shoes, prodding the tip of her umbrella into the dust with an air of faked determination...little grey top-knot wobbled on top of her head, her spectacles slipped down to the tip of her nose....and ancient purple ribbon looped over her ears...the grey rag of the petticoat gaped dismally beneath the lace him of her sari. (107-108).

She is a laughing stock in the society with her set of frailties and is often jeered at.

She suffers before being hired as a social welfare official, despite being compelled to find work at the age of forty as a lecturer at Punjab University and then being fired from this position. Despite the fact that life has handed her a poor hand, she refuses to let bitterness rule her life. Her dignity forbids her from begging, preferring instead to be hungry due to a lack of money. The hardships in her life have had no effect on her ability to persevere in the face of adversity or on her faith in herself. She becomes a staunch supporter of the poor and an outspoken opponent of child marriage and other superstitions. Ila Das realises that the education provided to females is meaningless and "handicapped" (139) only when she is compelled to survive in the real world.

When the family fortune is destroyed and the jewellery of the women is squandered by her brothers, her life takes a dramatic turn for the worst. Finally, she is left to fend for herself with no prospects for employment. The money has been spent entirely on her son's education and her survival is fall in jeopardy due to poverty. Her background makes it even more difficult for her to make ends meet on her little earnings. Ila eventually takes up a job as a social welfare worker to sustain herself after a shattered life with a broken self. In a feudal, patriarchal society, Ila Das was doing her best to combat illiteracy, superstition, and ignorance. However, she pays a high price for attempting to prevent the marriage of a seven-year-old girl to an elderly man. Preet Singh attacks her in the dark, strangles her, and then rapes her. Desai paints a vivid picture of it:

> Her eyes still swivelled in their sockets, two alarmed marbles of black and white, and quickly he left the scarf, tore at her clothes, tore them off her, in long screeching rips, till he came to her, to the dry, shrivelled, starved stick inside the wrappings, and raped her, pinned her down into the dust and the goat droppings, and raped her. Crushed back, crushed down into the earth, she lay raped, broken, still and finished (156).

Ila's rape and murder are emblematic of the punishment meted out by a male-dominated society to women who strive to defy social norms.

She deserves to die calmly after a life spent attempting to sustain herself and fighting with conviction for a just cause, but even that is denied to her. Her sexual violence and assault have significant meaning because she has been silenced for daring to speak out against Preet Singh, a patriarchal authority. The rape's ferocity is a reflection of the sexual violence that silences women and confines them to conventional spaces. Her existence is snuffed out by a society that reacts violently to her attempts to improve it. Nanda Kaul weeps as soon as she learns about Ila Das's murder, "No, no, it is a lie! No it cannot be" (158).

Ila Das represents every Indian woman who is left to fend for herself. If no man is present in their lives, they are seen as easy prey. She is not permitted to live a dignified life or to contribute to society. Only financial independence would have allowed her to live her life as she sees fit. Even though, there is uneasiness and worry because many evils, such as rape and murder are commonplace.

Raka, Nanda and Ila are the nuances of victims who have been stifled by psychological and physical restrictions, as well as the male domination. Ila Das, on the other hand, is shown as a misfit who is brave enough to confront life and aid others in the process. She is very aware of society's marginalised women as she works to change their ways. Her struggle for survival is both pitiful and inspiring, as she, like Nanda, attempts to maintain a coating of dignity and cannot bring herself to ask for the support she desperately requires from Nanda.

The title *Fire on the Mountain* too, carries with it a lot of meaning. The fire represents not just the forest fire but Raka's ultimate self-expression, but also the fire that burns within the souls of the three ladies. The fire within them yearns to be let out through self-expression and solitude, away from familial connections and on the outside of civilisation. The fire has erupted, and it has a different possesses: calm, solitude and isolation. Inner turmoil and violence are fueled by patriarchal restrictions, infidelity, hassles of children, parental abuse and of course, the curses of society described as "custom." As a result, the 'fire' stands here as a metaphor of repression that seeks release in the form of a quest for individuality.

Such predicaments of women is well understood in Beauvoir's *Second Sex,* which tells:

> It is not surprising that the woman torn between these contradictions often spends her day in a state of nervousness and bitterness; she always loses on some level, and her gains are precarious, they do not count as any sure success. She can never save herself by her work alone; it keeps her occupied, but does not constitute her justification: her justification rests on outside freedoms. The wife shut up in her home cannot establish her existence on her own; she does not have the means to affirm herself in her singularity: and this singularity is consequently not acknowledged. For Arabs or Indians, and in many rural populations, a wife is only a female servant appreciated according to the work she provides, and who is replaced without regret if she disappears (Beauvoir 647).

This reflects the futility, anger and despair accumulated over years of oppression and repression, as well as the conventional role-playing mandated by patriarchal mores. As a result, post-colonialism bred tension, self-doubt, and unhappiness among post-colonisers got projected in Desai's this novel. Ananya Bhowmick rightly put it, "Though the colonisers left, yet their presence could be felt for the next fifty years and *Fire on the Mountain* which is a product of 1977 clearly portrays this element" (Bhowmick 260).

Conclusion

To sum up, Anita Desai has portrayed distinct perspectives of Indian women in Indian society through her women trio: Nanda Kaul, Raka, and Ila Das in *Fire on the Mountain.* Furthermore, Tara and Asha's hidden presence adds to the novel's depiction of various aspects of Indian women. Desai's these three women characters are enslaved by social pressure and are unable to be free. This pressure isolates them from their surroundings and from what would have been their own reality, i.e., their perspective of life and the world. They are alienated by society and this deep sense of solitude manifests itself in a variety of ways in the novel.

In the *Fire on the Mountain*, Anita desai has faithfully shown the plight of Indian women, including the hardships, trials, traditional constraints, male abuse, isolation, alienation, professional discrimination, and bondage in the name of marriage, all of which are still widespread in our society. In it, Desai "foreground the conclusion that marginalised and "othered" women are necessarily only victims of gender-related violence" (Kaur 4). Under the harsh glare of reality, sensitive women like Nanda wither away, Raka fail to blossom as early in her life, Ila Das pays the price for criticising a male-dominated society's norms in form of rape and death. The penalty meted out to Ila Das reveals the most hideous face of male sovereignty. As a result, the society in which the novel's female characters live is biased, with the odds significantly stacked in favour of male species. However, bravery and dignity projected by Desai in these women trio – Nanda Kaul, Raka, and Ila Das is matchless. These characters, in their own brave and dignified way, oppose the cruel strength of a world dominated by patriarchal norms. Ila's awful death is, without a doubt, quite depressing. However, she can never be branded a failure because she has tackled life's most difficult challenges with amazing bravery. If Ila Das raised a banner of rebellion during her lifetime, Raka's setting the mountain on fire gives the reader hope that the next generation will not take things lying down and that change is on the way. Nanda Kaul maintains her dignity at all times. Life has not treated her fairly, yet it has not managed to entirely subdue her. She has a great elegance in dealing with her husband's extramarital affair. She strives to live independently, on her own terms, after settling down in Carignano.

The modern Indian woman has likewise gone on a quest to discover the true meaning of life and her sensitivity and struggle to face the truth, as represented in Anita Desai's work *Fire on the Mountain*, gives one hope that the quest will one day be realised.

Works Cited

Beauvoir, Simone D. *The Second Sex*. 1st ed., First Vintage Books Edition, May 2011 translated by Constance Borde and Sheila Malovany Chevallier., Vintage Books, 2011.

Bhowmick, Ananya. "Ambiguity in Empowering Women in Post-Colonial Fiction: Analysing Anita Desai's *Fire on the Mountain*." *International Journal of English Language, Literature and Translation Studies (IJELR)*, vol. 7, no. 3, 2020, pp. 259-260.

Chahal, Sonia. "A Feminist Approach to Anita Desai's Fire on the Mountain." *IJRAR – International Journal of Research and Analytical Reviews*, vol. 5, no. 2, Apr.-May 2018, pp. 1955-1957.

Desai, Anita. *Fire on the Mountain.* Random House India, 2008.

Emara, Maha Abdel Moneim. "Anita Desai's Fire on The Mountain: An Ecofeminist Reading." *Advances in Social Sciences Research Journal*, vol. 4, no. 2, Jan. 2017, pp. 195-207.

Kaur, Gurpreet. "Women, Animals and Violence: Anita Desai's Fire on the Mountain and Lee Yew Leong's "Honey, I'm Off To Be A Jellyfish Now"." *Journal of Ecocriticism*, vol. 8, no. 1, Mar. 2018, pp. 1-9.

Krishnaswamy, Shantha. *The Woman in Indian Fiction in English, 1950-80.* APH Publishing, 1984.

Singh, M. R. "Gender Discourse and Stereotypes in Literature." *International Journal of Creative Research Thoughts (IJCRT)*, vol. 6, no. 1, Mar. 2018, pp. 887-889.

CHAPTER 2

The Plight of Women at Urban Spaces

Itishri Sarangi

Abstract

The complexity of space has always been shaped and reshaped by our reminiscence and living occurrence. The present paper is an attempt of reflexive venture. A brief review of international and national is done in order to experience the superficial life of the women in a situational context as a subjective experience. The study will explore the connection between mobility and space in the case of urban women. The research examines the impact of space on women living in urban areas. The concept of space has always been a gendered issue. A review of feminist literature is essential to understand the concept of space in relation with feminine subject. A peep into globalisation bring forth the notion of space has both a connotative and denotative meaning that affects the general relation to a large extent. Hence, it is important to comprehend the symbolic meaning of physical body. The main problem of space arises not only for the safety of the women but rather the fear created towards the same. The purpose of the research is to examine the experience of an individual at urban spaces. Following this decisive factor, our study is constrained to the urban environment.

Keywords: women; urban space; place; mobility, female subjectivity.

Introduction

Urban spaces across cultures has proliferated and flourished immensely in the field of literary studies. The concept of freedom in urban spaces is limited to the notion of safe and unsafe areas. It has been a constant struggle between the rigid and routine arrangement against the male-female dichotomy that is being opposed or entirely different and a repeated branching into two sections as two opposed classes. Male chauvinism is one of the oldest fixtures in the earth. The presence of women in a street without a male counterpart has always been a subject of suspicion and discomfort. The women ought to act or react in order to continue to exist, to escape, or transform their circumstances where the city faces full of obstacles. Feminist often questions the standard model of sex/gender when undue emphasis is given on sex as a biological aspect where female desirability is based on sex appeal and male desirability on wealth. Women, who were once rarely involved in spaces outside their homes have broken existing boundaries to enter new economic, social, and educational environments. However, the gendering of space for these women has been profoundly changed and challenged by a variety of factors namely state obstruction and modernisation. It is more of a gender experience where space has played a major role in the process. There seems to be a growing visibility of women that gives an insight into gender and their commodification. The role of cinema has a major impact in the cultural creation of the city life that depict the urban life and points towards a new intellectual framework for debate. The movies depict the urban sustainability as a dialogue of value and experiences faced by women. Space is dynamic, full of life constructed, and challenging. There is an urgent need to rediscover women history and renovate the female dimensions to reflect her experiences and achievements in proper perspective and adequately compensate the distorted and forgotten past of the woman world which has been neglected by the standard textbooks and mass media.

Significance of Research

Both men and women are exposed to different set of environments. Both the theoretical and empirical evidence suggests that women development both in personal and professional development is influenced by natural environment. The research will provide a deeper understanding of the problem faced by women at urban spaces as the predicament is less understood and grossly misinterpreted. The findings and result of the research will be a great contribution to urban studies especially for the migrants. The study will address concerns regarding urban planning and development catering to the needs of women at urban spaces.

Rationale behind The Study

Women in comparison to men suffer comparative more at workplaces. There is a need to design the qualitative and quantitative analysis of women's experience at urban places that speaks about the reality of women lives.

Research Questions

What are the kinds of risk a women faces at urban areas?

What happens to a women when she tries to expose the sexual or any other harassment she faces?

How widespread are these abuses related to women?

Why does the social stigma let women to keep silent and who should be held responsible for the same?

Is social media the right kind of platform to speak?

Is the relationship between violence against women and mental illness been adequately explored?

Objective

To access the kind of risk women faces at urban spaces.

To identify the consequences that a woman undergoes while she tries to expose the harassment she faces

To explore how widespread are the abuses related to women

To educate women to overcome the social stigma that upholds women to keep silent.

To delve into the pros and cons of social media.

To find out the relationship between violence against women and their mental illness?

Methodolody

The primary data was collected through well trained staff. In order the collect the data the staff had to develop a relationship with the respondents and taking them into confidence. The secondary data was collected from the government data base.

Literature Review

- *Sexual Harassment of Working Women,* this book emphasises on how sexual harassment concept has become common and at the same time ignored thoroughly. The controlling tendency of men concerning the job of women leads to the deterioration of material survival of women. The author has first tried to conceptualise the definition of sexual harassment in the context of a pervasive social issue. Secondly, the author has put a legal argument to clarify the concept of sexual harassment is discrimination based on gender. The book concludes on legal action on sexual harassment would strengthen women economic conditions and bring socio-economic equality. (Catharine A. MacKinnon. 1979)

- *Sexual Harassment: A Debate* book is a collaborative effort to highlight sexual harassment debates in the contemporary context. The readers will find two viewpoints to tackle with the issue of sexual harassment. The authors have focused on a wide range of educated audience who often get puzzled while understanding the complex concept of sexual harassment. (Linda LeMoncheck & Mane Hajdin. 2000)
- *Sexual Harassment of Women: Climate, Culture, and Consequences in Academic Sciences, Engineering, and Medicine* book stimulate the concept of sexual harassment in different levels of academia such as scientific, technical and medical employees. The content of the book extends to explain how sexual harassment negatively impacts on various important aspects of their career advancement. It systematically ascertains the preventive measures to prevent in curbing these problems in academic settings. (Paula A. Johnson, Sheila E. Widnall, and Frazier F. Benya. 2018)
- *The Women's Movement against Sexual Harassment* book is extensively well researched to indicate the magnificent role played by the women working in the United States. This carefully-researched book also concretes the idea of efforts such as enactments, interpretations and litigations which have been brought in the US to limit sexual harassment. It's a good education as well as a motivational book about the movement against sexual harassment. (Carrie N. Baker. 2008)
- *What is Sexual Harassment, and how to conduct Inquiry as per service rules?* Book deals with the laws on the issues of sexual harassment. Specifically, it brings clarity about the procedures for piloting inquiry on such vital issues so that the culprits do not get away due to routine infirmities. It extensively examines the sections prescribed under the Sexual Harassment of Women at Workplace Prevention, Prohibition and Redressal Act, 2013. Referring to both National and International case-laws, different Government policies and

service rules this book is found useful for both academic and non-academic purposes. (Mukesh Chaturvedi. 2019)

- *Reconceptualising Sexual Harassment* article focuses on sex-based harassment in the working sector. It has dealt with the issue from the feminist's perspective signifying sexual harassment as a social problem. The author categorically highlights the role of movies, newspapers and television in depicting the character of women who are forced to get into sexual abuse. (Vicki Schultz. 1998)
- *What's Wrong with Sexual Harassment?* The article argues that the connection between sex discrimination and sexual harassment has been hypothesised by the Supreme Court of America. Here the author emphasises on the fact that how sex discrimination has been dominated by the laws enshrined by the lower courts to deal with sexual harassment. This article clearly describes how there is a gap present in the existing concept of sexual harassment which is inconsistent with sex discrimination. (Katherine M. Franke. 1997)
- *Sexual Harassment as a Gendered Expression of Power:* the author of this article tested the theory given by Catharine MacKinnon on sexual harassment of adult women. This article compares the behavioural syndrome in sexual harassment cases of males and females during adolescence. It also emphasis on the fact that financial vulnerability also leads to such situations. Finally, the article concludes with the viewpoint that adult women are easily targeted and become victims of sexual harassment. (Christopher Uggen and Amy Blackstone. 2004)
- *A Theory of Tort Liability for Sexual Harassment in the Workplace* is a well-researched article to systematically describe the two types of sexual harassment, first is a physical form like touching against the will of a woman, brushing the body of a woman, physical assault – rape etc. and second is a verbal form like filthy remarks, double meaning comments, direct demand for sex etc. This article explains three vital aspects (economic, physical and emotional) on sexual harassment. (Krista J. Schoenheider. 1986)
- *Resisting the Enforcement of Sexual Harassment Law:* In this article, the author describes how the people of the United

States believe that sexual harassment is illegal and prosecution is needed. This research reveals the micro-level methods that trigger contradict about the implementation of sexual harassment law. It also focuses on how the role of law is significant to bring social change and reducing inequality. (Justine E. Tinkler. 2012) Milbrath (6) states that "...if quality of life is defined as happiness or well-being or satisfaction, it is necessarily subjective", thus, the objects which we value as positive provide that value to our life quality. Rapoport (7) points out that the evaluation we make of the environment involves more than a detailed interpretation of it; it is a global and affective reaction which is strongly influenced by ideal images that are of a subjective nature. Gender perspective becomes useful, in evaluating how the gender relations that occur in a particular context affect quality of life.(Annas 1996) Theorists like Grosz (1992, 1995) and McDowell (1980, 1999) help us understand how spaces can orient or organise family, sexual, and social relations. Everyday language is packed with preconceived opinions and value judgments that act as obstacles to understanding. (Haug 1987 p. 61) space has been a highly debated concept in the humanities, but a specific moment in time when the fascination with space and spatiality began and initiated what has come to be called the spatial turn cannot be pinpointed. Damayanti and Kossak (2015) Spatial identity is a result of a connection between people, physical elements of places, and activities associated with them. The development of identity occurs through the psychological process place attachment. Choudhary (2014) tries to discuss the process of formation and reformation of spatial identities in the aftermath of globalisation. The basic premise of the paper is that identities are more often remain attached to space and these are direct outcome of the culture if the culture is taken as sum total of one's interaction with the given surroundings.

Discussion/S

Risk faced by Women at Workplaces

There is a dearth of research to analyse the risk faced by women at urban and metro spaces. In a country like India that is largely patriarchal, it is difficult to expose the abuses. It is definitively not an easy way out for women. Almost 28 percent of women face sexual harassment within the first year of the employment. And almost 70 percent of women do not report it because of the patriarchal power structure along with their threat to job. Most of the time, it is women who has to quit the job than the accused himself. #metoomovement has really changed the face of the country. The cases which were earlier there like Bhavri Devi who outed a child marriage case in the village was raped and assaulted by a group of men that subsequently led to the Visakha guideline 1997 and the subsequent prevention of sexual harassment policy which was implemented in 2013. But despite all of these cases its not been easy and the me too campaign has given a momentum for young people for women to speak out against violence rape culture, sexual harassment. It has enabled women to have a space, support of other women and men to speak about the issues in public space. It has given a strong warning to the perpetrators saying that is is not alright to sexually harass and violate the people and create a space where they can talk about it properly. A lot of organisations is trying to implement the policy around sexual harassment which was not the case earlier. There has been a change in the way of people are seeing the sexual harassment now, while earlier it was connected to honor of a person. But now it seems women are feeling comfortable talking about it openly and there is support from them.

metoo is not the first feminist right movement in India. India has a long history of women rights movement. The campaign is a significant and crucial step. It is a kind of change in International narrative that people have in women around India that they are extremely victimised by gender based violence. Women now think that they are survivors and that they can challenge the perpetrators.

The government has lost a sense of crucial opportunity to stand by the women of India. As opposed to see many parts of the world what the government would have done to set an example bringing about the system change. As the movement is limited calling it a hash tag movement it does not reach out to rural women. The movement requires more sensitisation program (government sensitisation program.) where NGO, s ought to be involved where women need to come out and complain.

A lot of men have also come out and supported this movement and have said that we stand by you and what you say. Men can play huge role in that.

Abuses at Workplace

Harassment at workplace is a global concern in terms of public health. The #metoo and #times up are wake up calls and strong demands change in the policy of sexual harassment. The workplace demands a safe environment. Not all the organisation in India has a sexual harassment policy. The guideline of appropriate conduct must be specified and the consequences may be outlined. The workplace must show its dedication to implement the policies clearly and unambiguously. The decision taken by the organisation should be examplary so that such cases can further never occur.

Work Life Imbalances

Working women faces lot of challenges at workplaces often trying to strike a balance between family and workplace. She faces double jeopardy from two sources simultaneously. Women toil hard to negotiate with their multiple roles to achieve freedom and purpose of life in order to add their contribution to society.

Social Stigma

There is a huge social stigma women find courage and strength coming forward in this me too campaign. It is really interesting to see that twitter in particular is used by media and is not a safe place at all. Women are trolled and threatened. It is crucial for the women to come out in large numbers. Women are struggling top come out with these kinds of stories because there is a huge legal threat where women can be prosecuted in these defamatory cases. Legal help in India is very difficult to get.

Pros and Cons of Social Media

The social media has given a platform for the people to speak out against any kind of violations. It has also gathered lot of support from the common public where women feel that they have a number of people supporting them and standing by them. Sometimes there is a series of trolls and then there is a series of support. This is how the social media works that subsequently leads to mental illness as a harsh stigma that leads to serious consequences making the victim uncomfortable.

Harassment at Workplace

A safe workplace is a woman legal right free from any sort of discrimination in order to ensure that there is equal protection under the law for women's right and dignity. Most of the cases are unreported. There is a requirement of ground-breaking redressal mechanism to counter harassment at workplace. After interviewing few women it was found the every woman at workplace have faced harassment in some way or the other.

Sexual advances without consent of an individual.

Stalking

Invading the personal zone.

Inappropriate touch

Ostracising an individual at workplace

Making highly inappropriate lewd remarks

Grapevine communication without any rhyme or reason

Prank calls to sexually harass them for arousal

Sexist remarks.

Burdening with workload

Body shaming

Belittling women at public spaces.

As per the latest data published on 8th Feb 2019 by the Press Information Bureau, Government of India, Ministry of Child Development, the cases registered under the category of insult of women at workplace we see a steady increse in the cases from the year 2014 as per the National Crime record Bureau.

Year	2014	2015	2016
No of Cases	57	119	142

The above table depicts that for the last three years the cases registered has been increasing.

The Ministry of Women and Child Development has opened The Cyber Crime Reporting portal under Nirbhaya Fund named as She-box which is an online Complain Management system where any women facing sexual harassment at workplace can register an online complain. The portal is an initiative to ensure women that a safe workplace is every woman's right.

As per the record presented at Lok Sabha, Uttar Pradesh recorded the highest number of cases followed by Delhi, Haryana, Madhya pradesh, Maharastra and other states.

State	No. Of Cases registered
UP	726
Delhi	369
Haryana	171
MP	157
Maharasdtra	147

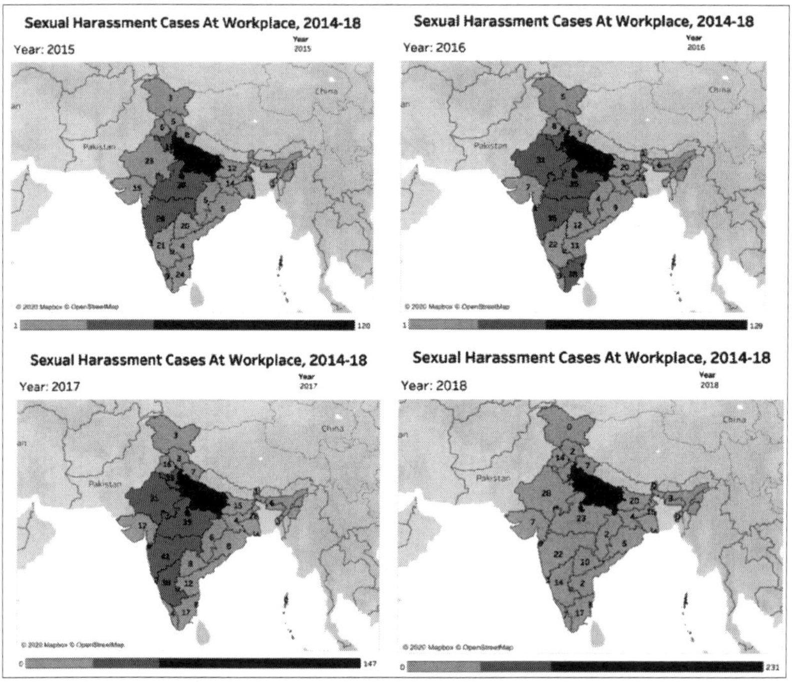

Source: Source: Lok Sabha July 27, 2018; December 15, 2017; 2018 figure as on July 27, 2018

A panel discussion titled "The Red Change: Reach and Impact of Sexual Harassment policies in India" that was carried out with 200 women from 80 different organisation from Urban workplaces in Mumbai, Delhi, Chennai and Bengaluru. The report was released by Brinda Sarkar in the Economic Times Bureau, on June 19, 2019. From the panel discussion it was believed that the companies hiring women employees must increase awareness by defininf certain code and conduct and must sensatise the issues of women harassment in different workshop, forums, talk etc. in order to ensure women a safe workplace. It also revealed that though more than 80 percent women are aware of the policies related to harassment yet 30 percent of them were reluctant and hesitant to complain against such occurrences.

Campaigns that has triggered to highlight issues of sexual harassment at workplaces was the #metoo movement (2014-17) where we see a 54percent rise in the reported cases. In Mumbai alone the cases registered in 2014 were 340. But in 2017 the cases jumped to 570 as per official figures. The movement seems to have empowered the voices of women where they started being vocal about their issues they faced at personal level. The movement exposed prominent personalities from various fields including media music, entertainment, advertising and accusations were unbelievable.

Findings

A primary survey was conducted with working ladies. 36 respondents agreed to participate in the survey. A questionnaire was also prepared to collect their response.

What kind of emotional response does sexual harassment evoke on you?

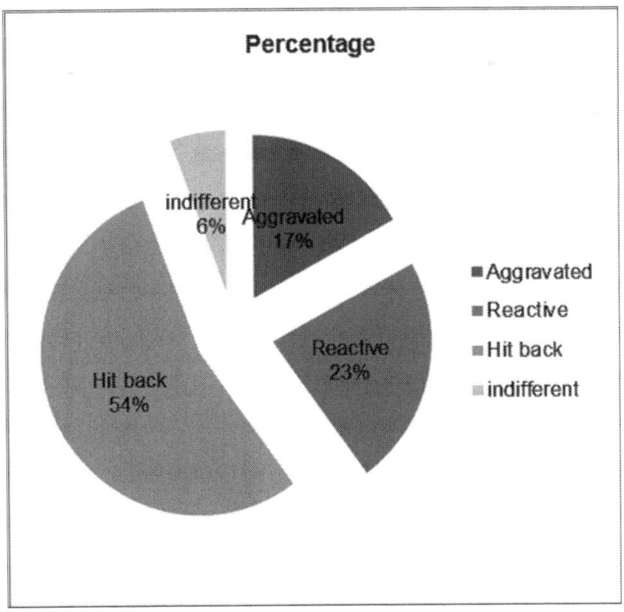

Do you find it difficult to trust and have friendship with men at work place?

1

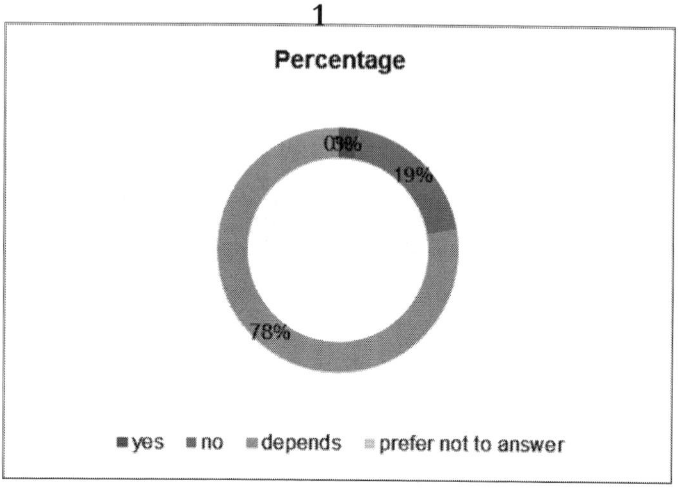

Has respondent harassment ever affected you personal life?

2

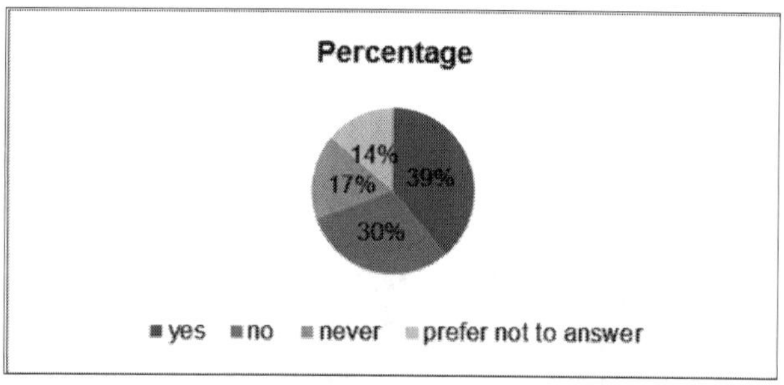

Would you complain to police of any kind of harassment to you?

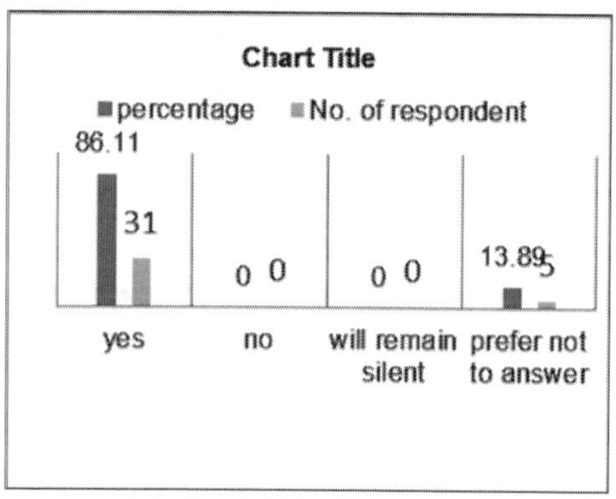

Do you believe there is a need for a policy on sexual harassment?

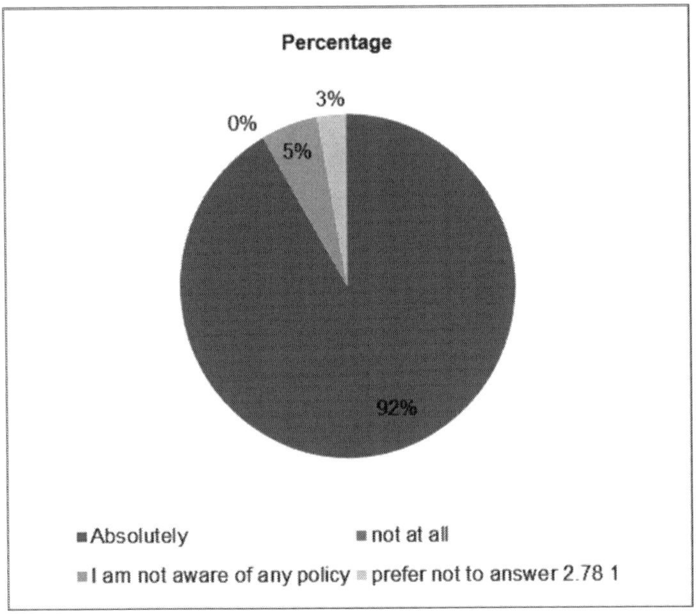

Do you think women should raise issues of sexual violence at different forums?

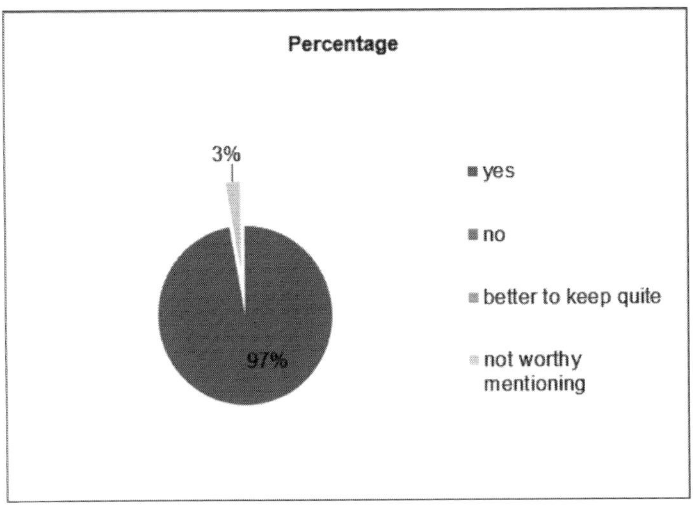

Do you think complain mechanism in India works properly?

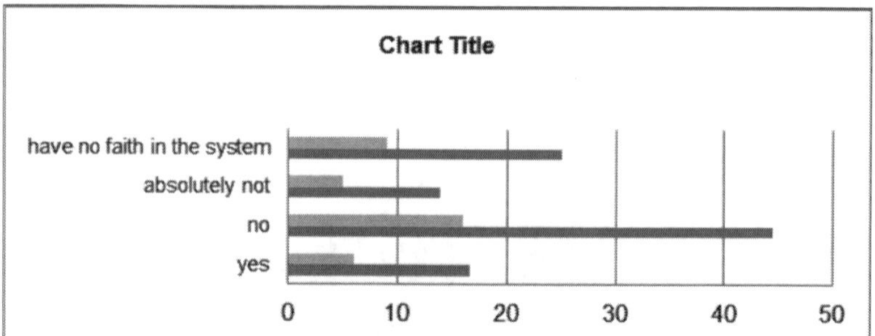

	yes	no	absolutely not	have no faith in the system
No. of respondent	6	16	5	9
percentage	16.6	44.44	13.89	25

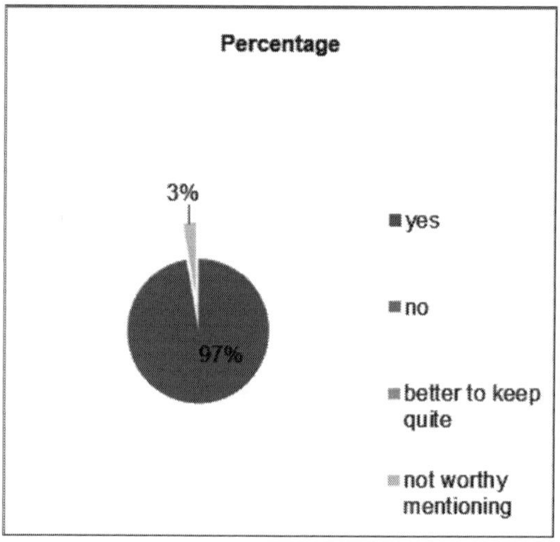

From the primary survey it is evident that women these days are aggrieved when it comes to sexual harassment at workplace. Many remained indifferent to such issues thinking. There was a huge gap in the thought process due to social stigma.

Limitations

The primary survey was a hard nut to crack. The questions were of basic understanding. Several women refused to take the survey which become a deterrent factor. Therefore, the women selected for research were from different regions of India.

Conclusion

The code of silence ought to be broken by women. Time has come for a social change. Previous data reveals that powerful men who are accused of sexual harassment at each and every place starting from newsroom to judge chamber. (From Justice A. K. ganguli to Tarun Tejpal). The finding of the study tries to fill a gap in order to have a deeper understanding of the issue. The above research can play an important role to rethink of the existing laws and its amendment with a deeper scrutiny. Government has still a long way to go to address such cases in fast track system so that the victim will have a faith in the system as the laws related to harassment are not effective in its implementation a takes a long process. Therefore women often prefer to remain silent in most of the cases. Justice delayed is justice denied. She is the power that has been domesticated and ostracised for the benefit of man. Feminism is a concern not a concept. Unfortunately, despite of exemplary contributions in all walks of life women have often been relegated with ease to the footnotes of the footnotes of history which requires strong condemnation. Our ignorance of these women is greatly compounded by the exclusion of information on societies which acknowledged female's power in public life, diplomacy, religion, medicine, the arts as well as backbone of the family structure and inheritance. Both prejudice and male chauvinism are mixed up in these deliberate silences and gaps. Woman is empowered by nature to give life yet the society is tacitly unwilling to recognise her worth and give her due credit. Woman' power on the other hand is unfailing and inevitable. Over the years women have been systematically deleted from history, their stories discarded, distorted and identities replaced.

Works Cited

Primary Sources

Milbrath, L.W. (1978), "Indicators of Environmental Quality" in *UNESCO*, "Indicators of Environmental Quality and Quality of life", reports and papers in Social Sciences No.38, pages 3-56.

Rapoport, A. (1978), *Aspectos humanos de la forma Urbana. Hacia una confrontación de las ciencias sociales con el diseño de la forma urbana*, G. Gili, Barcelona.

Annas, J. (1996), "Las mujeres y la calidad de vida: ¿Dos normas o una?" in Nussbaum, M. and A. Sen (editors), La calidad de vida, Fondo de Cultura Económica, Mexico D.F.

Grosz, E. (1992). *Bodies-cities.* In B. Colomina (Ed.), Sexuality and space (pp. 241-253). New York: Princeton Architectural Press.

McDowell, L. (1980). "Towards an understanding of the gender division of urban space. Environment and Planning," 1, 59-72. McDowell, L. (1999). *Gender, identity and place: Understanding feminist geographies. Cambridge*, UK: Polity.

Haug, F. (1987). *Female sexualisation: A collective work of memory.* London: Verso Classics.

Schultz, Vicki. 1998. *Reconceptualising Sexual Harassment*, Yale Law School,

Franke, M. Katherine. *What's Wrong with Sexual Harassment*, Columbia Law School, 1997.

Christopher, Uggen, (2004) *Sexual Harassment as a Gendered Expression of Power,* Amy Blackstone, SAGE publication, Vol 69, Issue 1.

Schoenheider, Krista J. (1986) *A Theory of Tort Liability for Sexual Harassment in the Workplace*, U. Pa. L. Rev. 1461.

Tinkler. Justine E. *Resisting the Enforcement of Sexual Harassment Law*, Published online by Cambridge University Press: 27 December 2018.

Books

Sexual Harassment of Working Women: A Case of Sex Discrimination, Catharine A. MacKinnon, Yale University Press, 1979

Sexual Harassment: A Debate, Linda LeMoncheck, Mane Hajdin, Rowman & Littlefield, 1997

Sexual Harassment of Women: Climate, Culture, and Consequences in Academic Sciences, Engineering, and Medicine, by Johnson, Paula A., National Academies Press (16 August 2018).

The Women's Movement Against Sexual Harassment, Carrie N. Baker, Cambridge University Press, 2008.

What is Sexual Harassment, and how to conduct Inquiry as per service rules, by Mukesh Chaturvedi, Notion Press; 1 edition (29 November 2019).

CHAPTER 3

The Dynamics of Belonging and Its Implications for Recovery from Trauma of the Women Characters in Safia Elhillo's *Home is not a Country*

AV Koshy and Debdatta Mallik

Absract

The present paper traces whether the young adolescent girl, who is called Nima, the protagonist in *Home is Not a Country*, which is a novel in verse, will forge a reactive relationship with those around her leading to a situational identity, or find a way to achieve a mythic triumph over her sense of trauma through her developing sense of belonging in shared customs, language and a kind of ethnic hybridity with her people, one that stands apart from the hyphenated identity she is bound to embrace.

Keywords: Immigrants, trauma, home, hyphenated identity, semi-corporeal, community-bonding, recovery, belonging, first generation.

Introduction

Stories of immigrants have common themes of separation and the rebuilding of the self through the dynamics of belonging to communities. This applies to first-generation children of the immigrants too. The fact that this also takes into consideration gender issues like that of how being a woman impacts all this and hoe she is in turn impacted by all this and the novel in verse under the microscope here is written by one and that there are no studies on it so far make it interesting to take a closer look at the novel.

The objectives of the study are to show that the following complex and interwoven strands are what the author deals with, including women and gender:

1. Nima, the protagonist of the novel, has the choice of re-capturing the knowledge of the older generations who were the initial immigrants to America, of people like her mother Ayesha, Khaltu Hala, Haitham's grandmother, and making it her own; but whether she wishes to abandon the old ways to generate a new identity based on her adoptive culture is questionable.
2. Lack of proper cultural assimilation leads to severe trauma amongst the first-generation American youth who while attempting to straddle borders and boundaries become a part of multicultural practices, leading to questions of national loyalty to the adopted nation being directed at them.
3. The shifting racialisation of first-generation Americans, and the historical backdrop against which it unfolds leads to alienation, isolation and unsettling trauma, and they often respond to trauma by replacing, integrating or hyphenating cultural identity.
4. Ambivalence, and trauma are showcased in the book. What society's attitude towards the ambivalence and hybridity of these first-generation youngsters as revealed in the book is, is also probed.
5. Nima as a first-generation American does not forge a reactive relationship with those around her but she tries to develop a sense of belonging in her shared customs, language and a kind of ethnic hybridity that stands apart from the hyphenated identity she feels bound to embrace.
6. There is a clearer understanding by Nima, though it is not fully realised in actuality, of the role of belonging, community identification for individual healing and to validate that developing of a sense of belonging by rebuilding decentred communities is an organising principle towards the resolution for separation and trauma, addiction and depression, towards the end of the text.

The question or hypothesis is how a first-generation youngster responds to trauma – trauma that is personal, cultural, historical, and ancestral in its varieties, through developing a sense of belonging and of community. Accordingly, the paper explores the issues of trauma, the search for home and a sense of belonging, and the crisis of a hyphenated identity in the young girl Nima and her imaginary twin Yasmeen in Safia Elhillo's *Home is not a Country*.

Elhillo addresses a modern understanding of trauma amongst the first-generation Americans who are women, and through her narration of the progressive experience over generations – of the immigrant mother Ayesha and the first generation American Nima and her imaginary twin Yasmeen in the book, – she reveals a new perspective on migration, trauma, family and belonging. Trauma and marginalisation determine the complex relationships of the young girl with her host country, society in the school and other decentred groups she interacts with. The perspective of re-examining the trauma in the first generation American and to validate the possibility of recovery from it by developing a sense of belonging and through community bonding is highlighted.

A Brief Literature Review

Safia Elhillo is a Sudanese American writer, born in the United States (1990). Currently, she is a Lecturer at Stanford. She has been nominated for and won many awards for her writing including an honourable, special mention for the Pushcart Prize. She explores themes of belonging and identity, particularly in the context of migration and nationality. Safia Elhillo's "*The January Children*" is an example that retells the experiences of the Sudanese diaspora. The book is an unfolding of the effect of migration upon one's identity, conceivably experienced by many Sudanese people, especially the women and diaspora. In "*Home is not a Country*", she relates the trauma of a young adolescent girl, a first generation American caught between two cultures and her gradual, unfolding awareness of the importance of belonging and community bonding.

Elhillo who rose to fame with her *The January Children* (University of Nebraska Press, 2017). had already dealt with the issues of migration, identity, belonging, issues the first – generation of children of the migrants face, trauma and recovery from it through finding a sense of community from the past to an extent in that book and her other works like her poems published her and there. Her other books, apart from these two, are the "Chapbooks:

- *Ars poetica* (MIEL, 2016)
- *A suite for ol' dirty* (MIEL, 2016)
- *Asmarani* (Akashic Books, 2016)

- *The Life and Times of Susie Knuckles* (Well & Often Press, 2012)" (Wikipedia)

What little critical attention Elhillo has garnered primarily deals with *The January Children.* In the novel in verse under consideration, *Home is not a Country*, she continues her exploration of the earlier, above-mentioned themes. It has received a number of engrossing reviews. "Her story captures a familiar wistfulness for the places we come from but have never truly known. It's a tapestry of life in small moments, and the revelations we have about our pasts over time." (Dutta, 2021) According to Maya C. James (2021), "nostalgia and wishful thinking make for compelling reflections on identity… "in the novel. In *Kirkus Reviews* (2021) an unknown reviewer says of the novel accurately, leaving out only the nationality… "a Muslim girl traversing post–9/11 America with the baggage of a past she does not yet fully understand", and ends the review with this fragmentary sentence, "Movingly unravels themes of belonging, Islamophobia, and the interlocking oppressions thrust upon immigrant women." All these goes to show that the novel can be studied in the arc of Nima's character as being about the themes outlined in the study which these reviewers only touch on but can be gone into depth here as befitting of research in the light of larger studies happening in the field of theory on these same pressing themes that have swum increasingly to the forefront in recent years due to the influx of migrants, of gender and race and class, of first generation writings, of trauma as increasing, of the question of identity politics, belonging, community building, one's relationship to one's past, history and time, and of 'imaginary homelands' to borrow a title from Rushdie – all in relation to women's studies.

Nima's Trauma and Its Causes

Trauma is defined in psychiatric and psychological terms, as "Psychiatric trauma is essentially a normal response to an extreme event. It involves the creation of emotional memories about the distressful event that are stored in structures deep within the brain. In general, it is believed that the more direct the exposure to the traumatic event, the higher the risk for emotional harm." (Davies, 2021)

People who suffer trauma include war victims, rape victims, victims of school shootings who survive in USA who then go for therapy due to developing mental illnesses, victims of depression, anxiety and panic attacks and other traumatic disorders like PTSD that need medical intervention too as otherwise it leads sometimes to suicide from increased suicidal tendencies or aggression, self-harm in some cases etc.

However, in literary studies on trauma, as we are dealing with fictional characters, different or lesser forms of stress can be included in the reckoning, although one has to take into account the biography of the writer. Thus, in Elhillo's case, in the novel in verse under consideration, Nima can be seen partly as an alter-ego of the narrator/author as also coming from Sudan, being Muslim, being 'Arabic' in the sense of having adopted Arabic culture, tribal in the non-pejorative sense, dark-skinned, again in the non-pejorative sense, first-generation, out of place and struggling to find her identity, all stressful overtones of experience even if not strictly traumatic as in the case of PTSDs or those needing medication.

Nima's trauma starts with the death of her father which she does not remember properly, with her mother's memories of it which she can only be part of tangentially, and more familiar ones like being a child with an advance sensitivity in a land that considers her a stranger as yet and where her mother is not at ease, a land that has not accepted them both fully. This is especially so in the aftermath of 9/11, where she is bullied and suspected to be a 'terrorist', friendless, having no siblings, though she tries to adopt Haitham and fails there too to have him as a kind of brother figure. Thus we can say her trauma is of being a victim of racism, age-related being only a teenager and child (14 at the time of her narrative in the book), of gender bias and religious discrimination, and of not belonging either to the community of her past which she can only imagine, or the present one she belongs to in America, of school which fails to satisfy her as a foster home, or of home as her mother is too busy struggling to survive. She is forced to turn inwards and bring into being for her survival a form of self-therapy by imagining or creating Yasmeen, a being or entity she imagines she herself should or could have been and who she believes can make and keep her happy as the self's friendly other and companion/sister. Such self-therapy can either go wrong, and does begin to before she snaps out of it, as it is self-administered, or help her out of the dead end she feels her life is or is becoming. Much of her characterisation may be drawn from Safia's life itself but that is reductive reading as she is not just that but something more, showing that Safia is a writer worth her salt in her strength of creating a woman character such as Nima, as pointed out by Maya C James.

In *Home is not a Country*, Safia Elhillo's focal character, the 14 year old Nima, carries the weight of an exacting and austere solitariness due to lack of having friends at the outset, an inescapable world of pain and suffering, a personal trauma.

However, even before the beginning of the story, there is separation from her father (dead in a "car crash") (Elhillo 15) and from her country, presumably Sudan, though unnamed in the novel, which forms the root of a deeper trauma. As the story develops, there are active challenges in the present that are threatening to such a small girl. The book chronicles Nima's revisiting her past through a set of photographs, a catastrophic beginning remembering her parting from her dad, and then the challenges of single parenthood for her mother Aisha who "mostly she goes to work & comes home tired … her eyes make tears that do not fall" (Elhillo 17).

Nima feels an intimate sense of proximity to her father through the pictures, but the longing and desire to have known her father in reality has its edge; the cuts and wounds of the mind make it fiercely difficult for her to bear the pain of her father being "impossibly far away" (Elhillo 15). With this comes the thorny realisation of what life should have been, which instead is always going to remain an impending non-arrival as in the photographs, "In the one on the coffee table he stares awestruck at his bride", "a passport picture in Mama's wallet." (Elhillo 15)

Nima's loss is in the past and her break, rupture or discontinuity is in her no longer belonging to her origins. Growing up fatherless in a new country, Nima is quick to hide in the shadowed shelter of her aloneness, appearing as if numbed by the past and the uncertain present and thereby internalising her unhappiness. Hiding the past by internalising it is represented by her replacing the old photograph of her mother in wedding finery in the spectacular headdress in the protected shelter of a used tin box hardly opened anymore, "I keep this photograph in an old tin box" (Elhillo 17)

Internalising her sadness, Nima transforms her hurt at not having the life she could have had. This thought of loss appears and reappears in the first half of the story and as her response to the trauma of having lost a father and country reveals itself through fragile vulnerability, she looks out at the outside world and becomes too scared to participate in it, a world which she feels she cannot inhabit. This fear resurfaces mostly at the beginning of the journey of her transformed trauma as she wishes for. "a different country, a different life & the story hushed to memory." (Elhillo 15).

In the section "Mama," Nima's understanding of her mother deepens and intensifies as the novel progresses to show an indissoluble bond between them. She shows a striking maturity in understanding her mother from an early age that the life her mother had hoped for was taken away at the time she had begun to appreciate it "eyelashes painted dark beneath/ a headdress of silver coins" and then "my mother is alone as I will come to know her." (Elhillo 16). She understands her mother's epicentre of pain and how she struggles to create a home for herself and her daughter in a new land and embraces its newness "speak shy quiet English testing new words" (Elhillo 18) and strangeness (only suburban America" (Elhillo 18) and yet does not achieve the contentment or joy she had imagined she would acquire in a new land. As the impetus of life changes for her, and she grapples with new experiences, Nima notices "the worry lines stamped into her brow". (Elhillo17) She sees that "the headdress has been sold and my mother is alone is at work is rushed / in her headscarf and blue jeans." (Elhillo 17)

Nima has few options to experience the beckoning new life at school and she chooses to retreat behind Haitham who seems to her with all his awkwardness, helplessness and mischief, a necessary friend; more like a brother. Nima's friendship with Haitham at the beginning of the story is that of blind allegiance stemming from the fact that their mothers are connected by "some ancient sisterhood of grief" (Elhillo 18) and as she says about Haitham "we've always known each other" (Elhillo 18) a statement which documents their shared common past, the common land or country of origin, the sameness of religion, age, and race, and experiencing the sameness of a situation in a new land.

Their friendship becomes easy and filled with banter and mischief, and the closeness reveals he is a sociable young boy who loves Nima as his sister. She gets to know Haitham for his mischief, "stealing candy", harmlessly cracking jokes regarding the Arabic teacher. teasing her for her rigidity in staying isolated, his difficulties, his trespasses, and tries to bring out the best in him not through critique but by addressing the better part of him. However, Haitham is apparently unaware of Nima's problems, especially that of the now increasing sense of trauma. Nima has by now alienated herself from children of her age at school "barely passing grade in social interaction/ muttering and burdened by a shadow of an accent that I cannot manage to make charming" (Elhillo 20), scared again to participate in a life that may result in hurt. School too with its "assortment of others. All citizens of the social margin and though assembled we do not talk" (Elhillo 20) is a place where learning Arabic (which is "so boring") and English, she feels herself to be the composite of a generation caught between two or more cultures who even if they individually have not faced the anxiety of loss and erasure, oscillate between rootlessness and rootedness, alienation and belonging. Suburban America with its harsh artificial Walmart lights and polished floors appear in stark contrast to the tales of the date palm trees and riverbanks, weddings that went on for weeks, cafes crowded with poets and lush gardens humming with insects in their land of origin that she has never, paradoxically enough, seen.

The desire to fit in in the new society of Walmart and Starbucks makes her discard her lunch of stale "okra, lamb, rice" for tasteless sandwiches with "plasticky cheese" "between them.

The dilemma Nima faces is that she has the option of recapturing the knowledge of a land of origin and making it her own or abandoning the old ways to generate a new identity based on her adoptive culture. This dilemma causes a myriad of emotions from numbness to sadness and a deepening sense of alienation. The alienation deepens as a girl from her class comes home to work on a project and returns only to berate Nima's fleece shirt and home's smell of rice and dirty plants and wonders whether her mother was bald beneath her headscarf. Whatever be the choice of those like Nima, their widespread influence on American society prompts the question whether differences in national origin and cultural background negate in a fundamental manner the overcoming of her sadness. Nima transforms her hurt at not having the life she could have had by imagining Yasmeen. She looks out at the outside world she inhabits and becomes too scared to participate in it. This fear resurfaces mostly at the beginning and in the middle of her journey in the novel.

Nima faces a novel predicament that of maintaining cultural and communal distinctiveness and keeping herself away from what she considers mainstream. The alienation is strengthened by the thought that is she being forced into the position of a racial minority at school and in the suburbia she inhabits. These thoughts which bring with it a horrifying sense of puzzlement and dilemma and yet more vulnerability with a profound sense of unworthiness that are not shared with or by Haitham who for all his concern, brotherly love and protective nature fails to understand the shadows of Nima's mind and in that sense remains a flat character, paving the way for the arrival of Yasmeen.

Recovering from Trauma

Having explained the roots of Nima's trauma, we need to look at how she goes about trying to resolve it. Her first attempt is through imagining a geist, a doppelganger, a twin, a female djinn, a qareen. This is to alleviate her loneliness and make it bearable but, much more, it is a form of self-therapy that is both admirable as it draws on her 'roots' and also risky as it is being done by a novice at the art of self-healing.

Yasmeen appears throughout Home like an unresolved parallel. At first, she seems to be emblematic of a longing of Nima for a finer version of herself. "I imagine her yasmeen this other girl bright & alive mouth full and dripping with language easy in her charm & in essence she looks like me but of course better..." (Elhillo 24) and "I imagine her back home fathered beloved. .... called to from across the street by classmates by teachers jewel of the neighbourhood. ... like everyone knows her name & I ache to have been born her instead" (Elhillo 25) Nima's challenge at this juncture is her vulnerability and her sense of unworthiness through which she must pass in order to evolve into the next phase of her life. At this stage, she is even in retreat from her name Nima that seems to have caught and imprisoned her.

> "my mother meant to name me for her favourite flower. .... instead I got this name & I don't even know why maybe named for some unknown dead relative some dreary ghost so no one wants me at their party..... of course I fade to the back of the classroom. ... teacher glances and squints like she isn't quite sure who I am" (Elhillo 24)

Nima's hiding from others, by trying to remain invisible and feeling unworthy and unloved when the outside world avoids her consciously or unconsciously, but which she considers a conscious act on their part is at this point an act of freedom of being misunderstood by others, from ideas about herself and from outside interference taking refuge in nostalgia and as Haitham calls her "nostalgia monster" (Elhillo 26). It is when the trauma of being oppressed by the sense of the self and sense of others seems complete and makes her feel yet more invisible "In the hallway no one looks my way. .... the bus driver does not see me at the stop". (Elhillo 27)

Yasmeen's appearance, though frightening for her, as she appears as a visitation, can be seen as also the first sign towards the fulfillment of a need. Later it is a call for help and that is when the change is imminent. To consider Yasmeen as help, can be regarded as a transformative dynamic that holds the possibility of resulting in her emancipation at a later stage of her journey.

Oppressing the self by oneself and retreating from the other systems of oppression at school where she is berated more and more for her "terrorist father and terrorist mother" manifests as an escalating sense of unworthiness and non-acceptance leading to distress. Nima takes more and more refuge in the stories and songs and life of a bygone land of origin which they inhabit no more. Nima tries to find a sense of connectedness through shared history, culture, a sense of belonging, the fulfillment of needs and effective mediums of communication. So the poems where she relates with Haitham, his mother Khaltu Hala, the grandmother of Haitham, and her own mother is her exploration into a semblance of a community as a collective change agent, "unit of solution in society" through which people can proactively address trauma-related problems within their locality and relational groups.

An important reference on belonging and storytelling for healing is in "Community Healing and Resistance through Major Storytelling: A Framework to address Racial Trauma in African Communities" (Chioneso, Carla, Gobin, Robyn, Smith, Sharde, Ruby, Helen) where three major components of the framework of recovery from trauma are delineated. "

a) Justice as both a condition of and an outcome of community healing;
b) Culturally syntonic processes (i. e. storytelling and resistance) that direct the re-narrating of trauma and act as conduits for transformation
c) Psychological dimensions (i.e. connectedness, collective memory, and critical consciousness) that promote justice informed outcomes." (Chionesco et al102/103)

In the C HeARTS framework quoted above, community is advanced as an agent of change while centring justice and the important role of cultural practices to facilitate community healing.

Conclusion

While Nima does not reach there, she starts the process towards this. In intuiting this, Elhillo matters as a new and significant young literary voice in the field of women's writing that has something remarkably new to say about the first generation black/coloured Muslim in USA who is a woman born of an immigrant and on her methods of coping and survival and transformation and eventual journey into being phenomenal and triumphant through creating a memorable character like Nima who achieves a walk on a road to recovery in her creation of the mythic Yasmeen and her reconciliation with the identity of her ancestors and being a woman in a new land.

Works Cited

Davies, Charles Patrick. "Medical Definition of Psychiatric Trauma" M*edicine Net*, March, 2021, https://www.medicinenet.com/psychiatric_trauma/definition.htm-.

Dutta, Nayantara. *'Home is Not a Country' Imagines the Lives We Could Have Led.* npr, March, 2021, https://www.npr.org/2021/03/04/973389493/ home-is-not-a-country-imagines-the-lives-we-could-have-led.

Elhillo, Safia. *Home is not a Country*, Make Me a World, 2021. "Home Is Not A Country." *Kirkus Reviews*, www.kirkusreviews.com/book-reviews/safia-elhillo/home-is-not-a-country/.

James, Maya C. *Home is not a Country by Safia Elhillo.* LOCUS, September, 2021.

https://locusmag.com/2021/09/maya-c-james-reviews-home-is-not-a-country-by-safia-elhillo/.

"Safia Elhillo." *Wikipedia*, the Free Encyclopedia, Wikimedia Foundation, Inc, 11 May 2017, en.wikipedia.org/wiki/Safia_Elhillo. Accessed 18 Dec. 2021.

Nkechinyelum, *Chioneso A, Hunter, Carla*, Gobin Robyn L, Smith, McNeil,

Sharde, Mendenhall, Ruby, Neville, Helen A, *Community Healing and Resistance Through Storytelling: A Framework to Address Racial Trauma in Africana Communities.* 2020.

CHAPTER 4

Portrayal of Women's Oppression in Select Indian Fiction

Sukanya Saha

Abstract

In the globalised society with increased impact of the west, significance of several orthodox practices is being now questioned and sought to be kept at bay, over past few decades. Contemporary Indian literature is showcasing not only the women's oppression but also the women liberating themselves from the imposed shackles. The traditional image of ideal and coy Indian women is undergoing radical transformations. Indian writers are adopting changing and challenging perceptions about women which promote new ideologies and perspectives. The narrations and themes are altered in accordance with the women as lead, and their achievements are being celebrated. The premise of this article is laid over highlighting how fictions over the decades have treated the idea of women's oppressions and have depicted them as liberating themselves from the society's biases.

Keywords: Indian women writers, oppression, internalized oppression, subjugation, marginalisation

Introduction

Simone de Beauvoir famously claimed, "one is not born, but rather becomes a woman". She brought in the phenomenon of biological rejection. Woman does not have any autonomy. The problem is that the man is considered as 'self' and woman is the 'other' (Beauvoir).

Oppression is an age-old reality woman have been confronting constantly being denied of opportunities. In "Exploitation, Extortion and Oppression" (1987), Alen Carling says, "Exploitation is the unfair use by one person of the excluded situation of another", (Carling 173). Women being oppressed in patriarchal society is expressed in number of ways. Regardless of family's societal status and education, oppression of women is evident. Women have been struggling for their rights worldwide. They seek equality in right to vote, in wages and workloads, in politics and above all, in families. Surveys conducted around the world, reveal that women in the western world enjoy comparatively more rights than their counterparts in southern, eastern and northern spheres of the world. Such studies direct towards the factors which influence women's marginalised status. Women's movements have brought down the cases of exploitation on domestic and professional fronts to some extent, however the society's bias against women's equal status remains a flagrant reality.

Contemporary women walk through the double-edged sword of family and profession, constantly subjected to the judgments. This juggling of career and family and multitasking with expectations met, exerts a pressure that drains them psychologically and physically. Women are labelled with tradition and culture hallmarks to make them 'acceptable'. Those who flout the rigid norms and claim emancipation, are declared immoral or identified with some derogatory connotations.

Iris Young in her book, *Justice and the Politics of Difference* (1990), identifies, "Five Faces of Oppression". She writes, "oppression [...] represents a family of concepts and conditions, which I divide into five categories: exploitation, marginalisation, powerlessness, cultural imperialism and violence" (Young 1990) Women are fettered with ties, both external and internal. This accounts for their exploitation, marginalisation also powerlessness. The paper quotes from the select texts to strengthen the argument about how oppression of women have been a constant subject of fiction writers. Certain prominent theorists have been cited who have written with focus over women's marginalised status.

Analysis and Discussion

In *Lamps In The Whirlpool* (1995), Rajam Krishnan narrates how social mores oppress women in grinds. The Madi culture prevalent in Brahminical society lays rigid rules of sanctity for its followers. The female protagonist, Girija toils tirelessly day-long to cater to her mother-in-law's needs for holy rituals. She is barred from the privileges of entering her own bedroom during daytime. She must refrain from touching her children for dressing them up or making them ready for their schools. Pharr. S writes that "self-hating" and "self-blaming" eventually surface in women as psychological reactions to constant oppression. Rathna, Girija's cousin, says that the latter has become a "kitchen insect", "Don't you think, it is a blatant flushing of your rights?". (LWP 40). Girija is apparently a victim of "internalised oppression" enduring a battle within her. Her true self has been crushed and she has been reduced into a slave. She has lost her essential self to the extent that she starts fearing a life in case her husband dies. However, eventually she breaks herself free from these seventeen years long drudgeries by throwing away her Mangal sutra, the sacred string worn by married Indian women. Girija thus becomes an example of oppression through culture.

The Temple Is Not My Father (2014), underlines the malaises of 'devadasi system' practiced in certain temples in India. Godavari is pushed into this wretched practice at an early age by her father. Rasana Atreya, the author, renders the sufferings of an innocent woman. Godavari's mother could not stop her husband from pushing their daughter into this ill-fated life. The poignance in little innocent Godavari being dressed in new clothes and jewels and taken to temple and getting her married to the temple God is intense. The lecherous glances of males would send cold shivers down the spine as the women in the crowd watch haplessly.

The irony lies in Indian women being idolised as embodiments of dharma, chastity, subordination. For instance, Shashi Deshpande writes in *That Long Silence* (1988), "Sita following her husband into exile, Savitri dogging Death to reclaim her husband, Draupadi stoically sharing her husband's travails". Indian women reel under the suffocating ideals of Sita, Sati, and Savitri. In *The Thousand Faces of Night* (1992), Githa Hariharan ridicules the common notion of exemplifying women from mythology. Such idol worship is suffocating. Impact of these images haunt women and affect their subconscious. This complicates their existences. The intricate, orthodox, and self-contradictory ideals about love, sex, and marriages, inspired by mythologies apparently wreck the psychological and physical being of women in Indian society. Such myths travel through generations and women are subjected to frameworks prescribed by mythology. Devi, a nineteen-year-old girl is pushed into matrimony with a stranger without her consent. Sita, (Devi's mother), Mayamma (Devi's servant maid), Lakshmi (Devi's grand ma's maid), are other women in the novel, subjugated in one or other ways irrespective of their social status, education, and economic conditions. Sita is denied her Veena playing, an activity which she cherished. Instead, she must devote herself to the caregiving of her mother-in-law and husband.

In *One Indian Girl*, (2016), Radhika Mehta, an educated girl, gets her dream job in New York. She earns well. The book's cover projects the image of an ideal Indian woman. In the cover of the book, it is clearly seen the image of an 'ideal' Indian woman in sari. All men in Radhika's life expect her to be a self-sacrificing, submissive, and house-wifely in nature. Iris Young says that the cause of women's oppression is not only the inequality of power, wealth and status but also abstaining women from the activities which privilege them (Young). Debashish, wants her to appear less intelligent and earn less than him. Neel Gupta exhorts her to be a working woman and stay away from the temptations of motherhood.

I said I want to have a family. Have kids, be a good mother and look after them well. That's not thinking clearly? (*OIG* 208),

> Say what you wanted to say, Neel?'
>
> Neel deceitfully praised her, "'You are a star at work. What is all this mundane stuff you are talking about? Any woman can do all this." (*OIG* 209).

Radhika's mother compares her with Aditi, the elder sibling, who is passive and submissive to her in-laws. Aditi, however, yearns to have a life like Radhika, who is an achiever. Radhika's mother pesters her to get married and fears that increasing financial independence will transform her daughter completely. The mother blames Radhika for not inculcating the qualities of a good girl.

Anuradha Roy's *All the Lives We Never Lived* (2018) is an anguished delineation of the pain of abandoned child. However, in Gayatri, Roy portrays a rebel who was a misfit, torn between incessant calling for an artist and the society's expectations from her, indeed, she "had stood on the rim of a volcano, seen the fires below and taken the lunge" (320). She could be easily subjected to criticism for abandoning her nine year old who had no role in any of her deprivations, especially after little Myshkin's venting of his anger, "for not writing to my father, for going away, for not taking me with her' and agonising yearnings for her, 'I saw anything I associated with her – an empty vase that always had fresh flowers before, a white sari drying on a line-a giant fist of pain squeezed my chest hard enough to break my ribs." (151)

Despite that, Gayatri's fleeing act validates arguments about marginalised, subjugated status of women, a commodity which is meant to be owned and exchange hands at will. Following are few sentences from the book that would underline the typical stature society adopts towards its women.

"My mother owned me, she transferred me to NC & then he owned me", "the way he made me feel guilty about every expense" (220).

"you are no more than a foolish deluded woman if you don't agree with him…" (222)

"he humiliated me every chance he had' (223).

She epitomises women reeling, after giving over their passions and pursuits for social security and acceptance, "there was a bird trapped inside me beating its wings' (223), 'I want to eat life, grab everything new and taste it." (224) In fact, Myshkin too admits that, "she was turning into the concentration of all that I longed for in my life and did not have. I wanted to do what she was doing.' (188)

Nek Chand's aura as accommodative yet domineering husband emanate contrasting shades. He willingly accepted Gayatri's hand in marriage who apparently had less options with her ways of the world. His self-proclamations as a tolerant and progressive are evident in Myshkin saying, "Being a progressive man (he said)" (46), suffocates Gayatri. He fumes, 'Everyman admires me as a progressive man. Allows his wife every freedom…lets her do anything she pleases", as if wives are meant to be tamed with "Propriety, sobriety, obedience" (40).

The nonconformist in Gayatri grew larger and soon discovered a way out with the appearances of Spies and Beryl, who identified her as, "young, beautiful, gifted, tortured, stifled – was an obvious subject for rescue." (68).

Nek's bend for nationalism was superior to tending the emotional wounds of Gayatri. He takes pity at Lipi in marrying her and rescuing her from the cursed widowed life of hers, yet the chauvinist in Nek deprives her of all pleasures which a woman naturally cherishes. He enforces his nationalistic ideals over her with which he failed in Gayatri, reducing her merely into muted, being confined to corners. She is not allowed what she fancies and must be clad in handspun saris and turn into an archetype of simplicity and purity staying put from social gatherings. The scars of Lipi's wasted life are so disturbingly deep that Nek's guilt nursing to her could not salvage her old self.

Gayatri and Lipi are two disparate facets of womanhood, rubbed against the same touchstone to make assertions about the unreasonable or arbitrary fates women are pushed into and their offspring Myshkin and Ila's fates entwined, "bought together by the disappearance of [...] two mothers." (205) Arjun Chacha's wife is rarely allowed to step outside let alone her being instrumental in affecting lives. Of what material women like Mukti Devi are made up of whom men Nek idolize. If the rhetorical speeches of Mukti Devi are revolutionary and affecting for Nek then why the artistic impulses in Gayatri are deliberately suppressed by him which had the same potency. The binaries in the characters of Gayatri's father Agni Sen, an ardent traveller and art lover, and Nek Chand; Myshkin's grandfather Batty Rozario, a gentle patron, and son Nek; Myshkin's neighbours, Arjun Chacha, an affluent yet pretentious aristocrat, and his brother Brijen Chacha, an over-indulgent vocalist, present two extremes of the male world, that were vital in constructing or deconstructing the lives of Gayatri, Lipi and Myshkin directly or indirectly.

Conclusion

Lamps in the Whirlpool, *The Temple is not My Father*, *The Thousand Faces of Night*, *One Indian Girl*, and *All the Lives We Never Lived* are publications on a span of three decades. The settings of these novels and characters in them have entirely different circumstances. However, the underlying thread that binds them is oppression. Multiple waves of feminism have not brought any significant difference in the general scenario. Any set of novels can be randomly chosen that are published post-independence highlight the dilemma of women. The culture based Indian society makes women to comply with the anarchy of deceitful patriarchy. In these four novels, women face the agony of aching culture machination and reel under the consequences of internalised oppression.

Work Cited

Atreya, Rasana. *The Temple is not My Father.* Kindle Edition. Smash words. 2014.

Beauvoir, Simone. *The Ethics of Ambiguity.* Translated by Bernard Frechtman, Citadel press, 1949. Print.

Bhagat, Chetan. *One Indian Girl.* New Delhi: Rupa Publications, 2016. Print

Carling, Alen. "Exploitation, Extortion and Oppression". *Political Studies*, Vol.35, Issue 2. 1987, p. 173-188.

Deshpande, Shashi. *That Long Silence.* New Delhi: Penguin Books, 1989. Print.

Hariharan, Githa. *The Thousand Faces of Night.* New Delhi: Penguin Books, 1992. Print.

Krishnan, Rajam. *Lamps in the Whirlpool.* Translated by Uma Narayan and Seetharam. Chennai: Macmillan, 1997. Print

Pharr, S. *In the time of the right: Reflections on liberations.* Berkeley, CA: Chardon Press. 1996. Print.

Roy, Anuradha. *All the Lives We Never Lived.* Gurugram: Hachette India, 2018. Print.

Young, I.M. *Justice and the Politics of Difference.* Princeton, NJ: Princeton University Press, 1990. Print.

CHAPTER 5

Deconstructing Gender and Diaspora in the Poetry of Sujata Bhatt

Hitesh D Raviya and Rohini Sharma

Abstract

The research paper majorly engages with the examination and depiction of the theme of gender and diasporic sensibility in women in the poetry of Sujata Bhatt. The recurrent dominant essence of alienation and double exile undertowing in her poetry has been identified and investigated. The research paper deconstructs the significance and impact of history and culture in constructing identity in Bhatt's poetry. She relentlessly holds a conviction to undo the physical, cultural, and moral violence done on female body, which is decoded in the research paper. Her poetry is an acrid depiction of cultural violence on women which she believes is stronger unjust than any other severity. Apart from above said, Bhatt's poetry is also a reflection on her intense attachment to homeland and an unbroken continual relationship to it. The research paper analyse the poetry of Sujata Bhatt under the lens of gender and diaspora, understanding Bhatt's view on feminism and her voice of revolt.

Keywords: Diasporic anxiety, Memory, Identity, Self, Gender, Feminism, Sujata Bhatt

Born in Ahmedabad, Gujarat in the year 1956, Bhatt spent her infancy and early childhood at Pune before immigrating to America in 1968 where she received an MFA degree from the University of IOWA. Bhatt worked as a writer-in-residence at the University of Victoria, Canada. Sujata Bhatt has been a recipient of numerous prestigious awards like Commonwealth Poetry Prize and Alice Hunt Bartlett Prize for her first poetry collection *Brunizem*. Traveled across various countries Bhatt currently stays in Germany. Since she traveled extensively Bhatt has a multicultural perspective on art and literature. Bhatt has translated various Gujarati poetry collections into English. Her paramount poetic achievements include *Brunizem* (1988), *The One Who Goes Away* (1989), *Monkey Shadows* (1991), *The Stinking Rose*

(1995), *Point No Point* (1997), *Augatora* (2000), *The Colour of Solitude* (2002), *Pure Lizard* (2008). *Brunizem* is a deliberation on authors close connection to both Indian and western culture. In this poetry collection bhatt uses metaphorical references of various mythological legends, animals, erotic love and political satires. *Monkey Shadows* exposes and contemplates on the ferine nature, the naked savage desires of humans. The poetry collection is a resultant of Bhatt's extensive travelling and amalgamation of education and knowledge of different cultures apart from Indian culture. In this poetry collection she engages with the duality and contradictions in the world comparing scientific laboratories and mythic landscapes in the same framework. *The Stinking Rose* has a collection of a few experimental poems where Bhatt has experimented and celebrated bilingual poems which collaborates Gujarati and English language together. Thematic concerns of this poetry collection explore "the various mythologies and the magical aspects of garlic in a sequence of twenty five parts, is also haunted by places, especially Vancouver Island (where the author lived and worked for six months), and her native India. Europe is also present, a place of sometimes reluctant abode." *Point No Point* is a collection of poetry dwelling upon the theme of diaspora, Bhatt's connection with the native land. "Language, politics and gender, place and history are key themes that emerge in this work". *Augatora* is a German word when translated in English means eye gate or windows of the soul. This poetry collection is a corollary of Bhatt's wide ranging travel experiences which includes Durban, New Orleans, Jerusalem, Riga Amsterdam, Barcelona, and the other small islands of German North Sea coast. The subject of the poetry collection includes love, history, culture, memory, language and science. In *Color of Solitude* Bhatt dwells into the psychology and motivation of an artist, particularly painters and their paintings. She not only investigates their language but also other devices which add to its ambiances like music and the landscape. *Pure Lizard* is the latest written poetry collection of Bhatt. The underlying theme of this poetry collection is transformation. The poetry collection is an inspiration and in a way response to music by composers like Telemann, Bob Zieff, and Philip Glass. It also has its roots in the poetic correspondences that Bhatt had with the Welsh writer Gillian Clarke about home and belongingness. Bhatt has innovatively made use of animal and plant imagery to depict the toxic reality of human life in the poetry collection.

From time immemorial, humans have been travelling, migrating in the quest of better living conditions within a nation and across borders. When there is such movement, people not only carry with them their adeptness and expertise but also their culture heritage and memories attached to it. Uprooted from their own culture, traditions and, people they experience a lack of belongingness and a troubled relationship with host nation, trying to adapt and adjust to the host culture, negotiating identities. The Term "diaspora is derived from Greek, meaning dispersal or scattering of seeds. Today, the term diaspora describes the experience of moment or displacement and social, cultural, and political formations that result from it."(Carment 2). The pain feeling alienated and disconnected at the foreign land has been described by one of the poet Satendra Nandan in his poetry *Lines across Black Waters* in a section called "Travelling into a Far Country". The poet in this context remarks

> Home less I had come in search of paradise.
> This house of hell was now all mine.
> Survival is a life sentence.
> Routine becomes a spiritual ritual (1-4)

One of the very prominent critic of the postmodern times Homi Bhabha has described Diasporas as 'unhomed' in his work *The Location of Culture* (1997). The corollary of voluntary migration is the ultimate feeling of lack of belongingness and loss further resulting in identity crisis. The image of self is displaced resulting from suppression of one's culture from the other which brings a sense of homelessness and loss upon the subject. Kim Butler explains the difference between forced and voluntary exile as:

> Types of relationships between the diaspora and the homeland will depend on changes in homeland conditions and the timing of those changes in homeland conditions and the timing of those changes' the forced exile is essentially expelled from and by the homeland, while the voluntary exile has the opportunity to return. (189-219) (12)

Sujata Bhatt's in her poetry majorly focuses on the condition of women and diasporic sensibility. Apart from Sujata Bhatt, Meena Alexander and Chitra Banerjee Divakaruni have also worked on similar lines. Bhatt in her poetry deliberates the conflict of transnationals corollary in flexible identities. She reflects upon how these diasporic people cannot neither completely leave their homelands nor can refashion to the host culture, always swinging back and forth between their authentic identity and the influence of the host culture to which Edward Said describes as "the unhealable rift forced between a human being and a native place, between the self and its true home" (173). These transnationals "serve as the bridge between homeland and their host state. This link to the 'homeland', however, does not only have to be physical, but also includes imagined representation of time and space." (Carment, 4). By the means of her poetry Bhatt elucidates that these diasporic conflicts are a resultant of the political, cultural and the psychic processes. Sentiments of loss, loneliness and nostalgia which communicate diasporic sensibility are the dominant thematic concerns depicted in the verses of Sujata Bhatt. Since travelled extensively Bhatt uses a transnational lens to analyse the way the diasporic groups construct their 'homes' through their involvements with the host culture. Her own state of diaspora manifests in her metrical compositions by the means of her characters and how they negotiate between their cultural values with host culture and still maintaining and carrying along her own authentic identity wherever she goes expressed in poetry *Point no Point:*

> I am the one
> Who always goes
> away with my home
> which can only stay inside
> in my blood my home which does not fit
> with my geography.

Bhatt in her poesy critically dissects the theme of diaspora voicing the struggles of the immigrants in perplexed relationship with tradition and modernity yet not adhering to the culture of hybridity. She associates the issue of home not just to the geographical identity but a part of self, which is deeply engrained in her conscious. These sentiments are expressed in her poetry while she writes:

> But I never left home
> I carried it away
> With me-here in my darkness
> In myself.

The concept of home and nation is not only just recollection of cultural memories, traditions and rituals but story of history in broken narrative, disintegrated by the post-colonial consciousness. In an interview with Vicki Bertram, Sujata Bhatt explains her distress when for the first time she realised, she had to learn English when she moved to New Orleans at the age of five. She also reveals that leaving India made he feel devastated and miserable. "I missed the climate, the atmosphere, the spirit of the place"(14). This experience of Bhatt has been shared in her poem "History is a Broken Narrative". She proclaims her pangs of displacement as

History is a broken narrative.
Pilka story and see where
It will lead you.
You take your language where you get it
Or do you.
Get your language where you take it?
I got my in New Orleans.
In New Orleans, when I was five.
A whole new alphabet to go with the new world.

A similar dilemma is voiced in another piece of poetry "*The One Who Goes Away*" where Bhatt delineates her lose of contact with Indian culture triggering anxiety, depression, feeling of marginality, alienation, and loss of identity.

Sometimes I'm asked if
I were searching for a place
That can keep my soul
From wandering
A place where I can stay
Without wanting to leave. (22-27)

Further on the similar lines Bhatt expresses her cultural shock, a feeling of emptiness, frustration, disillusionment, home-sickness and ultimate multiculturalism lived as an expatriate while negotiating between two incongruent cultures grappling with the question of hybrid identity, pluralities and multi-layeredness. Setting down her thoughts in the poem "*The Multicultural Poem*" avers:

It wants to be read at the border
to the person who checks your passport
The multicultural poem does not expect
the reader to 'understand' anything.
After all, it is used to being misunderstood (52-56)

It is a common predicament experienced by migrators that although they move away from motherland, they can neither adjust to the new world's culture nor can they return to the native, they remain uprooted and cannot become one with their original self. In spite of adopting the new worlds culture there is a sense of otherness that prevails resulting in Identity Crisis. In her poetry Bhatt delineates this diasporic anxiety existing as concomitant to experience of disengagement and displacement. In her poetry she not only enshrines nostalgic memories but also adapts to the new world sharing her experience of different languages and multicultural meanings.

Gender and Feminism in The Poetry Of Sujata Bhatt

Apart from the diasporic anxiety the other themes which are predominant in the poetry of Sujata Bhatt are gender and feminism. Gender differences are a social construct. Simon de Beauvoir, a French philosopher states in her book *The Second Sex* that one is not born as a women, but rather becomes one. For millennia it is believed that women are the carriers of ideologies of cultural roots, tradition, religion but also it is fact well known that by the means of cultural ideologies the identity of women is manipulated, suppressed and constructed. It is the male world which perpetrates the social responsibilities and political stature of women, a politics of sex and power. Culture of a given society effectuates the gender differences:

Gender relationships among the people are determined, in a culture, by a number of different operating authorities like family relations, legal systems etc. These operating authorities are the reason that are responsible for creating certain rules or regulations to control and manipulate Social Institutions. Even the history reveals the fact that women were marginalised and were not given equal rights to use their power to bring changes in the social sphere. (Reeve and Baden 18)

Literature written is evidence of the psychological turmoil women undergo because of cultural identity crisis. Their peripheral existence of women have become a subject of writing of many women writers across the globe and India. To name a few Indian women writes who have worked on the subject are Bharti Mukhrjee, Kiran Desai, Chitra Banerjee Divakaruni, Sujata Bhatt and Jhumpa Lahiri. Sujata Bhatt in her poetry deconstructs the phallocentric ideology which has reduced woman to a kind of an object to whom the right to make choice and subjectivity is refused, rather their identity is treated as a subject to be decided by the society/ men/ patriarchy. Bhatt through her verses transcends the boundary of gender. Adrienne Rich in her book "Of Woman Born: Motherhood as Experience and Institution" avers on the similar context:

> Patrairchy is the power of the fathers: a familial-social, ideological, political system in which men – by force, direct pressure, or thought ritual, tradition, law, and language, customs, etiquette, education, and the division of labor – determine what part women shall or shall not play, and in

> which the female is everywhere subsumed under the male. It does not necessarily imply that no woman has power, or that all women in a given culture may not have certain powers. (57)

The subversion of women often happens by the means of gendered language. Women are usually defined by what they lack. The concept originated from the discourses of Ferdinand de Saussure where in an example he defines 'Darkness' as the absence of light. Saussure elucidates that the word does not have any inherent meaning of its own but rather originates in binary opposition. Sujata Bhatt does not endorse the gendered theory of language and through her poetry tries to reverse the roles. In "The Blue Snake Who Loves Water", the 'river', which is usually gendered as male/he takes the connotation 'she', the only one who can comprehend the poet:

> No one will ever
> Believe me.
> No one, expect maybe the river.
> Last week the river was a muddy slur.
> But now full of blue sky
> The river bends and smiles and Becomes a 'she'. (53-59)

Bhatt disdains the practice of gendered language politics. She has not only labored on the diplomacy of words but also on the cultural violence and culture of violence. The predicament of gender violence is not new. Looking into history it is undeniable that gender violence has taken place virtually in all societies, in the form of violence happening with in the family or culturally fabricated in the form of rituals or traditions. Understanding gender violence requires to analyse the effects of larger social contexts on gender performances. Gender performances are nothing but roles associated to a particular gender embedded into their psychology by phallocentric cultural ideologies. Denying or challenging these traditions or rituals undermine their ethnic identity. These forms of gender violence are concomitant of hierarchical structures of power shaped by cultural meanings. Bhatt reflects and undermines such gendered cultural violence. In fact she denounces any 'culture that encourages violence against women'. In her verses Bhatt openly condemns the well-known sati ritual which endorses the act of woman immolating herself after her husband's death as cultural corollary. In her poem "Buffaloes" she anathematises the ritual of sati:

> The young widow
> Thinks she should have

burned on her husband's funeral pyre.
She could not, for her mother-in-law
Insisted she raised the only son
of her only son.(1-6)

India is a country where we can find contrasting images of women. Culturally women in India are associated with image of Great Goddesses, who are regarded as the ultimate power slaying demons. On the other hand "is the clouded face of the domestic handmaiden trailing behind men in life expectancy, nutrition, health, education, pay, and other rights on the subcontinent" (21). It is surprising how in a country which treats women in reverence also reports high cases of female feticide, which is selective abortion of female fetuses. Daughters of the family are seen as social and economic burden whereas sons are considered to be bringing social security to their parents. Sujata Bhatt strongly objurgate such crime against women. In one of her poetry she describes the devasting reality:

A women kills
her newborn granddaughter
Because She has four already.
A women kills Because
There's not enough money
Not enough milk.
A women kills her newborn daughter
And still eats dinner
And still wears a green sari. (1-9)

A similar essence is carried in another poetic verse by Bhatt called "Voice of the Unwanted Girl", in which the unborn girl is the speaker talking to her mother

Mother, I am the one
You sent away
When the doctor told you
I would be
A girl – In the end they had to
Give me an injection to kill me.
....
Mother, I am the one you sent away
When the doctor told you
I would be a girl-your second girl. (1-7, 20-22)

Bhatt's poetry is a response against the hegemonic assumption of women as subordinate and an object of patriarchal laws. The predicament of sexual harassment, restricted freedom, violence and rape has voiced in her poetry. In another poetry "Reincarnation" Bhatt delineates how women are subject to male dialogue and expected to be heeded to.

> The wise old men
> of India say
> there are certain rules.
> For example, if you loved
> Your dog too much,
> In your next life you'll be a dog,
> Yet full of human memories.
> ....
> The wise old men of India say
> One often dreams
> Of the life one led before. (1-7, 13-15)

Conclusion

Sujata Bhatt's poetry is a reflection of the hypocrisy of Indian culture where at one extremity women are worshipped as divine, as Goddess, as the ultimate power whereas at the other extreme women's body is subject to cultural violence expected to adhere to patriarchal norms about sexuality, marriage, widowhood. Instead of accepting the feminine identity as natural and essential, their identity is rather fabricated. By the means of her poetry Sujata Bhatt stimulates the question of women's unequal position and deliberates on how patriarchy impedes women's action.

Apart from the theme of gender and feminism the other major theme that underlies the poetry of Sujata Bhatt is diasporic sensibility. It is evident that her poetry exhibits a sincerity of feeling which roots from her own diasporic experiences. The research paper is a careful study of her poetry to understand the struggles and challenges of diasporic people by deconstructing it layer by layer. As an immigrant poet Bhatt describes the feeling of nostalgia, alienation, lack of belongingness and negotiating identities. The sentiment of uprootedness, exile, memories, displacement and search of identity which manifest in the poetry of Sujata Bhatt have been analysed from the lens of diaspora.

Works Cited

Bertram, Vicki. "Interview with Sujata Bhatt." *Carcanet Press*, https://www.carcanet.co.uk/cgi-bin/scribe?showdoc=4;doctype=interview.

Bhabha, Homi K. *The Location of Culture*. Routledge, 1994.

Bhatt, S. (n.d.). *Brunizem.* googlereads. Retrieved December 5, 2021, from https://www.goodreads.com/book/show/2049588.Brunizem.

.... (n.d.). *Monkey Shadows.* Carcanet Press – One, two. Retrieved December 5, 2021, from https://www.carcanet.co.uk/cgi-bin/indexer?product=9781800170193.

.... (1995, February). *The Stinking Rose.* Carcanet Press – the stinking rose. Retrieved December 5, 2021, from https://www.carcanet.co.uk/cgi-bin/indexer?product=9781857540482.

.... (1997, January 1). *Point no point: Selected poems by Sujata Bhatt.* Goodreads. Retrieved December 5, 2021, from https://www.goodreads.com/book/show/2049587.Point_No_Point.

.... (n.d.). *Augotora.* Carcanet Press – augatora. Retrieved December 5, 2021, from https://www.carcanet.co.uk/cgi-bin/indexer?product=9781857543810.

.... (n.d.). *Pure Lizard.* Carcanet Press – pure lizard. Retrieved December 5, 2021, from https://www.carcanet.co.uk/cgi-bin/indexer?product=1278

.... "Reincarnation." *Brunizem*, Carcanet, Manchester, 1988.

..........Point to No Point: Selected Poems. Carcanet, 1997.

.... "Buffaloes." *Brunizem*, Carcanet, Manchester, 2012.

..........*The One Who Goes Away*. Carcanet Press, 1989.

.... "History Is a Broken Narrative." *Augatora*, Carcanet, Manchester, 2000.

.... "The Multicultural Poem." *PN Review*, vol. 25, no. 5, 1999.

Butler, Kim. "Defining Diaspora, Refining a Discourse." *Diaspora: A Journal of Transnational Studies* 10.2 (2001): 189-219. Project Muse Web. 10 Dec. 2013.

Carment, David, and Ariane Sadjed. *Diaspora as Cultures of Cooperation Global and Local Perspectives*, Springer International Publishing, Cham, 2018.

Carment, David, and Ariane Sadjed. *Diaspora as Cultures of Cooperation Global and Local Perspectives*, Springer International Publishing, Cham, 2018.

Hazel, Reeves, and Sally, Baden. *Gender and Development: Concepts and Definition.* London: Institute of Development Studies, 2000.

Nandan, Satendra P. *Lines across Black Waters.* CRNLE, Publ. in Assoc. with Academy Press, New Delhi, India, 1997.

Rich, Adrienne, et al. *Of Woman Born: Motherhood as Experience and Institution*, W. W. Norton & Company, New York, NY, 2021.

Raman, Sita Anantha. "Introduction." *Women in India: A Social and Cultural History, Volume 1*, p. 11.

Said, Edward, *Reflections on Exile and other Essays,* Harvard University press, 2002, Pp-173

CHAPTER 6

Feministic Reading of Shiva Trilogy and The Palace of Illusions

Saroj Bala and Rajiv Ranjan Dwivedi

Abstract

Feministic reading of myths and ancient stories has gained traction in our time questioning the concept of patriarchy that often includes all the social mechanisms reproducing and exerting male dominance over women. Mythology helps us to relate to our past, present and future, providing subjective basis to our identities but is at times coloured with shades of patriarchal supremacy. If we trace the contours of the status of women in Indian society, we find that the Vedic era lent due space to women when compared with the times of the Ramayana and the Mahabharata. In fact, the role and status of women has always been a dynamic affair, and therefore, it would be unwise and myopic to draw a line objectively. The Feministic interpretations of our mythical stories are in vogue these days that explore this grey area. Some retellings are subversive and acceptable but some are outright inversive and contrary to the mainstream discourse. Amish Tripathi's characterisation of women in the *Shiva Trilogy* represents their power, skill and authority and Chitra Banerjee Divakaruni's *The Palace of Illusions* treats the epic character of Draupadi as secretive and revengeful. She is aware of her extraordinary fate and the tribulations in her journey. Her advice in administrative matters to Yudhisthar is not disclosed but her say in political and personal affairs is well known. Chitra Divakaruni has narrated the epic from Draupadi's perspective lending it a feminist consideration. The paper aims to analyse and critique the feministic take of these two authors in the *Shiva Trilogy* and *The Palace of Illusions* respectively.

Keywords: Mythology, feministic, women characters, patriarchy, retelling

Introduction

The emergence of mythology inspired literature has raised many women characters to the height of protagonists who were otherwise minor or less important than their male counterparts. Some of these retellings like *The Palace of Illusions* and the *Shiva Trilogy* are subversive but some go beyond subversion, rather tilted towards inversion like short story *Dopdi* of Mahashweta Devi. As feministic perspective of the epics has become quite popular among critics and readers, many writers are trying their luck in this field. Kavita Kane, Chitra Banerjee Divakaruni, Sara Joseph, Devdutt Pattanaik and Mahashweta Devi are familiar names in this genre. In fact epics are not the static details of our history, rather many versions of the same epic are available in different languages. These versions inspire and provide space to the feminists to challenge the patriarchal set up. Feminist theory typically characterises patriarchy as a social construction, which can be overcome by revealing their analytical manifestations. Feminism is a range of social movements, political movements, and ideologies that aim to define and establish the political, economic, personal, and social equality of the sexes. Most forms of feminism characterise patriarchy as an unjust social system that is oppressive to women.

Feminist theory has explored the social construction of masculinity and its implications for the goal of gender equality. The Patriarchal cultures like Indian and South Asian countries' are criticized for oppressive forms of masculinity which limits their horizon of representation. As for Indian mythology, it is full of examples where women are relegated to subordinate positions. Mythology has played an integral role in every civilisation across the world. It has reflected the society's consciousness by revealing inner realms of human mind. It strengthens, empowers, elevates and enriches the ordinary existence of the common folk. The reinterpretations and retellings of epics have been part and parcel of our culture and literature of different Indian languages. Time and again for different reasons re-examining of mythologies has revived the tales of yore. These tales also carry guidelines of morality for the young generation. Although literature ingrained with mythical characters and episodes have always magnetised readers but a new surge of retelling of myths, especially from a feminist perspective has questioned the age old patriarchy. These feministic retellings of the myths have transformed the understanding of the epics like the Ramayana and the Mahabharata. Divakaruni's novel *The Palace of Illusions* is based on the epic the Mahabharata. It is a modern version of the Mahabharata from Draupadi's point of view. The retelling is narrated in the first person and writer has given ample space to other women characters to share their personal experiences. *The Palace of Illusions* presents Draupdi's inner tribulations regarding important contribution of women in personal and royal/ administrative arena/affaires. Chitra Banerjee Divakaruni's compelling protagonist Draupdi is powerful, courageous and determined being who is capable of changing the course of history. The feminist approach is more appealing to the readers as it has modernised the conventional attitude towards women and their roles in the society. *The Palace of Illusions* has presented Draupadi as a woman who raised her voice against the patriarchal norms and the set standards for women characters. She clarifies her position by saying:

> "I'm a queen. Daughter of King Drupad, Sister of Dhristdumna, Mistress of the greatest palace on earth. I can't be gambled away like a bag of coins or summoned to court like a dancing girl."(Divakaruni 190)

She remembers lines from the Nyaya shastra and reminds them; "If perchance a man lost himself, he no longer had any jurisdiction over his wife." (Divakaruni 194)

Amish, a banker turned writer has gained fame through his debut novels of the Shiva Trilogy. His character delineation of women is unique as he finds them without any flaw. Princess Sati, Queen Kali, Ayurvati, Kankhala, Renuka, Krittika, Anandmayi, Veerini etc. are prominent women characters in Shiva Trilogy. They are presented as powerful persons with principles who dare to take plunge and prove their worth through actions. Sometimes, even the Neelkanth is surprised at the determined will of Sati. Sati is the princess of Meluha and the daughter of Emperor Daksha. Despite being a princess, she is discriminated against as a Vikarma who are considered as a carrier of bad fate. Undeterred by this, Shiva accepts her as his soul mate and the better half. Sati is shown as a paragon of virtues who is ready to fight her own father when he strays from the right path. As a law abiding citizen she performs all the duties in spite of being a royal personality. Sati's hidden twin sister Kali is the Queen of the Nagas. Ayurvati, the chief of medicine in Meluha is meticulous and dedicated to her profession. Kankhala, as the prime minister is laudable for taking care of administrative affairs. Amish has been partial in making all the women characters positive and duty bound. He has portrayed all his women characters as bold and intelligent. There is no trace of any negativity in them as if they all are angels. This kind of representation is unrealistic and exaggerative as in actual life we find shades of goodness and evil in men and women.

Review of Literature

Patriarchy is a social system in which society is organised around male authoritative figures. In this system, fathers have authority over women, children and property. It implies the institutions of male rule and privilege and is dependent on female subordination. Our mythology carries the burden of patriarchy in the Indian society. The moral guidelines provided by mythology are time tested and reliable. The patriarchy that has existed since time immemorial is being challenged and writers have been revisiting the past literature and giving voice to the deprived and the marginalised. History bears proof to the fact that women have always been relegated to an inferior position in the society. Their representation in literature and other art forms, too, has been nothing more than being a devoted mother, wife and sister or as an enchantress, a wicked witch, that too only in relation with the protagonists. Recently in literature there has been an upsurge of retelling of myths, especially from a feminist point of view. These retellings of the myths have transformed the understanding of the epics like the Ramayana and the Mahabharata as many modern retellings of the epics have been from perspective of the vanquished characters like Raavan and Duryodhan. Similarly women characters' view point has also become very popular among readers. This shift in the contemporary literature is a result of the Feminist movement throughout the world. Writers are revisiting the past works in order to contemporise the modern human predicaments and preferences.

These writers oppose the conventional boundaries of gender and class, and reinterpret (mis)representation of certain events as reflected in the ancient epics. Devdutt Patnaik's *Sita: An Illustrated Retelling of The Ramayana* (2013), *The Goddess in India: The Five Faces of the Eternal Feminine*(2000), Amish Tripathi's *Sita – The Warrior of Mithila* (2017), Utkarsh Patel's *Shakuntala: The Woman Wronged* (2015), Kavita Kane's Karna's Wife: The Outcast Queen (2014), Sita's Sister (2014), Menaka's Choice (2015) and Lanka's Princess (2017), Chitra Banerjee Divakaruni's *The Palace of Illusion* (2008) are few works which present women characters as the protagonist and give the reign in their hands to draw the picture of their life as they want. These works are famous for retelling the tales from the women's perspective, thus giving a critical insight into the life and longings of female characters. As for Chitra Banerjee Divakaruni's style of retelling, she strongly condemns the shackles of the androcentric society and shows the way for women to come forward and speak about their ambitions and expectation from the society. *Sister of My Heart: A Novel* (1999), *The Conch Bearer* (2003), *The Palace of Illusion* (2008), *Arranged Marriage* (1995) and *The Forest of Enchantment* (2019) are some of the famous works which portray women as the hero, rather Shero and give them enough space to speak up about their lives by providing them a possibility to bring a change in the patriarchal society. The feminist treatment of mythology has generated diverse literary responses from the research scholars and critics from India and abroad. Chitra Banerjee Divakaruni and Amish Tripathi's representation of women characters in *The Palace of Illusions* and the *Shiva Trilogy* respectively has attracted the attention of the critics as their feministic leanings are close to the heart of young readers. Consequently retellings of myth have attracted many a creative and critical representation in the recent times. Two of the major writers who have coveted interest in dealing with the roles of women in myth are Chitra Banerjee Divakaruni and Amish Tripathi.

These works are famous for retelling the tales from the women's perspective, thus giving a critical insight into the life and longings of female characters. While in the epic Draupadi many times remain in the shadow of the male characters, she also revolts against the oppression which symbolises the rise of feminism in Hindu mythology. Menaka, the famous mythical *apsara* (celestial maiden) in Indian mythology, had to make certain life choices and give up her daughter in order to lead a life dictated by patriarchal norms. Similarly, Sita and Ahalya had to undergo severe penance throughout their lives in spite of being pure and innocent. History has been cruel to such women of prominence, but the recent developments in the genre of fiction have given a considerable space to such women whose voices have been suppressed for a very long time. Those who were side-lined for so long have now come up with ideas and dreams of their own. Finally, they are being given a chance of representation in the contemporary mythical fiction. These women are not just epitome of beauty and compassion, but they are also commendable examples of bravery, leadership, strategic competence and – survival of the fittest instinct in the midst of staunch hegemonic practices.

Draupadi of Divakaruni rejects stereotypes set for women by the society and the people around her. She creates a comfortable space for herself by recognising her self-worth and rejecting the society's definition of beauty. The institution of marriage is often seen as a means of attaining political stability and child bearing; it has very little to do with the softer emotions of love and desire for these women. In fact, the marriage for Draupadi is nothing more than a conquest for the heroes to prove themselves worthy in the eyes of the various kingdoms present. But for Draupadi things got harder with the involvement of her mother-in-law Kunti; she had to marry Arjuna (the hero who won the competition) as well as his four brothers to keep Kunti's words. Even though it was unethical for a woman to marry five husbands, this union was justified by sage Vyasa in *The Palace of Illusions*:

> "To keep me chaste and foster harmony in the Pandava household, Vyasa designed a special code of marital conduct for us. I would be wife to each brother a year at a time, from oldest to youngest, consecutively. During that year, the other brothers were to keep their eyes lowered when speaking to me. (Better if they didn't speak at all.) They were not to touch me, not even the tips of the fingers... Each time I went to a new brother, I'd be a virgin again." (Divakaruni, 119-120)

In another retelling of the powerful eponymous character from the Mahabharata, Mahasweta Devi's Draupadi – or Dopdi as she is called – is a rebel who is cornered by the police trying to put down the forces she represents Thus she subverts the narrative of the original plot and instead of acting as a victim becomes an agency to leave the men 'terribly afraid.'

On the other hand the women in the Shiva trilogy set the traits of feminine virtuosity. Shiva takes Sati's counsel and wages war against the evil with her advice. Her twin sister Kali is a wise queen of the Nagas who travels to Egypt to avenge the murder of Sati. Amish has created Kali's character to celebrate the feminine power and glorified her ability which is hidden in her disability. His portrayal of mythical women show their devotion, purity of being and indomitable strength. These qualities make them popular icons of the Sapt Sindhu.

Shiva Trilogy

Influence of feminism on Amish Tripathi is reflected in the portrayal of women characters in his books under Shiva Trilogy and Ram Chandra Series. Feminist theory has explored the social construction of masculinity and its implications for the goal of gender equality. The social construct of masculinity is seen by feminism as problematic because it associates males with aggression and competition, and reinforces patriarchal and unequal gender relations. Sati is the heroine of the Shiva Trilogy who is a Vikarma as she gave birth to a still born child and became a widow. She is ostracised but as a royal person she keeps herself involved in dancing and martial arts. She is no less than Shiva in valor. In *The Oath of the Vayuputras*

Sati's fight with Swuth, the leader of the Egyptian assassins shows her knowledge of war strategies and her confidence. According to the Aten cult every assassin has a belief that one day they will meet a magnificent and worthy opponent and it would be impossible for the man to kill ever again. At that time his duty will be to give his victim an honorable death and give up his profession for the rest of his life. Her last fight with an Egyptian mercenary Swuth, forces her opponent to give her an honorable death. Swuth who considered women as

> 'stupid baby producing machines' and 'only a little better than animals' (477) whispered, when he was going to kill Sati 'Killing you shall be my life's honor, my lady' (478). The dumbstruck assassin is forced to accept her as: his "Final kill" (The Oath of Vayuputra 477)

In her case masculine quality of bravery makes her sacrifice herself for the people of Meluha in one on one dual of Aten. Amish's women characters seem to be inspired from the Sanskrit quote: Yatra Narystu Pujyante ramante tatra Devta (Gods reside where women are respected)

His reverence for women as epitome of goodness is reflected in a non-mythical character called Kankhala who is the prime minister of the Suryavanshi Kingdom, Meluha under King Daksha. Her introduction given by King Daksha reflects her important position in the country. She takes care of the administrative, revenue and protocol matters besides other duties. She commits suicide when she is ordered to go against Dharma and the savior, the Neelkanth. For her Dharma protects those who protect it. Same is the case with Ayurwati, the chief of Medicine in Meluha, a nearly perfect empire. Her marvelous and diligent work saves life of Shiva and Sati from poisonous fatal wounds and weapons like Agniban. Her faith in the legend of Neelkanth makes her a very devout follower of Shiva who is the savior of Meluha from the evil. Yet another character named Tara suffers stoically and devotes her life for the welfare of others. As a Parihan scientist she helps in the production of Somras as well as Daivi astra, Pashupatiastra and Brahamastra. Despite learning about her fiancé Brihaspati's death she continues her work silently. In the vengeance of Neelkanth against evil she convinces others for the use of Pashupatiastra which leads to massive destruction. Acceptance of male dominance by queen of Meluha shows the passive side of feminine nature. Veerini is Princess Sati's mother and wife of King Daksha but in spite of her royal status she is not allowed to keep her

Naga daughter Kali and Naga grandson Ganesh, with her. She opposes Daksha in all the sins he committed for his own happiness. She thanks General Parvateshwar for saving lives of scientists who are repositories of the knowledge of Somras.

Kali's plight as a Naga represents the oppressed Nagas who suffer due to their physical deformities. As the Queen of Nagas she is a fierce fighter who is not ready to give up her cause. As Sati's sister she gives all her support to fight against the evil. She is assertive in challenging ancient rules which discriminated and excluded Nagas from the mainstream. She appoints another brave Naga woman Suparna as the commander of the Naga army in her absence. Major Uma is a dutiful Branga officer at the gates of her country who cannot be bribed or forced to break the law. In spite of losing her only child to plague she is ready to sacrifice her own life for the safety of her country. The Neelkanth gives her solace and comfort by showing the path to victory over the evil. Krittika is a Vikarma as she is a widow whose touch may contaminate others. She is the constant companion to another Vikarma woman, princess Sati. Neelkanth and Sati consider her as the second mother of their son Kartik for her support. As a commoner she knows her role and speaks her mind at the right time without fear. Anandmayi is the Chandravanshi princess who openly woos General Parvateshwar in spite of his being a Suryavanshi, who are their enemies. She represents passion and freedom. She decides to stay with her husband in crisis and goes against her own brother without fearing death. Her faith in the Neelkanth and safety of her life does not stop her from her duty as a wife. She is critical of Suryavanshi's possession of the Neelkanth and consequent arrogance which makes them consider Chandravanshis as evil:

> "The legend is not false and we are obviously not evil. It is just that you are naïve. You have been misled by evil Suryavanshis" (*The Immortals of Meluha* 380)

Unlike the mythical spaces lent to the women, non-compromising in so far all the women characters here are assertive and ready to sacrifice their life for honor. In Shiva's mission to fight for the oppressed, to be the voice of the voiceless almost all women characters are supportive. They are not rigid and ready to change for the sake of Dharma and humanity in general. No woman character is on the side of evil of Somras, discrimination and oppression. Amish's positive approach towards womanhood is laudable as righteousness is their hallmark. Instead of being miserable and wretched in the face of adversities they calmly accept their fate and fight for justice.

The Palace of Illusions

Divakaruni's *The Palace of Illusions* intricately puts forward the voice of women in a world where they need to be heard the most. By putting Draupadi as the narrator, she tries to highlight the unimaginable strengths and capabilities of woman and how they can change history. Women, in general, have never been treated as equal to men since ages. Women were entirely controlled by patriarchal society where they faced suppression and subordination to a great extent by the male domination. But many women raised their voices and fought for their identity and equal positioning in the society. Mythology is full of women characters whose assertion and courage have been guiding examples for the womenfolk. Draupadi is one such character from the *Mahabharta* who stands for resistance against the patriarchy.

The popularity of the epic has encouraged writers to explore the new perspectives of the same old tale. In Divakaruni's *The Palace of Illusions* 'Mahabharata' has become Queen Panchaali's personal narrative which exposes the stereotypical perception of women in the Hindu social setup. In the original epic, Draupadi is secondary to the male characters, whereas in Divakaruni's work Draupadi has been placed at the centre, highlighting her fiery wit, wisdom, courage as well as her flaws. The Palace of Illusion is a novel known for portraying Draupadi as a real human with emotions and ambitions and not merely as a princess. The Guardian's reviews Divakaruni's reimagining as – 'weaves myth into a modern idiom.' Women were asked just to give a helping hand to men, as appears from this comment by Drishtadyumna's tutor in order to stop Draupadi from having the education with his brother. He says:

> – A kshatriya woman's highest purpose in life is to support the warriors in life: her father, brother, husband, and sons. If they should be called to war, she must be happy that they have the opportunity to fulfil to a heroic destiny…' (Divakaruni 26).

Bold and stoic, Draupadi entirely disagrees with these kinds of thoughts and decisions made by the controlling men. She proves her disagreement by saying: – And who decided that a woman's highest purpose was to support men? (Divakaruni 26). Despite the suggestion to focus on feminine chores, she was stern about her aims and learnt everything which a king should know. She used to learn the war skills and take political lessons secretly.

Just like Dopadi of Mahasweta Devi, Draupadi must know that "there isn't a man here that she should be ashamed." Dopadi outrivals Draupadi of Mahabharata in articulating her 'indomitable laughter' after the rape episode rather than being a woman who waited for a male to rescue her. Unlike Draupadi, Dopadi Mejhen knows to execute herself directly without any need of an agency to act for her.

Divakaruni's heroine is an extraordinary woman who from early childhood was very clear about her needs and desires. She had the ability to assert her uniqueness, pride and longing for self-identity which was challenging for the patriarchal society. She was a woman who refused to hold onto a man's identity and desired to create her own. She rejects the name given by her father, Draupadi, which meant daughter of Drupad, as this showed her father's control over her. She says she wanted a more heroic name which would have defined her qualities instead of his father's ownership towards her. Her anguish is seen in these lines:

> – …But daughter of Drupad? Granted he hadn't been expecting me, but couldn't my father come up with something like less egoistic? Something more suited to a girl who was supposed to change the history? …I needed a more heroic name. (Divakaruni 5)

Draupadi was very clear about her decisions, even though if it seemed impossible at that point of time where men were the decision makers of women's lives. She was determined about her education despite the fact that his father as well as the tutor made fun of her. She wasn't allowed to sit along with her brother, Drishtadyumna, as women were devoid of education and was indulged in activities like weaving, dancing, sewing, singing, cooking and works which will help in pleasing men.

Her beauty and womanly attributes were given much more importance than her intelligence and wisdom. At the time of her marriage, when the decisions of women were not at all considered, she spoke up fearlessly during her marriage ceremony where she was to choose her husband. Even though astonished by the hands of destiny when she is divided between the five Pandavas brother, she never gives the control of her life in their hands. Draupadi was much looked down upon because of getting married to more than one man. She was questioned and fingers were raised by society on her character. Karna, even addressed her to be a *whore*, during the game of dice for having several husbands. Despite all the transgressions and horrific experiences, she never lets her courage and confidence shaken. Instead, she takes all the ill treatment as an experience which will help in building her stronger and empower her. In a world where women were not allowed to see a war, Draupadi became the reason for war. Not just Draupadi, other women characters as Kunti, Gandhari, Shikhandi and Uttara have shown that women are much stronger than men and have the capabilities to achieve anything they want. This work shows that even in the ancient times women were bold and determined enough to set standards for them and lead their life on their own terms. Mahasweta Devi, through the character of Dopdi, shows us the other side of the picture. Dopdi embodies all those lower caste women who haven't found a voice in the midst of the men of their own caste as well as the high end officials and police personnels. She is shown in contrast to Draupadi, who had five husbands, thus making her a complete woman with desirable men. Dopdi, on the other hand, was raped by several men for a stretch for many days, thus rendering her voiceless.

Conclusion

Thus, what emerges from the critique is the fact that the two writers, namely Amish Tripathi and Chitra Banerjee Divakaruni have conceived the myth and the characters thereof in different perspectival mould. The feministic take of both the authors is effusively positive across the Texts. Amish justifies their actions and decisions by citing logical reasons. The depiction is slightly idealistic and the unblemished characters of women seemingly lack shades of grey or hints of evil. In order to make the character of Kali acceptable, her revengeful and impulsive nature is justified by the elaboration of her past grudges and injustices done to her by her own father. His portrayal is reverential and as receptacles of power women ably execute duties while abiding by principles. Sati is admired and respected by the Neelkanth who gives Meluha new laws for an equitable society irrespective of the social identities of gender and caste. In case of Divakaruni's *The Palace of Illusions* it is Draupadi who is the protagonist. She is one of the most talked about characters of The Mahabharata yet this novel goes further as it revolves around her struggle and assertion to live life on her own terms. Draupadi, a fire born princess, wife of five Pandavas, is a fierce fighter in the male dominated world of warriors, gods and never ending politics of Kaurva clan. Her assertiveness is unique as she resists her disrobing in the court for self-identity in an overpowering patriarchal setting. In her retelling, Divakaruni deconstructs and rejects the subservient existence of the epic women and her focus is on Draupadi who is seen to have changed the fate of an entire dynasty. However, Draupadi is overly secretive, suspicious and stubborn at times. Yet, there is visibly a very close affinity between the 21st century woman and Draupadi for many Draupadis are trying to survive in this crisis-ridden world.

Works Cited

Divakaruni, Chitra Banerjee. *The Palace of Illusions*, The Doubleday Broadway Publishing Group, Random House, New York, 2008.

Tripathi, Amish. *The Immortals of Meluha*, New Delhi, India: westland ltd. 2010.

Tripathi, Amish. *The Oath of the Vayuputras,* New Delhi, India: westland ltd. 2013.

CHAPTER 7

Breaking Silence: Sufferings of an Afghan Woman in Atiq Rahimi's *The Patience Stone*

Ashwini and P. Kiruthika

Abstract

This paper deals with the sufferings, abuse and mental violence as a means of domestic oppression in the novel *The Patience Stone* by Atiq Rahimi. This novel revolve around the family abuse between a husband and his wife in a single room. The employment of abuse, insult, and rudeness leads to a psychological distress and dissatisfaction to the mainstay character. Rahimi imposes that a husband's abusive manner towards his wife has a large psychological impact affecting her performance, and causing her to lose the value of life. The unnamed protagonist of the novel is oppressed by the male characters and they made an effect on her well-being. The Unnamed woman in *The Patience Stone* is the victim of male oppression. She tells about everything which exemplifies her condition in a patriarchal society. It is an astonishing confession, without constraint, about sex and love and her anger against a man who never realises and understands her. This work uses the complex emotion of a women who is in need of a real partner. This paper accounts the burden of oppression of marital, social, and religious norms of the afghan woman who is fronting to have her basic rights.

Keywords: Afghan woman, Abuse, Mental violence, Male oppression, Rights.

Afghanistan, a landlocked and mountainous terrain is often referred as the "Heart of Asia" and "fulcrum of unprecedented strategic significance." The country's population is, ethnically speaking quite mixed, though the native Afghan retain their indigenous character. "The country has two national languages of Pashtu and Dari which are spoken by majority of Afghans". (Manas VS, 2006). Even though Afghan is highly rich in both natural resource and population, the people of the country are always facing a tautness situation throughout the period from then to till date. Afghans began to take flight their country in April 1978, when the Marxist People's Democratic Party of Afghanistan (PDPA), toppled the government of Muhammad Daoud. The trickle of refugees speeded when the Soviet Union entered in December 1979, seemingly to reinstate order to the country as the PDPA became gradually shattered. While political squabbling was undoubtedly a problem, some bystanders also noted that Afghanistan's leadership had begun bothering the world leaders. "The Soviet attempt to subdue the Afghans was at times predominantly brutal, including the assumed use of torture and collective punishment. By the beginning of 1981, some 3.7 million refugees had fled to Iran and Pakistan". (Samay Ram 2004, p.39).

Smaller numbers of refugees continued to flee Afghanistan for the decades, and this is still in progress, specifically the educated fled for the Taliban's vision of Islamic respectability, with its undecorated restrictions on women's activities, education, social and cultural life. Three decades of war prepared Afghanistan one of the world's most hazardous countries for women and children. After three decades of war and subjugation, an overwhelming number of women remain illiterate in Afghanistan. "Afghan girls are also discouraged, sometimes seriously, from seeking education. More than half of all brides are under 16, and one woman dies in childbirth every half an hour. It is the country with the highest maternal mortality rate in the world" (Khan, 2012). Furthermore, violence against girls or women in Afghanistan reached record levels in 2013, according to the Independent Human Rights Commission of Afghanistan (AIHRC). War in Afghanistan has a disproportionately negative influence on women. Afghan women have borne the brunt of the oppression and are subjected to practices that reflect gender biases. While the international community still expects to liberate and authorise Afghan women in supposed post-conflict Afghanistan. "Afghan women are struggling to inverse awareness that they have no help and that they are victims as they are facing enlarged levels of violence. In spite of being four years beyond conflict and into peace in Afghanistan, violence against women appears to be increasing" (Abirafeh, 2006). Afghan women have been regarded as uninformed, untreated, and voiceless for ages.

This research paper focuses on the novel *The Patience Stone* by Atiq Rahimi, an Afghan citizen, who himself is a refugee. Atiq Rahimi is a French-Afghan writer, director, photographer and translingual author who has published in Dari (Persian) and in French since 1999. As an outspoken author, Rahimi did not withdraw from narrating loss, trauma and fundamentalism already in the 1990s. For his first publication in French, *Syngué Sabour. Pierre de patience*, (*The Patience Stone*) he was awarded the highest literary prize in France, the Prix Goncourt. Rahimi explores challenges of the global Afghanistani diaspora. Propelled by his own encounters of going from Kabul to Paris, Rahimi investigates, with his Kafkaesque accounts, subjects of misfortune, enduring and endurance, all situated in a conflict torn country. This work is an analysis of political violence and the condition of women in the country. This novel is written in the setting of Afghanistan. So, the study is concerned with how Afghan people especially women who have been hegemonised, repressed and killed by Russia, Taliban, America and other ethnic groups. In the novel, many characters have been associated in the politics of Afghanistan directly or indirectly. They were subjugated by Soviet Union in the name of communism and later on they encountered dreadful violence by different religious and ethnic groups like Taliban and Mujahidin. In the last segment of the event as shown in the novel, Afghans are facing the cultural domination and their conservative religious minds has promoted terrorism and violence.

The novel evolves around the perspective of woman, for whom war carries only suffering and the woman is awaiting for freedom. The novel tells about the frantic dilemma and unjustified cruelty done to the woman in Afghanistan. *The Patience Stone* depicts the social, economic, religion, and political aspects of Afghanistan. It shows how beliefs and ethics are degraded politically, socially, economically, and sexually in Afghanistan that can alter any mindful citizen in the world against immorality. The novel tells about the wife of a soldier who is lying unconscious with a bullet in his neck, the unnamed protagonist of *The Patience Stone* cares for her husband, changes his drip and puts drops in his eyes, all the while confessing herself of the truth about her feelings toward him against a situation of mortar fire and gunshots. "His eyes, even smaller now, have retreated into their sockets. His gaze is fixed on the ceiling, on the exposed, blackened, rotting beams." (Rahimi, 2010, p. 2). Thus he becomes her – Sang-e Saboor, a mythical stone that according to Persian folklore absorbs the pain of those who expose themselves to it, and then it ultimately explodes. Atiq Rahimi want to hold the readers stuck with a captivating account of the shocking conditions of the women in his country, ravaged by war, barbarism and under-development. The author tries to make it clear that Afghan women are facing hardships, the splodging of men, social taunts, and the fight against male oppression.

As Hosseini said in introduction of *The Patience Stone* – "For far too long, Afghan women have been faceless and voiceless." (Rahimi, 2010, p.1). The violence against the afghan women is the most universal yet least familiar human rights abuse in the world. At least one woman in every three has been beaten, forced into sex, or otherwise abused in her lifetime. Most often the abuser is a member of her own family known as the intimate partner abuse (The Population Information Program, Center for Communication Programs, 1999) Partner abuse can take a variety of forms including physical assault such as hits, slaps, kicks, and beatings; psychological abuse, such as constant belittling, intimidation, and humiliation; and forced sex. Abuse of women and girls, regardless of where and how it occurs, is best understood within a "gender" framework because it curtails in part from women's and girl's subservient status in society. In this novel, the unnamed protagonist shares all her emotions barely to her bedridden husband, but at the very end of the novel, she is attacked by her own husband as she told her intimate desires which according to him is taboo. A common form of violence against women around the world is abuse by their husbands or other intimate male partners.

The Patient Stone outlines a strong willed and obstinately firm Afghan unnamed woman whose rights had been impoverished in a male dominated society all her life. It exposes clearly about her hopelessness and unpardonable oppression. Her husband was paralysed by war injuries and nursed through a tube. She always did was to plead Allah to make her husband well again so that he could return to her and their two small daughters. "Her gaze wanders, joining his vacant gaze somewhere among the dark". 'Al-Qahhar, Al-Qahhar, Al-Qahhar. . . ' (Rahimi, 2010, p. 6). She favoured and cared for him at all hours of the day and night, adjusting the intravenous line, although she herself suffered from hunger and was threatened by the infrequent acts of war that erupted near their home. The woman appeared to be oblivious to her fate. On the other hand, she shown incredible bravery by allowing herself to confront her oppressive life at her husband's side in extended, soul-searching monologues. She gradually became aware of the severity of the disparities she had grieved as a result of this process. Through her bold and shocking confession, the woman revealed how she despised her husband, her dissatisfactions with him, her most intimate secrets, her wants and hopes, and the wounds and tragedies she had suffered at his hands. Her father handled her family in a disrespectful and unadorned manner throughout her upbringing. He enjoyed making wagers on the quail fights. He came home and beat up her wife and their seven girls after losing the bet. She was a rebel by allowing the cat to eat his exorbitantly priced quails. He had a habit of punishing her excessively. As part of the wager, he even handed up his second daughter to marry an elderly man.

> He had no money left to honour his bet, so he gave my sister instead. At twelve years old, my sister was sent to live with a man of forty!' Her nails leave the roots of her hair, and move down her forehead to finger the scar at the edge of her left eye. 'At the time, I was only ten. . . no. . . ' She thinks about it. 'Yes, ten years old. I was scared. Scared that I too would become the stakes of a bet. (Rahimi, p. 58)

When it came her turn to marry, she was encouraged to have a forced marriage in place of her younger sister. She had been engaged for almost a year and then married for three years to an uncaring man, as she had never seen or touched him before that day. She got her period a week before the wedding night because she was so afraid of seeing her spouse for the first time. Despite the fact that she was a virgin, she was so scared that what if she did not bleed that night because blood was evidence of her virginity. When he started touching her, she didn't say anything and claimed to be asleep. He became enraged when he discovered she had her period after the intercourse, and he began to beat her. The author aims to highlight how Afghan men's minds are veiled by their so-called culture in all of these instances, as the woman in the narrative are considered as subordinate. He left her to struggle alone in his house while he went to fight since it was his honour, and she felt quite forlorn. She was forced to live with her husband's relatives after he abandoned her. When she was bathing, his brother would constantly keep an eye on her. Only his father treated her with respect. Her husband's injuries condensed him silent, letting his wife to open up more and more and to speak openly of the problems in their marriage without fearing punishments. Rather than merely praying, she was able to bare her soul and make the confession. She took a stand beside her husband and confessed that she found him disgusting and called him "a monster" for all he did to her. At the same time, he felt a strong sense of catharsis and it rejuvenated her life spirit to finally be able to talk to him about it all, without being broken up, without being criticized. The man, who was just lying there mute but still breathing, was more to her like the "patience stone" in whom she revealed everything, who immersed all her pain, unhappiness and misery until one day it would burst. In the end it all, unexpectedly, came to head in desolation.

> He moves closer, grabs her again, heaves her up against the wall. The woman looks at him ecstatically. Her head is touching the khanjar. Her hand snatches it. She screams and drives it into the man's heart. There is not a drop of blood. The man, still stiff and cold, grabs the woman by the hair, drags her along the floor to the middle of the room. Again he bangs her head against the floor, and then brusquely, wrings her neck. (Rahimi, p.135).

Since the study tries to discover the domestic life experiences and sufferings of Afghan women in case of the depiction of patriarchy society, feminism approach is used. Feminism emerged as a natural reaction to society's deportment towards women. According to Holbrook (1989, p.48), feminism in general is a historical movement to give women equal politic, social, and economic right with men. Feminists try to struggle against behaviour given by patriarchal society. They propose to put away the images given to them by men and to prosecute the equality of politic, social, and economic rights. They also wanted to be able to rely on men and have their own independence from patriarchal culture. Furthermore, since the advent and development of feminism, which analyses and raises awareness among women, women's struggles to gain freedom have become a particularly prevalent issue in literature. Feminism is a critique of current socioeconomic conditions that have kept women out of male-dominated culture, social, sexual, political, and intellectual activities. According to radical feminist, they claim the patriarchal and gender are characteristics by power, dominance, hierarchy and competition. It must be over tuned on the way to women's liberation (Tong, 2018, pp.46-47). The novel *The Patience Stone* has been analysed from a feministic perspective and the feministic theory that is used in this study is radical feminism because the essential idea of this feminism is the patriarchy system that happens in the society of Afghanistan and becomes the culture of the people.

In the novel, oppression, powerlessness, cultural imperialism, exploitation, marginalisation, and violence are used to describe the hardships of Afghan domestic women. Male oppression of Afghan domestic women has physical and psychological consequences, including insults, beatings, sexual abuse, and murder. The socio-cultural context of the country in which the narrative is set influences this type of portrayal. The unidentified woman is insulted, beaten, and sexually abused in the selected novel. The unidentified woman is enraged by her husband's mental torment and power, and she curses him out of agony. The impact of all the accumulation brought her depression and made her a talk-active woman. The novel *The Patience Stone* ends when the unnamed woman dies by her husband who confessed all her desires and emotion. The novel shows the oppressed Afghan domestic women who is dominated by patriarchy system and the problematic and ethnic war of Taliban in Afghanistan. Afghan women subjugation occurs in the novel because of lack of power, jealousy, control, social stress and rearranged marriage. "To kill or to be killed are high impacts of male oppression towards Afghan domestic women in this novel". (Rahimi, 2014). There are few aspects which endow to high rate of domestic violence counter to women. One of the reasons are like economic factors which grounds women to be reliant on their husband enormously. In this novel, as the protagonist is in lack of education and due to her country's war atmosphere, she was effusively dependent on the male characters like her father and her husband. Other common factors are, patriarchy, high spiteful to each other and difference of opinion. In patriarchal society, women are deliberated as subordinate to men because of their place in the family and the society. When men feel they are greater to women, barbarism is more potential to occur.

The ideology of placing the male power above women has been long-standing, co-opted and imposed on the society in many government regulation or religious laws. According to Robinson and Bessel (2002, p.12), within a traditional culture, there is no room for women as individuals. She implies that women are continually reminded of their inherent nature, and particularly of their household and reproductive responsibilities, namely to clean, to cook and to raise children. The unnamed woman is expected to be happy in the role of a faithful companion of her husband and as good and caring mother rather than pursuing her own rights. In this novel, the woman is just a source material for the husband family and she is never asked about her dreams. In the meantime, the history of Afghanistan speaks the fact that, alongside the cruelty imposed by combat, this country is among the strongest patriarchal societies that creates more restricted, oppressed conditions for women. However, many scholars disclose that "Afghan women fight to survive during the war and take part in social participations to reclaim their rights, and further their enhancement over the history of Afghanistan" (Barfield, 2010). As Appel and Richter (2007, p.170) assert, narrative has an implicit influence on the way people view the world as well as shifting people's worldview. Much of the related literature on this theme speaks to the fact of the prevailing portrayal of Afghan women as submissive victims of war and violence, to be liberated only by the Western military intervention.

The brutal killing of women are seen till date in all Social Medias and in newspapers. A massive question mark hangs over the fate of Afghan women and their rights till date. The world must implement whatever control it has remaining to preserve the rights and try to protect the needs of Afghan women. The Taliban regime destroyed Afghan institutions and the economy, which was already distraught by decades of fighting and the Soviet scorched-earth counter-insurgency strategy. The resulting extravagances unfavorably affected women and children (WHO, 2019, p. 23). As in the novel the woman who is abundantly dependent on her husband, the women of Afghanistan are still fully reliant on men in their families for authorisation to access health care, attend school, and work. "Forgive me, as she strokes his arm. 'I'm tired. At breaking point. Don't abandon me, you're all I have left." (Rahimi, p.14)

Many Afghan men remain deeply conventional as the husband in the novel. Typically, families allow their girls to have a primary or secondary education, usually up to puberty and then will proceed with arranged marriages. A recent study showed that only fifteen percent of Afghan men think women should be permitted to work outside of their home after marriage, and two thirds of men criticize that Afghan women now have too many rights (Vanda Felbab-Brown, 2019). The woman feels side-lined, disregarded, patronised, and harassed on a regular basis, as if they're trying to persuade her to return to the kitchen, which is the place where women should be in the eyes of male Afghans. People all around the world should stand united to the women and children of Afghanistan as they too have DREAM and no other as the unnamed woman in the novel should die due to people's so called orthodox notions.

The very high prevalence of domestic suffering and violence against women in Afghan society is a strong evidence of this tragedy, as the protagonist is murdered by her husband. Because so much violence and suffering occurs in the novel, the house, which is supposed to be a safe and secure place for women, becomes a particularly deadly location for them. The anonymous woman loses her identity as a wife in her husband's house as a result of patriarchal systems in society and culture. Men must accept their responsibilities as offenders and endeavour to improve their attitudes and actions toward women before real and fundamental change can occur. If the anonymous woman's husband had radical thoughts, he would not kill her. As a conservative and culturally trained individual, he was forced to murder her wife when she revealed all of her deepest secrets. The paper aims not to generalise the experiences of all Afghan women, but rather to recognise the experiences and sufferings as valuable and important in understanding the nature of grief of most of them. The unnamed protagonist is also a worthy human being who deserved to have a free and fair life, without violence. In order to challenge and transform the oppressive gender relationships taught and reinforced in society, schools, and religions, a gender education is urgently needed in the educational and religious framework. Stereotypes of submissive, meek, and docile women are unjust and detrimental to women's self-esteem, justifying violent acts, and must be demolished.

Works Cited

Abirafeh, Lina. *Freedom is only won from the inside: 'Domestic violence in post-Conflict Afghanistan.'* 2006.

Appel, M., & Richter, T. "Persuasive effects of fictional narratives increase over time." *Media Psychology*. 2007. p.170.

Barfield, Thomas. *Afghanistan: A Cultural and Political History*. Princeton, NJ: Princeton University Press, 2010.

Holbrook, David. *Images of Woman in Literature*. New York: New York University Press.1989. p.48.

Khan, Ejaz. *Top 10 countries with highest rape crime*. 2012.

Manas, VS. *A Political Geography of Afghanistan*, Bookwell Publication. 2006.

Rahimi, Atiq. *The Patience Stone* (Translated from the French by Polly McLean). London: Chatto & Windus. 2010.

Rahimi, Atiq. "*Afghan Culture Now!* A Conversation with the Afghan Writer and Filmmaker." 2014.

Robinson, Kathryn, and Bessell, Sharon. *Women in Indonesia: Gender, Equity and Development*. 2002. p.12

Samay Ram, *The New Afghanistan, Pawn of America,* New Delhi, Manas Publication. 2004. p.39.

The Population Information Program, Center for Communication Programs. 1999. *Ending Violence against Women.* In Issues in World Health. Volume XXVII, Numbe December 1999. Maryland: The Johns Hopkins University School of Public Health.

Tong, R., & Botts, T.F. *Feminist Thought: A More Comprehensive Introduction* (5th ed.). Routledge. 2018. doi.org/10.4324/9780429495243

Vanda Felbab-Brown's interviews with several rural Afghan women and Ghazni, October 2019.www.brookings.edu/essay/the-fate-of-womens-rights-in-afghanistan/

World Health Organisation, WHO Afghanistan Country Office 2019 Report, February 2019, p. 23

CHAPTER 8

Unnoticed Whimper Voiced in Manju Kapur's *Difficult Daughters*

Manju Kumari K.

Abstract

Women writers have brought a new scope to Indian English fiction with their deep insight towards men and matters. The concept is to create a major trait of the present contemporary writing towards wisdom, fortune and rich understanding. The writers mainly deal with the habitation and position of women in the society, their patriarchal problems and plights from all the periods of time. The complexity of life, various histories, cultures and structures of values, the woman's question, despite basic solidarity, needs to be tackled in relation to the social-cultural situation. The impact of patriarchy on the Indian women novelists have tried to evolve their individual stream of feminism grounded in reality. The Indian women novelists have their individual anxieties, significances as well as their specific ways of dealing with the difficulty of their female protagonists.

Keywords: Patriarchy, rebel, emergence, individual self, fulfillment.

Introduction

In patriarchal, societal and cultural and religious constructs, the bitter experiences, the miserable humiliation, the helpless cries of women go unnoticed. The shame and the suffering they have been exposed to for years have made their situation even worse than beasts. Indian women especially have faced this miserable traumatic situation for long. Male domination tries to overpower her, and the society and culture suffocates her. Hence women are suffocated by both internal and external powers.

Women either suffer in a meticulous world dominated by men, who, in the guise of father, bother or husband or suffer under the ideologies of the society, culture and custom. But women endure all these sufferings and remain oppressed until the time comes for them to emerge from these oppressions and look out for their survival.

This emergence may result in success or failure. Women will either be the victim or the survivor, yet another group remain as endurers.

The portrayal of women as the silent sufferer and defender of the tradition and traditional values of family as well as the society has undergone a tremendous change and is no longer presented as passive character. Women rebelling against the traditional role, breaking the silence of suffering, trying to move out of the caged existence and asserting the individual self-go through untrodden and difficult path. The womanhood is trying to bring them and yet they don't wish to break up the family bonds. This feminine consciousness explored by women writers leads to self-discovery of the women characters, who realise their inner strength.

Among the path breaking women writers Manju Kapur who has carved a niche for herself portrays women who refuse to remain silent, are educated individuals who demand their own space, question traditions and project a self which is free if guilt and various stigmas. This Paper focuses on the woman character, Virmathi in Manju Kapur's *Difficult Daughters* whose struggle to become a New Woman in her life.

Manju Kapur in her debut novel *Difficult Daughters* depicts many generations of women. The major theme that emerges is the lives of women during India's struggle for independence. Kapur describes her protagonist Virmati as a 'new woman' who breaks many social norms to gain her selfhood. In all her novels traditional, transition and modernity are the stages through which the women are passing. The remarkable changing image of women to support the feminism viewpoint runs as a feeling through the novel.

Difficult Daughters, is Kapur's tribute to the country's celebration of 60 years of independence in which she asks the protagonist Virmati to fight against taboos, social and family restrictions and manmade rules for women. The novel sets against the back drop of the struggle for independence, the novel are divided into three generations, with the values, mind-sets and relationship. *Difficult Daughters* brings out the emotional attachment of almost three generations. Amritsar is the place where almost all the events took place from time to time. Virmati remarks about Amritsar as, "Amritsar was a place I associated with my mother. Without her, I am lost. I lost for ways to connect." (DD 4)

Since Virmati was eldest daughter of Kasturi, she was forced to look after all her brothers and sisters and she assisted her mother in the nourishment of all of them. During the pregnancies of her mother, Virmati was always busy in arranging the household affairs and managing the thing as far as possible. Virmati, in her early age was given the task to handle the household responsibilities. She was bound to assist her mother in her every pregnancy. On the other hand, the condition of Kasturi was also not better. She had to pass through the pain and agony in her every pregnancy. She has to hear the comments of her sister-in-laws every time when she becomes pregnant. Manju Kapur writes about such thoughts in a pensive manner. Virmati has to watch as a silent spectator.

Virmati has some different notions in her life. She does not seem to be of compromising nature. She seems to be always involved in tussle with Lajwanti. Even the small things disturb her too much. Her study in Amritsar also puts in conflicting situation. The incident is evident with Virmati's character where she suppresses her inner most feelings for every pain she undergoes in life one such incident is when, Virmati was offended by this implication of herself as a pleasure loving female, and did not reply. If Lajwanti was offended by her niece's rudeness, she hid this fact. She did not want to initiate a longish stay, was paying for with a quarrel. (DD 14)

Virmati's one visit to Lahore changes her attitude. She wants to fulfil her dreams by making her educated but her dream of going Lahore is still far away. Virmati returns to Amritsar along with her father with heavy heart and it was obvious that her family did not wish her to be further educated.

Virmati's meeting with Professor Harish provides him an opportunity to realise her dreams. Her family appointed Harish to look after Virmati's study. Virmati develops intimacy with him as it is quite natural. The professor also found the perfect student in Virmati who was quite eager to realise her dreams at any cost. The Professor also finds the perfect companionship in Virmati. He is now ready to grab the occasion with smartness. The glimpse of Virmati gives the professor a real pleasure and emotional fulfilment. The affair between the Professor and Virmati is deep. In the typical traditional society in India it is impossible to think about such kind of relationship between the teacher and the girl student. The professor is quiet aware of his own limitation. He knows the consequence of such of affair and the society which does not allow him to do so. Virmati is at a confusion whether the professor would be there for her, her mind is filled with questions.

Manju Kapur has considered the difficulties of the protagonist, Virmati as a Socialist. For Kapur, feminism is both a concept and movement in the present century and is a new dimension to contemporary thinking. She reflects the internal and external conflict of Virmati. On one hand, Virmati was aware of professor's love for her but on the other side, Virmati was not ready to betray her father's faith in her. Even though Virmati was sure about professor's position and status she had decided to marry and above all she had an idea, 'I would be lucky if I found a husband like my father.' (DD 2)

Kapur's Virmati is a new woman of colonial India and stand as a symbol to explore the possibilities for modern women in education and economic independence who experience disgrace and disappointment in their colonial life. The novel obtains greater significance when read from the point of women struggle for identity.

Virmati's entire life can be divided into three phases. The first phase begins when she deserts her family, her religious and political authorities that try to point her liberty and identity. Her relationship with Harish although provides an escape from a loveless traditional arranged marriage, is itself secret and disturbing providing her only a little togetherness behind 'curtained windows'. In the second phase Virmati makes a retreat to her family to be reunited with her mother but fails miserably and cries out, "Will there be any change in my life. I wonder" (DD 255). However, Veena Singh asserts that "in Virmati there struck the head and the heart, physical and moral Virmati gives way to her heart and body". (DD 168) In the third phase finally Virmati revolves her crisis and resumes her strength when the nation is on trial. Virmati decides to take a firm stand.

Thus, a woman like Virmati should basically strive towards a fine independent partnership. But if she feels suffocated, then voice ought to be raised and here should be a total breaking away. But merely transcending societal norms is not enough. A woman should be aware in the inner strength of womanhood. A significant revolution for a woman can be fetched only from inside by being independent in the deeper wisdom.

Work Cited

Kapur, Manju. *Difficult Daughters*, Faber and Faber, 1998. pp. 1-282.

Malik, Seema. "Crossing Patriarchal Threshold: Glimpses of the Incipient New Woman in Manju Kapoor's *Difficult Daughters*" *The Commonwealth Review*. vol 9 no.2, 1997-1998, pp. 132-137.

Mishra, R.K. "Indian Women's Assertion of Individuality and Identity in the Social and Familial Life: a Thematic Study of the Novels of Manju Kapoor." *The Atlantic Literary Review Quarterly* vol. 14 no. 2, Apr-Jun, pp. 111-118.

CHAPTER 9

Feminism and Post colonialism in the Perspective of Sri Aurobindo

Rajiv Kumar Singh

Abstract

The question of feminism and post colonialism doesn't seek an answer anywhere else, but in the Consciousness of Supramental beings. Frankly speaking, the human mind itself is not constitutionally capable of visualising the Subtle Conscient being unless it is under the command of the Supreme Consciousness. Sri Aurobindo, a great Yogi and literary giant of the Indian soil has clearly pointed out the scope for human beings to have oriented mental force for the realisation of the one Divine or one Cosmic force working on the principle of integrity. Although, Sri Aurobindo was a Yogi and his Yogic vision is a blissful blend of Science and poetry on the one hand and yoga and poetry on the other. It is his Yogic consciousness that visualises the Truth in the centre of the being of man. The Truth is being manifested in his epic Savitri in particular and in his other works in general as well. The present paper attempts to explore the tract for the human being as shown by Sri Aurobindo in his Evolutionary theory.

Keywords: Supramental, Supreme Consciousness, Yogic vision, Subtle Conscient, Integrity

Introduction

The present paper also attempts to seek and reveal about the different kinds of conflicting forces working in postcolonial minds. In this perspective, it is not too easy to understand the forces working behind the human minds since these forces work in posterity. Postcoloniality, feminism and theory like Dalit and Subaltern are essentially the product of separate Consciousness of human beings. In other words, the dominance of the separate consciousness is the root cause of all miseries. As such, these theories are the results of those forces, which weaken and break the chain of integrity. Admittedly, the postcolonial mind shows the separate consciousness and it is essentially a reaction to the acts of the divisive consciousness. Postcolonial mind is visible on the planes below the spiritual consciousness: "Whereas from a Masculine perspective, independence ushered in the defining new condition of postcoloniality, for women there was no such break."[1] "All political programs of today, weather feminist or fundamentalist are products of their own age……"[2]

In this context it is imperative to mention here that the consciousness of Euro centricity or to say, the Western world, denying the existence of others is certainly an egoistic consciousness or the divisive consciousness. In this context, it would be appropriate to mention here that European modernity dating back to the 15th and the 16th centuries emphasised the optimal use of resources in order to get maximum profits. It was not simply optimal use of resources rather a kind of exploitative act for the natives. It was the result of their separative and egoistic consciousness that compelled them to expand themselves in more and more countries outside Europe so that they could get labour and raw materials and markets for their products. So, being under the command of separative consciousness, structures of colonial domination were, of course, racialised in the sense that natives were created and administered by acknowledging and reinforcing the racial difference between the natives and the colonial masters. The postcolonial literature doesn't view life integrally, for which we require it to evolve to the spiritual planes of consciousness.

> "A Spiritual evolution, an evolution of consciousness in Matter in a constant developing self-formation till the form can reveal the indwelling spirit, is then the keynote, the central significant motive of the Terrestrial existence."[3]

Sri Aurobindo further explains:

> "This significance is concealed at the outset of involution of the spirit, the Divine reality, in a dense material in conscience; a veil of in conscience, a veil of insensibility of Matter hides the universal consciousness-force which works within it, so that the energy, which is the first form of the force of creation assumes in the physical universe, appears to be itself inconsistent and yet does the works of a vast occult intelligence. The obscure mysterious creatrix ends indeed by delivering the secret consciousness out of its thick and tenebrous prison; but she delivers it slowly, little by little, in minute infinitesimal drops, in thin jests, in small vibrant concretions of energy and substance, of life, of mind, as if that were all she could get out through the crass obstacle, the dull reluctant medium of an inconscient stuff of existence."[4]

In fact, the 'secret consciousness' which ultimately evolves out of the 'thick and tenebrous prison' is the Supramental Consciousness. Since, the Supramental Consciousness is the integral consciousness, it has no ego; hence no conflict, – the conflict which has given birth to colonialism and post colonialism. It sees and feels all as itself and acts in that sense. Sri Aurobindo says that the supramental being 'would act in a universal awareness and a harmony of his Individual self with the total self, of his Individual will with the total will, of his individual action with the total action'[5] on account of being the integral consciousness. The Supramental Consciousness is, in fact, the transcendent consciousness.

Certainly, post colonialism is a reaction against colonialism for the growth of the ignored arena of the rest of the world. It is against the egoistic consciousness of the Western world, which has an eclipsed vision of the truth. The denial of the existence of others by the Western world clearly indicates the lower level of consciousness for which Sri Aurobindo speaks of the Supramentalisation. Sri Aurobindo, a Yogi of unknown eternal height, paves the way for the right understanding and tries to end the different conflicting forces of human beings. He shows that the divisive consciousness has to take refugee into the Spiritual, and ultimately has to culminate into the supramental consciousness for an integral view of life, the vision of which for the first time comes into the being of Sri Aurobindo:

> "Feminist criticism's self-transformations over the past several decades as it engages with both critiques from within and encounters from without – encounters with psychoanalysis, Marxism, Poststructuralisms, ethnic studies, postcolonial theory, and lesbian and gay studies – have produced complex proliferation of work."[6]

When we go through the British literature such as TS Eliot's *Wasteland etc.* we find that the poet seeks to evolve to the Spiritual plane of Consciousness, for which he takes refugee into Lord Buddha, and the Spiritual consciousness of the Upanishadic Rishis having an urge for 'Shantihi', – the peace which, Sri Aurobindo says, is the foundation for the spiritual and the supramental evolution of consciousness. We have to refuse reactions to establish peace into our being resulting in our soul transformation which Sri Aurobindo calls 'Psychicisation'. It is the psychicisation of our instrumental selves, – body, life and mind. Psychicisation of body life and mind takes place when Soul, which is a portion of the Divine in our being at the centre of these instrumental selves, takes over their governance as a result of which they undergo a divine transformation, and come to be receptive to what comes down from the invisible divine planes of existence. The psychicisation of these instrumental selves is the foundation of the spiritual and the supramental evolution of man. Sri Aurobindo says:

> "This psychic development and the psychic change of mind, vital and physical consciousness is of the utmost importance because it makes safe and easy the descent of the higher consciousness and the Spiritual transformation without which the supramental must always remain far distant."[7]

Consequent upon the psychicisation of the instrumental selves there will be no gravitational pull of body, life and mind while ascending the spiritual planes of consciousness. In such an urge for peace, – 'Shanthi Shanthi Shanthi'[8] T.S. Eliot comes to be more postcolonial than the so-called postcolonial writers. No Euro centricity or the egoistic consciousness of the western world exists in him. In fact, he emerges as a true postcolonial as he wishes to move on the path of the essential Divine consciousness shown by the ancient Rishis who were born on the land of India. Restoration of such a 'Divine Consciousness' must be the sole objective of the postcolonial consciousness.

It is important to mention here that Shakespeare's principal tragedies also indicate the evolution of a spiritual consciousness as Othello, King Lear and Macbeth undergo evolutionary change of consciousness. Unless we realise the Transcendent of which life is a 'walking shadow',[9] life will continue to be 'a tale, told by an idiot, full of sound and fury, signifying nothing.'[10] Such a realisation takes place in Macbeth at the fag end of his life. It is in this realisation that evolutionary change of consciousness takes place in him. The same thing is seen in Hamlet's assertion that he loves Ophelia more than forty thousand brothers could do. He reveals love of the transcendent consciousness into which all, the different streams of human love go to merge to be indissolubly one. In his dying speech ' killing myself, to die upon a kiss'[11], – 'kiss' which symbolises his love for Desdemona –, Othello yearns to be one with her who continues to exist in her Divine Self on the invisible supraphysical planes of existence, – the planes which are seen by the Yogis and Rishis on their yogic planes of consciousness. In such a yearning, he is conscious of her divine self, which is beyond the mortal touch. Such a consciousness of Othello of her Divine Self-shows his consciousness rising towards the plane of spiritual consciousness. This spiritual consciousness culminates into the supramental consciousness for which we have to turn inward to look into our deeper selves for evolving our latent spiritual and supramental consciousness as Sri Aurobindo has shown in his epic *Savitri* in the yoga of King Ashwapati and Savitri's yoga. Further, "colonialism is a violent conjugation where the sense of self develops through a negotiation rather than a separation, a relation rather than a disjunction, with the other."[12] "Postcolonial theory is a method of interpreting, reading and critiquing the cultural practices of colonialism, where it proposes that exercise of colonial power is also the exercise of racially determined powers of representation."[13]

On having gone through the works of Sri Aurobindo we see that feminism is also a product of separative consciousness because the question of having proper rights in all respects in the society arises when the person concerned is deprived of the same. Feminist theory argues that the representation of women as weak, docile and seductive is rooted in and influences actual social conditions, where she does not have power, is treated as a sex object or a procreating machine, has fewer political and financial rights and is abused. Therefore, feminism is a worldview that refuses to delink art from existing social conditions and practices. Feminism explores the cultural dimensions of women's material life.

Generally, it is seen that cultural texts naturalise the oppression of women through their stereotypical representation of women as weak, vulnerable, seductress, obstacle, sexual object or procreating device. Further, it is a political and theoretical stance, which promotes inequalities between men and women. Both men and women are not natural but social. As such, religion, family, education, arts, and knowledge systems are all social and cultural 'structures' that enable the perpetual reinforcement of this inequality.

> "Sex is biological, but the values and meanings associated with the female and male body are socially ascribed. Gender is this system of values and meanings. If sex and biology is nature, then gender is about the social and, therefore, culture. 'Female' and 'male' refer to the biological characteristics, while 'feminine' and 'masculine' refer to the social values assigned to these. Postmodern theories of gender argue that gender is not a fixed or stable category across the world. Gender, like a text, is a performance, the playing out of roles, that has to be repeated and validated within specific social and cultural contexts, but which is also open to contest and negotiations."[14]

Hence, the woman has always been represented as a territory to be conquered and dominated. Equating the nation with the mother as motherland is an old trope in cultural practices across the world. This equation has been a source of contention among feminists because, as they see it, it enables the male to control the woman and the country, even as this control masquerades as protection. Anti-colonial movements appropriated the woman as the boundary figure to be protected against the colonial male. If the nation is gendered then nationalism is patriarchal nationalism. This is all about the lower level of consciousness or to say the egoistic consciousness for which Sri Aurobindo has spoken of triple transformation – psychic, mental and vital. Sri Aurobindo has viewed the dimensionality of this terrestrial existence in the perspective of the supramental consciousness which Sri Aurobindo has discovered on a very high plane of yogic consciousness, – the supramental consciousness which, as the very word 'supramental' itself reveals, exists beyond the plane of the mental consciousness, that is to say, beyond the plane of dimensionality. The mental consciousness which is the apex of the dimensional creation is the divisive principle of consciousness, – Consciousness which is the basic thing in existence as Sri Aurobindo finds on such a high plane of his yogic consciousness. But such an apex is having two regions of which the upper one is pervaded by the Spiritual consciousness. In other words, this upper region is the plane of the Spiritual mind consciousness, – the 'Superconscient' as Sri Aurobindo terms it. He has discovered four planes of the spiritual consciousness on the plane of Mind where we have the knowledge and realisation of the one Divine, One Cosmic Self, more and more as we ascend these spiritual planes of consciousness, – the High Mind, the Illumined Mind, the Intuitive Mind, and the Overmind as he calls them. The High Mind, which is the first plane of the spiritual mind consciousness, or to say, the Superconscient plane of our being, exists above the plane of the mental mind consciousness,--- the mental mind consciousness which is the apex of the lower region of the plane of the mind consciousness. The mental mind consciousness we can cognise as the plane of, what we ordinarily call intellectual consciousness. It is established that such a higher consciousness, the supramental consciousness, is the sole view for the Earth for her salvation. The scientists who are baffled to see the paradox of waves and particles in the subatomic world will certainly find solace when they first enter into the world of spiritual consciousness. In fact, the scientists, and the intellectuals of the other domains of knowledge are in the trap of the divisive consciousness, remaining below the plane of the spiritual mind consciousness. In addition, it is the need of the hour to get release from the trap. Such a release begins to take place when we evolve to the Spiritual planes of consciousness with the realisation of the One Divine and One Cosmic Self. However, we are finally released when we evolve to the supramental plane of consciousness, which is the integral consciousness. This is what we find in the conclusion.

For that very reason that such supramental consciousness manifests for the first time in his being, Sri Aurobindo's consciousness can unmistakably be identified with the supramental consciousness which we have found in the evolutionary culmination, and breakthrough as well. Such a manifestation we note in his works like *The Life Divine* and *Savitri,* – the only epic to have been written in the 20th century-, beside his other works which were also written from the higher planes of the yogic consciousness. Since, this supramental consciousness is the evolutionary breakthrough, thus, it is necessary for us to view the earthly phenomenon in such a higher consciousness to achieve the goal of this terrestrial existence. The supramental consciousness which is the integral consciousness,---- the consciousness of the principle of the one----, is destined to come into the vision of science as well in the view of what the scientists have found in the subatomic world as Eddington, a celebrated nuclear scientist has found 'mind-stuff' existing at the base of Matter.

Consequent upon the spiritual and the supramental evolution of consciousness the problems of the ignored ones who are at the margin as depicted in the postcolonial literature and feminine literature will no longer exist. An integral life, --- the Divine Life---, will evolve and be established into the earth's nature consequently.

> "Surely for the earth-consciousness the very fact that the Divine manifests himself is the greatest of all splendours. Consider the obscurity here and what it would be if the Divine did not directly intervene and Light of Lights did not break out of the obscurity – for that is the meaning of the manifestation" [15]

The words of the greatest Yogi and the Seer of the Truth of the present time, Sri Aurobindo, form the embryo of the significance of terrestrial existence. All human activities academic, political, social, economic etc., go to show this divine manifestation, for He is the only Existence. Literature, expressing the vision of the seers of the

Truth exclusively, aims at the concrete mystic realities, the Divine manifestation that lies beyond the sight of human consciousness. Such realities are now in demand for human consciousness to be explored. Unless they are brought to tangible experiences resulting in its own transformation of human intellect, an important corner of it will remain unsatisfied and problems unsolved. Life here ends in nothingness and chaos. No bright destiny of Humanity is promised. A dark future lies ahead. Therefore, a new light emanating from the words of Sri Aurobindo comes as the savoir of human consciousness that will lead to the realisation of the Divine.

Sri Aurobindo very explicitly points out that the reality of the supramental world is as concrete as of the world in which the present humanity is living. Life will continue to be an idiotic tale until supramental realisation enters into the veins of this humanity. That is why William Shakespeare has created a vital world full of fatal forces like ego reflected in jealousy, vain ambitions etc., in order to make us sense the existence of the higher force which will make life meaningful. The manifestation of such a higher force has to come up under the push of evolutionary force.

Works Cited

1. Robert J.C. *Young: Postcolonialism: A very short introduction*, OUP, P. 99;
2. Ibid., P.98
3. Sri Aurobindo: *The Life Divine, Sri Aurobindo Ashram*, Puducherry, P. 824
4. Ibid; Pp.824-25
5. Ibid; P.974
6. Julie Rivkin and Michael Ryan: *Feminist Paradigms, Literary Theory: An Anthology, ed. Julie Rivkin and Michael Ryan, Blackwell Publishers, P. 527;*
7. Sri Aurobindo: *Letters on Yoga, Part IV, Sri Aurobindo Ashram Puducherry, P. 1095;*
8. TS Eliot: *Wasteland*
9. Shakespeare: *Macbeth, Act V, Scene V, Line 27;*
10. Shakespeare: *Macbeth, Act V, Scene V, Line 29-31;*
11. Shakespeare: *Othello, Act V, Scene II, Line358;*
12. Pramod K Nayar: *Contemporary Literary and Cultural Theory*, 2019, P. 157
13. Pramod K Nayar: *Contemporary Literary and Cultural Theory*, 2019, P. 154
14. Pramod K Nayar: *Contemporary Literary and Cultural Theory*, 2019, P. 89-91
15. Sri Aurobindo: *Letters on Yoga*, Part-I, P. 401

CHAPTER 10

Grave Realities of Women in Meena Alexander's "Moksha" and "She Speaks: A School Teacher from South India"

J. Priyanka and R. Rajavelu

Abstract

The modern Indian women poets reveal the complexities of their feminine psyche and mirror the changing position of women with the modernisation in the Indian society. In their quest for identity, they show activism towards self-discovery, self-expression, and self-assertion. They show compulsive concern for emancipation from the bonds of patriarchy. The female voices, besides having a profound concern for the various social evils, treat the woman's predicament and suffering in gendered contexts. This paper examines the bold feminist views of Meena Alexander where she portrays the grave realities of contemporary Indian society through her poem named "Moksha" and "She Speaks: A School Teacher from South India".

Keywords: Feminine, Women, Indian, Gender, Society.

The early English poetry in India certainly had a wide range of themes. The pre-Independence poets were skilful in handling their themes with parameter of form and structure. They championed orderliness in their technique and style. They maintained great composure in their rhyme and rhythm. Their themes include mysticism, spirituality, romance, philosophy, truth, beauty, nature, love, life, and death. The 'New Poetry' or the post-Independence poetry shows strong evolutionary changes in terms of insolence of conventions, and in extensive experimentation. And this discrepancy has been recognised in critical jargon as 'modernism'. The post-Independence poets are different from the pre-Independence poets in ethos, values, and sensibility, reflecting the change in perspective and milieu after Independence. They present a spectacle of the predicament of man in the modern world. Their works are marked by an inner conflict, a sense of alienation and aversion to milieu, and defiance of tradition. The impact of the various western aesthetic movements and trends such as realism, imagism, surrealism, naturalism, symbolism, new humanism, feminism and communism can be seen in the writings of modern Indian poets.

Then comes the women poets who showed great affinity with nature and spiritual-mystical concerns and portrayed Indian milieu, culture and heritage with romantic exuberance and lyrical poise. The post-Independence women poets are concerned with their essential feminine sensibility and in a bold and candid manner, they articulate their protest towards gender discrimination. The modern Indian women poets reveal the complexities of their feminine psyche and mirror the changing position of women with the modernisation in the Indian society. In their quest for identity, they show activism towards self-discovery, self-expression, and self-assertion. They show compulsive concern for emancipation from the bonds of patriarchy. The female voices, besides having a profound concern for the various social evils, treat the woman's predicament and suffering in gendered contexts. The weal and woes of matrimonial relationship, of being a woman in the man-made and man-governed world, are therefore central to their concern.

Alluring post-modernist slogans like "Feminism is Dead" are not relevant in the context of developing societies like India where this 'ism' has not even born. Unlike the West, where excesses and eccentricities of some women libbers have resulted in backlash against feminism, India, with her spiralling skewed gender-ratio and increasing brutalities against women stands much in need of such consciousness-raising literature. The issue of female identity, in one form or another, becomes an inevitable part of the contemporary Indian literary and critical discourse.

Expression of feminism is not an imported concept for Indian feminine poetic psyche. Long before the influence of the west, Indian women have always attempted to evolve their own values since antiquity. Buddhist nuns wrote psalms about the joys of leaving behind the tedious household chores and husband, and the word 'liberty' occurs very frequently in their poetry. Bhakti saint poets were living in a way unacceptable to society. Regional poets like Akkamahadevi, Mirabai, Bahinabai and Janabai struggled against the pettiness of the roles of women and restraints, refusing to abandon their quest for truth.

The poetry written by the contemporary Indian Women Poets are commonly demarcating the evolution of Feminine poetic consciousness in one hand, and the shifting position of women in Indian society on the other hand. Their poetry expresses the cultural beliefs of the people which classify the women of homemaking and childbearing with femininity precede to an unavoidable effect on a woman's character, personality, and identity. Their poetry gives voice for the voiceless, and they resist towards the orthodox social and religious codes which hinder woman's spirit and wipe out their identity outside the role of a mother/wife/lover.

Meena Alexander was born in Allahabad and was raised in Kerala and Sudan. Though she was a diasporic and postcolonial writer, she produced poetry that flourished in Indian refrains and imagery, identity crisis and self-discovery. In most of the works Alexander discourses many issues of women that includes the servitude ranging from social and cultural to religious. This paper analyses the different levels and incomes of oppression encountered by women in the society, in the select poems of Meena Alexander.

The poem 'Moksha' dialogs the overthrow of women in society. It focuses the major themes of liberation, freedom and the position of women in an Indian context. The poem proliferates with imageries, references and symbols that openly points out the injustice done to women. In the poem there are locations to bus station and railway station which symbolise the social space where thousands of people come and go every day. The chief characters in the poem are the writer's sister-in-law and a young girl Nirbhaya.

> "Aged a few years, my sister-in-law...
> the one they called Nirbhaya..." (8-21).

Her sister-in-law is standing on a grimy platform. She is dressed in a wool sweater and carries a suitcase that contains a packet of powdered rice, a stainless-steel pot and morsels of coconut. She is waiting to board a train. The sister-in-law represents an Indian middle-class woman which is evident from her appearance, luggage and mode of transport. Suppression of women exist in many forms. A good section of Indian women is subjugated and restricted within the four walls. They are burdened with tiresome household tasks and overwhelmed by the male members of the family. While another section of women is physically harassed and often prey to cruelties like, physical torture, rape murder etc. Several incidents are shown in news where women are brutally raped and killed in the contemporary times. Nirbhaya, a twenty-three-year-old physiotherapy student is one among those women in the Indian society who was victimized. She has been brutally raped by six men in a moving bus. History displays how women's rights and parity are changing over time. Even though women are educated, empowered, and given momentous roles, subjugation of women and criminalities against them are continued daily. At the same time a large section of women was denied for their opportunities, education and fundamental rights even though they have equal admittance legally and constitutionally. In the poem 'Moksha', Alexander conveys an inevitable fate of women in the society in the following lines

> In a crush of women severed from their bodies/
> Drifting as slit silk might/ in a slow monsoon wind… (16-18).

'Moksha', the title of the poem is self-explanatory, and it wishes the liberation or Moksha, liberty from all chains and bondages. Apart from contrasting two dissimilar images of women's suffering, the poet expresses the need for the long-awaited freedom of women, and she decides to overcome that fear which is within her and no matter what comes along her way.

Another poem named "She Speaks: A School Teacher from South India" depicts the dowry system in India and its misery in the lives of girls and their parents. Meena shows how the three young girls were hanged themselves to relieve the burden of dowry for their parents. The poem begins with the reference to a mango tree that was cut down by the storm.

> Portions of a mango tree the storm cut down,
> A green blaze bent into mud
> And they come to me, at dawn. (1-3)

According to L.Z. Marie, "mango is the food of the Gods. It is symbolic of love and fertility for Hindus and is seen as a symbol of attainment when being held by Lord Ganesha". In the Indian culture, mango also signifies wealth and immortality. But here we see a mango tree is ruined and it was related to the three girls from Kanpur who hung themselves from fans. Being a South Indian school teacher, the speaker in the poem, who is supposed to be the poet herself, talks about the tragedy of three girls from another part of the country.

Slowly in the hot air they swung, three girls.
How old were they?
Of marriageable age certainly. (16-17)

The poet deliberately does so, to well-lit the fact that girls suffer everywhere irrespective of their language, culture, religion and even age in different ways. Dowry, rape, mental and physical harassment, and torture, restriction of rights, lack of freedom etc. are some of the dominant issues of women. The mango tree cut down by the storm symbolises the lack of wealth. Moreover, the storm hit mango tree also symbolises the death of the three girls.

Through these poems, the poetess expresses her languor and discontentment of the unfair conventions. The poetess longs for the dawn where women's feeling is valued and honoured. Women are burdened and subjugated by patriarchal norms at different levels. They are always exploited and tortured irrespective of ethnicity or other dictates. Patriarchy does not accept a woman's individuality or give her due social space or respect. The elements of native culture with gender issues are highlighted in this paper to prove how deep is the gender oppression are seen in the contemporary society. The poet nowhere overtly shows disgust on the patriarchal society, in place of she is aggravated of being a woman in male dominated society. The idiosyncratic feelings of the poet make the poems reaching the deepest harmony of the heart among the readers.

Work Cited

Alexander, Meena. "Moksha". *The Hindu – Literary Review* 7 Dec. 2014, Weekly ed., 2.

.... *She Speaks: A School Teacher from South India.* poetryfoundation.org. N.p, N.d. web. 28 January 2021.

Marie, L.Z., *Fruits of the Gods.* www.lzmarieauthor.com.

Abrams, M.H. and Geoffrey Galt Harpham. *A Glossary of Literary Terms.* Cenage Learning India Pvt. Ltd., 2015.

Solaman1 Christy and Dr. Amutha Dhanaraj. "The Social Space of Indian Women in Meena Alexander's Poems in feminist perspective", *Psychology And Education*, ISSN 00333077, Nov 2020.

CHAPTER 11

Depiction of Women in Literature(s)

R. Gandhi Subramanian

Abstract

Various literature have depicted women in various times. Women have been treated with respect in Indian Literatures. Tamizh and Indian English Literatures have given prominence to women and treated them with respect. Subramania Bharathi in Tamizh, Rabindranath Tagore in his short stories, R.K.Narayan, Raja Rao, Mulk Raj Anand, Kamala Das and Anita Desai have depicted women in their perspective. Anita Desai stands apart in her depiction of women. Extracts from research papers/unpublished theses submitted to Bharathiar University by R.Gandhi Subramanian, R.Krishnamoorthy, V.Brindashree and A.S.Mythili have been used to reveal portrayal of women in Tamizh Literature, Indian English Literature, Canadian Literature and African-American Literature. Poems of Subramania Bharathi by Prema Nandakumar has also been used in connection with Subramania Bharathi's poems.

Keywords: Women, Literature, Women issues/

Introduction

Women have been depicted variously by various people-men and women – in various times, in various literature. As far as our Indian Literature are concerned women have occupied high pedestals and were treated with reverence and respect. The triumvirate Hindu Gods Brahma, Vishnu and Shiva have their creative, sustaining and destructive powers respectively through Saraswathi, Lakshmi and Parvathi. Perhaps the term 'better half' to denote one's wife has been derived by having these Goddesses as examples. The temples at Madurai and at Concheepuram both in Tamilnadu have these temples named after the female deity-Meenakshi Amman Temple and Kamakshi Amman Temple-the female deity being Meenakshi and Kamakshi respectively. The temple of Viswanatha at Kasi (Benaras) has Visalakshi, as the main female deity there. Meenakshi, Kamakshi and Visalakshi are well known names given to female children especially in Tamilnadu. An extension of this-the concept of treating women with veneration – can be seen in the naming of the rivers, Ganga, Yamuna, Godhavari, Narmadha, Sindhu and Cauvery by our ancestors:"Gange cha,Yamune chaiva, Godhavari, Narmadhe, Sindhu, Cauvery Jalesmin sannidhim kuru." (Let the waters of Ganga, Yamuna, Godhavari, Narmadha, Sindhu and Cauvery make their presence here, in (this) water.) [Translation mine]. Mytreyi and Avvaiyar (அவ்வையார்) are two of the Indian women who come to one's mind as great poets. Another well-known Tamil poet was Kaakkaipaadiniaar (காக்கைபாடினியார்)

Even unknown women are treated with courtesy as mother, sister and daughter by Indians. It is to be noted that a woman can play all the three roles – mother, wife and daughter – and two of these are interchangeable: an ailing wife becomes a daughter; and a daughter looking after her parents becomes a mother; a wife looking after her ailing husband turns into a mother, but according to our Indian tradition a mother can never become a wife to her son. A legendary woman Saavithri is said to have fought with Yama (the Angel of Death) to retrieve her husband's life. Agni, the God of Fire could not burn Sita for she was protected by her faithful, unshakable, chastity to her husband Rama. Incidentally one has to remember that the abduction of Sita was the cause of war in *Ramayana*. Draupathi born of Fire and the dishonourable treatment given to Draupadi caused the Mahabharatha war in *Mahabharatha*. Mandana's wife, Ubhaya Bharathi, who sat as a judge for the debate between Adi Sankara and her husband, is said to be an incarnation of Goddess Saraswati, the Goddess of knowledge. ("Mandana's wife Ubhaya Bharathi…considered to be an incarnation of the goddess Saraswati in the folklore…" *Mandana Misra* from Wikipedia, the free encyclopedia).

As at the ancient times, at the times of recent past also women were treated with respect they richly deserve. Jeejabai, is said to have influenced Chatrapathi Sivaji during his childhood years resulting in his victorious wars against the expanding Mughal Empire. Rani Lakshmi Bai is another brave woman who fought against the British, as did Velu Nachiar of Sivaganga in Tamilnadu.

Depiction of women in Tamizh Literature

Thiru.Vi.Ka (Thiru Vi.Kalayanasundaram) wrote *Pennin Perumai (The Glory of Women)*. Subramania Bharathi, a great Tamil poet had held women always in high esteem. Prema Nandakumar mentions, "In Nivedita he saw Mother Shakti herself, the emerging, energising power that ruled India and the world." (Prema Nandakumar. *Poems of Subramania Bharathi*, Introduction 1-53, Sahitya Akademi, Ravindra Bhavan, 35, Ferozeshah Road, New Delhi 110001,1977). Prema Nandakumar observes later in her Introduction to *Poems of Subramania Bharathi*, Thanks to Sri Aurbindo, Bharathi entered into the spirit of Shakti-tattva, the identification of Shakti or the Divine Mother with the universal energising Creatrix. It was under the double influence of his Vedic studies and the Shakti-tattva that Bharathi's poetic genius found triumphant self-expression in his prose poetry and in his *Panchali Sapatham, Kannan Pattu* and the Shakti poems. (Ibid)

Bharathi realised that woman is a manifestation of 'Shakthi' (Power) and accepting and acknowledging the rightful role of woman will lead to the betterment of society. Bharathi declares in his "Pennmai" (பெண்மை), 'Womanhood': "Pennmai vaazhkenru koothiduvomadaa Pennmai velhenru kooththiduvomadaa" (பெண்மை வாழ்கென்று கூத்திடுவோமடா பெண்மை வெல்கென்று கூத்திடுவோமடா.) (399) ("Let's dance with joy saying "Long Live Womanhood, Let Womanhood be Victorious".) His poem "Penn Viduthalai" – "Women Emancipation"-remarkably brief, clinches the argument, and hits the bull's eye:

> … Pennukku viduthalaiyenringor needhi
> *Pirapitthaen; Atharkuria pe(t)ri kaeleer!*
> *Mannukkul evvuyirum Deivamenraal,*
> *Manaiyaalum Deivamanro?*
> *Pennukku Viduthalai neerillaiyen(d)raal*
> *Pinnindha ulaginilae vaazhkaiyillai.* (458)

> **பெண்ணுக்கு விடுதலையேன்றிங்கோர் நீதி**
> **பிறப்பித்தேன்; அதற்குறிய பெற்றி கேளீர்**
> **மண்ணுக்குள் எவ்வுயிரும் தெய்வமென்றால்**
> **மனையாளும் தெய்வமன்றோ?**
> **பெண்ணுக்கு விடுதலை நீரில்லையென்றால்**
> **பின்னிந்த உலகினிலே வாழ்க்கையில்லை.**

(I've promulgated a Law declaring the Emancipation of Woman. Listen to its glory. If all lives on the Earth are holy, is it not true that one's wife (home maker) be called a Goddess...If women are denied freedom, there will be no sustenance [Life] on this earth.) He states in his "Pudumaippenn":

Nimirntha nannadai near Konda paarvaiyum
Nilathil yaarkumanjaatha nerhalum,
Thimirndhagnanachchrukkumiruppathaal
Semmai maadhar thirambuvadhillaiyaam (397,398)

(The modern woman by her bravery and mastery of Knowledge will never ever commit any blunder.)

His "Penn Viduthalaikkummi" talks of woman freed of slavery, injustice and oppression:

Pattangalaalvathum sattangal seivathum
Ettumarivinilaanukkingae penn
Ilaippillai kaanennru kummiyadi. (396)

(Let's celebrate that [we as] women are in no way inferior in [our] knowledge to men in accepting [our] responsibility or in making Laws.)

பட்டங்களாள்வதும் சட்டங்கள் செய்வதும்
எட்டுமாறிவிநிலாணுக்கிங்கே பெண்
இளைப்பில்லை காணென்று கும்மியடி

Subramania Bharathi's "Paanchaali Sabadham" பாஞ்சாலி சபதம் ("Paanchali's Vow") is a symbolic representation of his vision for woman empowerment and he visions the catastrophe that will destroy the society that dishonours woman. "Paanchaali Sabadham" is Subramania Bharathi's pinnacle of achievement in the cause of the oppressed woman Paanchaali being the symbolic representative of the oppressed woman. The injustice done to Paanchaali cannot be undone and the injustice done to a woman has universal repercussions.

Arjuna's words to pacify Bhima's anger are noteworthy:

Dharumatthin vaazhvudhanai soodhu kavvum;
Dharuma(m) marupadi vellum… (367)

(Dharma [the Righteous] is oft defeated by deceit, yet the Righteous shall triumph finally.)

Prema Nandakumar states, It is Draupadi who dominates the scene, and the rest are nothing, less than nothing…Drauoadi is particularly the symbol of Indian womanhood in general…As the poet of patriotism, again, Bharathi saw in Draupadi the very image of Mother India, enslaved and oppressed, but resolute and defiant still. (Prema Nandakumar. Introduction 1-53) Bharathiar's "Viduthalai" ("Freedom") gives an emphatic proclamation:

"*Maadhar thammai izhivu seyyu(m)*
Madamaiyaikkoluthuvom" (185)

(Let's put to torch the ignorance of belittling women.)

மாதர்தம்மை இழிவு செய்யும்

மடமையைக்கொளுத்துவோம்

His poem "Vaenduvana" ("Requests") repeats, "Penn Viduthalai vaendum" (83) ([I request] freedom for women.) பெண் விடுதலை வேண்டும்

Depiction of women in Indian English Literature

After this discussion on the depiction of women in Tamizh Literature, this paper moves on to a discussion of the depiction of women in Indian English Literature. Indian English Literature is a developing one but "this development has not been achieved in a day, but it is the fruition of the talented work rendered by many a great writer". (Gandhi Subramanian. "Thoughts on Anita Desai's Novels.") Fiction gave anew freedom to our Indian writers, as Fiction is the modern 'Avathar' of Epic. Mention has to be made of great Indian stalwarts such as Rabindranath Tagore, R.K.Narayan, Raja Rao and Mulk Raj Anand. There are more like Arun Joshi, Anita Desai, Chaman Nahal and Kamala Das, just to mention a few. "Anita Desai stands apart …in many ways a representative woman novelist of India, making use of English as her effective tool of expression…Anita Desai can be considered as a woman highlighting the lives of Indian women with their innate problems and trying her best to improve their lot through her writings." (Ibid). Anita Desai has a "rare imaginative awareness" and "profound understanding of feminine sensibility", states R.Krishnamoorthy. (R.Krishnamoorthy. "Role of woman as a Daughter, Wife and Mother in select novels of Anita Desai: Cry, the Peacock, Where Shall We Go This Summer? Voices in the City and Clear Light of Day. Unpublished thesis. 15) Anita Desai's *Cry, the Peacock* (1963), *Voices in the City* (1965), *Clear Light of Day* (1980), and *Where shall we go this Summer?* (1975) present the plight of women alienated from their family, from their parents, from their partners, from the society and even from their true selves. It is not uncommon to see parents trying their best to satisfy almost all the needs of their children, especially so with daughters… Whatever the parents wanted to be, but missed in their lives are forced on the children… The doting parents thereby fail to train their children to face responsibilities as grown-up adults. (Dr.R.Gandhi Subramanian. "Thoughts on Anita Desai's Novels." p.4)

Maya, the protagonist in *Cry, the Peacock,* cannot exist independently thanks to her bad upbringing. Her marriage was "...broken repeatedly and repeatedly the pieces were picked up and put together again." (*Cry, the Peacock*, 126). She cannot solve her conflicts, thereby increasing her difficulties leading to a complete disintegration of her personality, sense of guilt and self-hatred driving her to murder her husband and end her life by suicide. "She destroys and self-destructs." (Dr. R.Gandhi Subramanian. "Thoughts..." p.5).

Voices in the City (1965), portrays Monisha and Amla, the sisters from an affluent family. Both are childless and sensitive. Monisha says, I see many women, always Bengali women, who follow five paces behind their men...Lives spent in waiting for nothing on men self-centred and indifferent and critical, waiting for death and dying misunderstood, always behind bars, those terrifying black bars that shut us in, in the old house, in the old city. (120), her words exemplifying the condition of Bengali women living in hell over centuries. Amla, on the other hand is more liberated and more intelligent. She is more than average; enjoys her new job and the independence she gets through her job. "Calcutta doesn't oppress me in the least...It excites me." (142). R.Krishnamoorthy mentions, "In the shadow of death she discovers the value of life. Amla grapples from Monisha's death her authentic self and maintains the poise she displays at the end of the novel." (R.Krishnamoorthy. Unpublished thesis, p78). She prefers horse race to art exhibition shows her regressive and symbolic "sickening view of life as a gamble". (R. Krishnamoorthy.77). She sustains growth unlike Maya in *Cry, the Peacock* or Monisha, her sister. She resembles Sita of *Where Shall We Go This Summer?* in her mental strength during her marital despair.

Sita of *Where Shall We Go This Summer?* Discovers her 'self' through her struggles. Sita is specific that life is a constant struggle and realises that existence and survival are more relevant to one's life than one's struggle. Bim and Tara, the sisters in *Clear Light of Day* (1980) provide another illustration of a study of contrasting sisters. Their experiences had failed to create a meaningful life for them. Tara redeems her past at her parental house; Bim who "considered her past as meaningless realises the inadequacy of her approach and realises that only through love for others one can have any life worthy of meaning." (Dr. R. Gandhi Subramanian. "Thoughts..." p.9). Uma of *Fasting, Feasting* (1999) leaves her home to achieve independence without marriage. Anita Desai has said, "My characters who appear like losers, victims show a kind of heroism, of survival. I think if you can come through the experience of life with the heart and mind intact, without compromising yourself that to me is a heroic act that needs to be celebrated." as mentioned by Ramachandra Rao in *The Novel of Mrs.Anita Desai* (*Anita Desai* 1977)

Ms.V.Brinda Shree's thesis, "Women in the novels of Anita Desai: Transition from Alienation to Identification" attempts the depiction of lives of Indian women in Anita Desai's novels and exposes the exploitation of women by vested interests. The thesis analyses through different chapters, "Aspects of Eternal Feminine Sensibilities"; "The theme of Exile and Ailing Aliens" and "The Female Quest for Identity". The researcher mentions in the concluding part of her thesis, "What Anita Desai suggests…is the necessity of an awareness that the power of love does not only help in finding the answer to one's quest-different though an answer may be-but that love and acts of love are the means of woman and womankind to prevent their own destruction and along with that of their own culture." Anita Desai's concept of reality is that of a tangible thought, perhaps distorted entity. "It is a woman's or the concerned individual's task to find one's own destination." (222-223)

The discussion moves on to the depiction of women in Canadian Literature and conclude with that in African-American Literature after the preceding discussion on the depiction of women in Tamizh Literature by illustrations from Subramania Bharathi and In Indian English Literature with illustrations from Anita Desai's novels.

Depiction of Women in Canadian Literature

The depiction of women in Canadian Literature will be shown through the novels of Margaret Atwood, a Canadian woman. Ms. A.S Mythili in her thesis "Predicament and Survival in *The Handmaid's Tale, Cat's Eye, The Edible Woman, Lady Oracle* and *Bodily Harm*: A study of Margaret Atwood's Novels" states that Canadian women writers write more as women and are engaged in finding more adequate ways of talking about women's experiences "to project more authentic images of how women feel and what they do through their protagonist." (Abstract).

Margaret Atwood as a post-modern feminist protest writer deals with women's experience in a male dominated society. Margaret Atwood emphasises that women be "aware of their exploitation and refuse to be a victim" and survive their predicaments. Survival for them is to be "free of dominance and submission, where all individuals are free to determine their own lives as equals." Atwood's novels desire for a real, healthy and balanced relationship between men and women. Atwood's feminist vision offers a "fresh perspective on women's problems." The female protagonists of Atwood gain inward victories while they experience outward defeat though, states A.S.Mythili. (Ibid).

The women writers of Canada took up the problems of women such as their predicament and their power. The sweeping changes promoted their status but their conditions had "not improved much." (A.S.Mythili. "Predicament and Survival in *The Handmaid's Tale, Cat's Eye, The Edible Woman, Lady Oracle* and *Bodily Harm*: A study of Margaret Atwood's Novels" Introduction. 1-35). The women writers took up "the question of female identity in a male dominated world…The women were disadvantaged both economically and legally…" (Ibid). The Canadian women writers project a new woman of self-awareness, of independence and trying to have her own identity. They firmly believe in having a "peaceful, caring world." (Ibid).

Margaret Laurence, Margaret Atwood and Alice Munro are eminent feminist writers of Canada. For Margaret Atwood her country becomes her world. The protagonists of *The Edible Woman* (1969), *Lady Oracle* ((1976), *Cat's Eye* (1988), *The Handmaid's Tale* (1985) and *Bodily Harm* (1983) endure varying degrees of victimisation and accept responsibility for their victimisation. Atwood feels that "accepting one's capability is the only way a victim can truly survive." (Ibid). All five protagonists in these novels succeed in their endeavour and are survivors in the true sense of the word.

The Handmaid's Tale written by a woman novelist deals with politically totalitarian regimes where the victims are women. The novel resembles Love *Camp* by Louis-Charles Roger. where the healthiest women are mated by the healthiest men to produce the healthiest children for a Nazi Germany to prove Hitler's theory of the Great Aryan Race. *Love Camp* is a different statement on the victimisation of women by politically totalitarian regimes such as that of Nazi Germany.

'*The Handmaid's Tale* is an evaluation of female degradation, a cautionary and poignant tale that dramatizes a futuristic, bleak, totalitarian society where women are denied their basic rights."

(A.S.Mythili. 47). Women are not human beings but mere objects. They are a "national resource" (*The Handmaid's Tale*. 75), "containers" (107) and two-legged wombs." The women are constantly watched and guarded. In this novel, "Atwood concentrates on the problem of woman's survival in a hostile male dominated world through Offred's refusal to be a silent victim" states A.S.Mythili. (A.S. Mythili. 59, 60). Atwood's *The Handmaid's Tale* is a "warning about the danger of a patriarchal society and the dogma of religious right." (Ibid 78).

Margaret Atwood's seventh novel *Cat's Eye* (1989)-fascinating and detailed – narrates women's achievements as an artist. *Cat's Eye* reveals that art promotes feminism and women's freedom and reveals the abusive power, issues in the struggle faced by women. Elaine does gather courage and moves away from her women tormentors. A.S.Mythili states, "for Elaine to recover from her past…she should be able to recover the broken pieces of her past and put them together again."(A.S.93). A.S.Mythili mentions, "Through Elaine's narrative, Atwood implies that a creative life can help heal deep wounds. By the end of the narrative, Elaine Risley is a successful artist." (Ibid 105).

Though Margaret Atwood is a feminist and though her writings have highlighted that her major concern is woman and her plight, only two of Atwood's novels have been taken, having in mind the limitations of space. Those interested in Atwood's writings are requested to refer directly to her writings and have a first-hand knowledge of Atwood's concern for women.

Depiction of women in African-American Literature

Women have been depicted in African-American Literature as they have been in every other Literature. African-American writers-men and women – have created memorable women in their writings. The writers like Tony Morrison and Alice Walker-being women-throw light on their women and the plight of women. Some of the short stories reveal openly the shocking plight of women. Such shocking narrations have the impact of a gun fired at point-blank range.

The earlier African-American Literature dealt with the oppression of African-Americans by the whites. Later writers like Richard Wright and Ralph Ellison took the next step of awakening the conscience of Americans. Women like Toni Morrison and Alice Walker underlined the pain of suffering oppression from their own men. The oppression unleased on men was physical whereas that on women had been physiological and psychological as well. "The pain and agony caused by the African-American turned oppressor make an integral part of their novels." (R.Gandhi Subramanian. "Voices of Anger: The Oppressor-Oppressed Relationship in African-American Fiction with special reference to the select novels of Richard Wright, Ralph Ellison, Alice Walker and Toni Morrison." Introduction,1-29 Unpublished Thesis, 2000.)

It cannot be said that African-American Male writers were totally unaware of the oppression suffered by African-American women by their men. Richard Wright's "Long Black Song", the third story in *Uncle Tom's Children* touches the aspect of African-American male overlooking and ignoring the rights of his female counterpart: By refusing to cater to the physical desires and by refusing even to acknowledge the existence of such natural desires of his young wife Sarah…he scarcely realises that female children. He resents being oppressed and exploited but he is not even aware of his own role as an oppressor on his own woman. (Ibid 53).

Toni Morrison's novels reveal her evolution as a writer and also her concern for the African-American, especially the African-American woman. Morrison's *The Bluest Eye*, reveals the effects of imposition of a 'Zero-image' on young African-American female children. Doreatha Drummond Mbalia asserts that "The thesis of the novel is that racism devastates the self-image of the American female in general and the African female in particular." (28) (Doreatha Drummond Mbalia. *Toni Morrison's Developing Class Consciousness.* Selingrove: Susquehanna University Press, 1994.)

Pecola of *The Bluest Eye* is abused not only by her family but also by the oppressive society making its negative contribution to hurt and damage Pecola. Cholly's incestuous rape of his daughter Pecola is the sad result of a strange African-American response to male-female relationship. "The male African-American, himself being a victim oppression, turns a heartless oppressor on his women." (Gandhi Subramanian.168).

In *Sula*, Morrison turns her attention to woman's rights in particular. In Mbalia's opinion *Sula* is a continuation of *The Bluest Eye.* Sula reveals from the very beginning that she is different and that she will not tolerate harassment. "This toughness, against the harassment and oppression by the males becomes one of the characteristic qualities of Sula." (Ibid, 177). Sula remains independent till she breathes her last. Sula's last, final moment is touching: "She was not breathing because she didn't have to. Her body did not need oxygen. She was dead." Jadine of Morrison's *Tar Baby* is not the poor, helpless Pecola and she has transcended Sula. Tony Morrison's portrayal of her women-from Zero-image to independent individuality-a portrayal showing her deep concern for women.

Alice Walker occupies an eminent place among African-American women writers. She has stated in one of her interviews that she is committed to exploring the oppressions, the insanities, the loyalties and the triumphs of black women. For Alice Walker "black women are the most fascinating creations in the world." Her collection of short stories such as *You Can't Keep A Good Woman Down* and *In Love & Trouble: Stories of Black Women* show her concern for her women.

You Can't Keep A Good Woman Down has stories connected with women, child abuse and exploitation of the female. "How Did I Get Away with Killing one of the Biggest Lawyers in the State? It was Easy." And "Abortion" can be considered as examples to illustrate the point. The narrator of "How Did I…" "looks like a grown woman." Her mother's employer, a lawyer 'legally' rapes her. A lawyer raping a fourteen-year young girl, threatening her with his words, "he hadn't forced" her and blackmailing the victim speak volumes of child abuse and exploitation of the female. On the day of her "seventeenth birthday", she signs papers in the lawyer's office and commits her mother to an insane asylum. When her mother dies, she kills Bubba, the lawyer who raped her and her tormentor. "How did I get away with killing one of the biggest lawyers in the state? It was easy. He kept a gun in his desk drawer at the office and one night I took it out and shot him." The narrator continues: "No one came after me and I read in the papers next day that he had been killed by burglars. I guess they thought 'burglars' had stolen all that money Bubba kept in his safe – but I had it." This short story reveals the unexpected, extreme reaction of the victim. "The exploited had turned the tables…for a change." (Gandhi Subramanian.205)

The theme of abortion occupies the centre stage in the short story "The Abortion." Imani's first abortion-while she was still at the college – though told "It's nothing, nothing", and after shelling out a thousand dollars she was not well again for a year. For her present abortion Imani finds that abortion has "entered the age of assembly line" and also that those "assembly lines don't stop because the product on them has a complaint." "There was no way to explain abortion to a man" feels Imani. This short story explicitly reveals "the psychological scar left on womanhood by unwanted pregnancy." (R.Gandhi Subramanian.206)

Alice Walker's The *Color Purple* is a novel exploring the exploitation of women, the exploitation, abuse and harassment commencing from childhood, leading to traumatic experiences and leaving psychic scars in the victim. Through female-bonding Celie discovers her creative and unique ability to bond relationships. Alice Walker's writings show her intention to champion as a writer especially the cause of African-American women. Walker's words stand testimony to her determination. "I am preoccupied with the spiritual survival, the survival whole, of my people. But beyond that, I am committed to exploring the oppressions, the insanities, the loyalties and the triumphs of black women."

Toni Morrison and Alice Walker, being women, are able to understand the plight of African-American women more sympathetically. They express their conscious concern for the abuse of African-American womanhood and inhuman acts of violence on these women. Toni Morrison's Pecola and Alice Walker's Meridian and Celie are the victims of the negative impact of this oppressive environment. It is equally important to realise that the solution for these has to come from within. The men and women must change themselves first, prior to their efforts to change the society. They must realise that light cannot come of darkness and compassion out of cruelty. People – men and women – must minimize the problems of the suffering to make this world a better place to live in.

Work Cited

Brinda Shree.V. "Women in the Novels of Anita Desai: Transition from Alienation to Identification." *Unpublished thesis*, 2016.

Desai, Anita. *Cry, The Peacock*. Delhi: Orient Paperbacks, 1963.thesis. *Voices in the City*. Delhi: Orient Paperbacks, 1965.

.........*Clear Light of Day*. New Delhi: Allied Publishers, 1980.

.........*Where Shall We Go This Summer?* Delhi: Orient Paperbacks, 1982.

Gandhi Subramanian. R. "Voices of Anger: The Oppressor-Oppressed Relationship in African-American Fiction with particular reference to the Select novels of Richard Wright, Ralph Ellison, Alice Walker and Tony Morrison." *Unpublished Thesis*, 2000.

Krishnamoorthy, Raman. "Role of Woman as a Daughter, Wife and Mother in Select Novels of Anita Desai: *Cry, the Peacock, Where Shall We Go This Summer? Voices in the City* and *Clear Light of Day*". Unpublished Thesis, 2008.

Rao, Ramachandra. *The Novel of Mrs. Anita Desai.* Ludhiana: Kalyani Publishers, 1977.

Mbalia, Doreatha Drummond. *Tony Morrison's Developing Class Consciousness.* Selingrove: Susquehanna University Press, 1994.

Mythili. A.S. "Predicament and Survival in *The Handmaid's Tale, Cat's Eye, The Edible Woman, Lady Oracle* and *Bodily Harm*: A study of Margaret Atwood's Novels" Unpublished Thesis, 2016.

Nandakumar, Prema. *Poems Subramania Bharathi.* New Delhi: Sahitya Akademi, Reprint, 2004.

(Subramania Bharathi). *Bharathiar Kavithaikal.* People's Edition. Chennai: Kavitha Publications, 2006.

CHAPTER 12

Portrayal of Women in Mulk Raj Anand's *Untouchable* and *Coolie*

Ratna Prabha Kalyan

Abstract

Mulk Raj Anand, a socially committed novelist, has produced a good deal about the portrayal of women in his novel. He is a distinguished writer of world acclaim who wrote sixteen novels with different issues, in the manner of women. In this paper, an attempt has been made to analyse Mulk Raj Anand's exploration in his two novels – Untouchable (1936) and Coolie (1937). In these novel Anand throws open a heterogeneous field where different kinds of exploitation are at work and different systems of domination such as caste, class gender and colonial operate in a crisscross manners. Here will mentioned about behavior with women and also behavior of women, because here talk about two different novel but the author same. Here somewhere showing women's boldness with women and somewhere weakness of women. We will see here the portrayal of women in this paper. In his first novel Untouchable, It is a study of depiction of women life, the miserable plight of woman has been best portrayal by him. Anand has stressed in his old myth new myth; recital verse novel, the need for affecting a synthesis between tradition and modernity in novel form. He conscious of the Hazards involved in keeping up the spirit of the old myths sustained in the n contemporary idiom. In coolie Anand mention, sympathy toward women. Here Hari sympathies with his wife who seems to suffer from the natural weakness of her sex. Mulk Raj Anand has, in his novel taken a bold stand behalf of millions of Indian women tortured and hounded by unsympathetic husband crafty in-laws, fault – finding and censorious kith and kin, and above all, by deep seated guilt-feeling and self-accusing remorsefulness on the part of the women, born out of centuries of psychological subjugation and bombardment.

Keywords: Portrayal, sympathy, weakness, women, differences, caste

Introduction

Many writers raised the issues about women right in their writing like Raja Rao, Bhawani Bhattacharya, R.K. Narayan and many more among them there was one more world famous novelist was Mulk Raj Anand. He wrote almost in his all novel about women life with different issues. But here I will discourse about his two Untouchable and coolie. According to Anand, a novel is not reportage about social conditions; it is in exploration of social realism and that social realism and that social realism should be in the nature of poetic realism. So Anand lays emphasis on the importance of the desire image, or the romantic will. His first novel of untouchable in Indian society and this untouchably is not only about low caste but misbehave with lower caste women too. In *Untouchable,* Sohini is one of the important characters in the novel. Anand used Sohini character to project the evil nature of some bad people in the society and the women position in the society. Actually we give women great respect in words and deeds but really we are not doing that. In India we worship Maa Durga, Maa Laxmi, Maa Kaali, Maa Saraswati but respect for women is nothing. It seems like she is only for using, such as do house work, sex, bring up kids and all. If she raised her voice, man will shows their power on weaker women and unluckily women protect herself it will call that how undisciplined girl is, she has no any manner his parents didn't teach her good things and all.

After finishing Bakha morning shift he goes back home and looks for water. He finds his brother has left to go play, his father is still sleeping and his sister Sohini is trying to start a fire. He helps her and then discovers there is no water in the house. Sohini sensing her brother's exhaustion and frustration, volunteer's to fetch some water from well Sohini leaves the house with the water pitcher and heads to the well to fill it. When Sohini reaches the well she sees out castes crowded around it, none of whom are drawing water. If any of the out castes were to draw water from the well, the high castes would consider the water polluted. The outcastes cannot afford to have their own well built. Therefore they must wait at the foot of the high-caste well for a high caste to come along, take pity on them, and pour water into their pitchers for them. Unfortunately when Sohini approaches there are ten outcastes waiting in front of her and not a high caste in sight. Depressed but not discouraged Sohini seated with the others in to wait.

Among those already waiting is Gulabo washer woman and the mother of ram Charan, Bakha's friend, had observed sohini approach.

> She was a fair-complexioned, middle-aged woman, the regularity of whose supple body bore even in its decay the evidence of a form which must, in her youth, have been wonderful, but although her face was now covered with wrinkles she had pretensions to beauty and was now notorious as an assertive hussy who thought herself superior to every other outcaste, firstly because she claimed a high place in the town who had been her lover in her youth was still kind to her in her middle age. (*Untouchable*, 27-28)

Jealous of Sohini, even though as a sweeper the young woman is the lowest of the low within the caste hierarchy Gulabo begins to bully Sohini. There no any doubt that women's big enemy is woman. By jealousy and back bitter. Some women never want to help but ready for stop her path. Gulabo calls Sohini a bitch, a prostitute, and other derogatory names. Sohini, oblivious to Gulabo's jealousy laughs at the abruptness of the older woman's attack, thinking it is a joke. At this Gulabo's ire increases in frequency and vitriol. Soon Sohini realises that Gulabo's anger is very real and wonders women's fury. Suddenly Gulabo moves to strike Sohini but is stopped by waziro, the weaver's wife. She calms Gulabo down shocked silent, Sohini sits still and thinks about Bakha waiting at home for the water.

Coolie is a term for an unskilled laborer, though it can also be used as a pejorative. In this novel he mentions that the women coolies are compelled to work as rigorously as male coolies. The supervisors do not hesitate to punish women. The picture of a mother who is chased to the work spot, even she is her child shown how in human being, the rulers are even towards the women. The white compel the coolies to hand over their wives and daughter to them for the sake of fun and frolic and many a time to satisfy their sexual passion. The young officers like hunt are always in search of young girls and woman. Narain tells Gangu that hunt comes to the work sight, he tries to exhibit his boasting personality on the women "the coolie woman shuffled like hens at the arrival of a much dreaded cock" (*Coolie,* 49)

Most men do not find anything wrong with his standardisation of women. In coolie, A Hari sympathy with his wife who seems to suffer from the natural weakness joins her husband in the factory and works for the same hours. But in that time lower caste women have to face a lot of difficulties. She has to pay by sexually to upper caste and by abusing. Upper caste knows that these lower caste women never be aggressive and raised their voice, and they were masters and can do whatever they want with these women and their husband has no power to say anything against them. They will be punished and have to send their women to upper caste. Being the masters, they expect that their slaves should after their wives and daughter to them willingly. Sometimes they bribe the poor husband by 'Bakshis' to win their wives, if they protest they use their guns to terrorise them. Hunt offers five acres of land to niyogi for his wife where as he lashes one of the coolies, for not giving up his wife to him. When they fed up with them, they throw them away in order to set the new ones. In urban areas, the British behave like cunning imposters. But in the remote part like the valley of Assam they behave like wild animals. Here they are not afraid of the poor coolies because they know they will not raise their voice against them.

I have studied about one very cruel rule on the women by website about the breast tax (Mulakkaram or Mulakaram in Malayalam) was a tax imposed until 1924 on the lower caste and untouchable Hindu women by the kingdom of Travancore (in present day Kerala state of India) if they wanted to cover their breasts in public. The lower caste and untouchable women were expected to pay the government the breast. Travancore tax collectors would visit every house to collect the breast tax from any lower caste women who passed the age of puberty.

The village –legend nangeli is about women who lived in the early 19th century at cherthalu in the erstwhile princely state of Travancore in India and supposedly, cut off her breasts in an effort to protest against the caste-based breast tax. According to the legend she cut off her breasts and presented them to the tax collector in a plantain leaf, then died of blood loss. Following the death of nangeli, a series of people's movements were set off soon the people where she lived had come to be called as mulachiparambu (meaning place of the breasted women)

Everywhere women have to face trouble. Trouble is not like troubling but it's hurting on her respect women are in danger everywhere even in womb. If people know that there is girl in her worm, other insists her to abort that girl. If by lucky she safely came from there then the world here waiting for like haiwan and even 6 month girl have to raped. Even after seventy six years of independence, Indian society has not been able to deliver justice and dignity to Indian women. Atrocities' against them are still increasing. Every two hours, one woman is assaulted, every day women are raped, murdered and burn alive.

In *coolie*, somewhere men polite to women and here women shows her power to an orphan boy Munoo. He torture by her aunty she don't want him anymore, she want her own son and always shouted at Munoo but his uncle is very polite to him and bring up them but here his aunty shows him her cruel face. He says-

> My aunt wants me to begin earning money, said Munoo and she says, she wants a son of her own. My uncle says I am grown up and must fend myself. He has got me a job in the house of the baby of the bank where he works in Shampur. *(Coolie*, 2)

Anand has included in untouchable about Sohini that Sohini's assault in his novel for a specific purpose. He was trying to give his audience a clear picture of the pain any untouchable went through in his life in pre-independence India. The stigma of being born an untouchable does not die until the person's death. The Varna or caste hierarchy that has the Brahmins at the top and the Dalits or the untouchables at the bottom, even a touch of an Achhoot meant violation for an upper caste. Hindu required ablution. Bakha and his sister Sohini are untouchables. The Brahmin that tries to assault Sohini sexually is an upper caste Hindu. He tries to molest her but because of Sohini's protest is afraid of getting caught. He shouts polluted, trying to lay the blame on Sohini. Bakha wants to take revenge but he can't touch the Pandit or even enter the temple since this would turn the entire society against him. As an untouchable, neither Bakha and nor Sohini are allowed to enter the ample premises as they will violate is sanctity. Bakha is bound to lead the life of an underdog. The incident is just a reflection of the reality of Anand's times. The novel was published in 1935 when India was still not independent. Life was an ugly reality for the poor and downtrodden untouchables who could not dare to revolt against their oppression by the upper class Hindus. Being born an untouchable was like living accurse. The assault on Sohini portrays the ugliness of the caste system in India. The upper castes would not touch the untouchables or sit with them. Even if a man from an upper caste assaulted or violated the dignity of a lower caste woman no one would sympathy with her or help her. Bakha despite being from the untouchable class is a proud man at heart. There is no love, no happy, no good things, not good behavior with the women. It's like they live only hopelessly without their own perdition.

> "A life without love, Mohini mused with an unaware smile; a life without love is like jasmine without scent. It is like a tree without leaf, grass

> without green, clouds without rain, the bowl of the night sky stripped of stars, empty funereal, needless."(*Bhattacharya*, 26)

He cannot bear someone casting a dirty glance at his sister but he has to keep all that anger in his boundaries and the Pandit lives beyond those boundaries for from his reach. He has to bear all the frustration as he is just a poor underdog. There were millions of untouchables in the same oppression. The Pandit who would not touch a lower caste girl in daylight becomes a lustful dog, finding her alone. Had Bakha not been the son of a fatrine cleaner, he would have killed the priest, he could contain his fury with much difficulty. Bakha's love for sohini is unmistakably seen in terms of colonisation and appropriation. His love for her is presented in images which verge on incest and signalise his repressed sexual desire for her. He could not think of her brutalised by anyone even by a husband married other according to the rites of religion. He looked at her future life seemed to come before him. She had a husband-

> "a man who had her, possessed her, he loathed the ghost of her would be husband that he conjured up. He could see the stranger holding her full breasts and he responding with a modest acquiescence. He hated the thought of that man touching her. He felt he would be losing something" (*Coolie*, 55)

Mulk Raj Anand here, through Bakha seems to be castigating the nation of viewing women only in items of their body and a tool for sexual gratification thus. Making the beauty of a woman her greatest enemy and a burden of the family. Sohini has many admirable qualities. She is a modest girl who waits patiently for her turn at the well. She remains calm even when Gulabo, the washer woman upbraids her for no reason.

> "Sohini was a bit frightened at first and grew pale, but she kept intensely still and avoiding the shock, subsided into a listens apathy. As she looked away, however, and caste her eyes up to the blue heavens overhead. She felt a sort of dreariness a pain which though she accepted it resignedly, brought usefulness with it" (*Untouchable*, 17-18)

The incident intensifies the pain in the novel and makes the audience's sympathy in India is an anathema. The assault on sohini was a part of Anand's attempt to expose the ugly reality of the caste system. Being treated worse than animals is a part of Bakha and Sohini's daily life but this incident was something worse. Bakha felt the most intense pain of his life. Untouchability reduced the lower class people to the position of animals. They had no rights in the society and their existence was a burden upon others. Anand has brought out this pain very well through the characters of Bakha and Sohini. The two siblings cannot do anything but feel helpless over their status and console each other. Anand has portrayed the assault on Sohini to pull away the mask from the face of the Hindu society at whose top are the Brahmins, who call themselves descendants of gods and serve as priests in the Hindu society. Bakha and sohini are living the same curse. Every untouchable lives. However this is the limit for, Bakha beyond which the pain becomes in human and unbearable. If we talk about lower caste women problem than can see in coolie, how the worker types of wives and daughter suffer if their men person die or leave women.

He had heard of how the landlord had seized his father's five acres of land because the interest on the mortgage covering the unpaid rent had not been forth coming when rains had been accent and the harvests bad. And he knew how his father had died a show death of bitterness and disappointment and left his mother a penniless beggar to support a young brother-in-law and a child in arms. The sight of his mother grinding grain between the scarred surfaces of mill-stones which she gyrated round and round. Round and round by the wooden handle, now with her right hand, now with her left, day and night, had become inaudibly imprinted on his mind. Also, the sight of her as she had lain. Dead on the ground with a horrible yet sad, set expression on her face, had sunk, into his subconscious with all its weight of tragic dignity and utter resignation (*Coolie*, 2-3)

But somewhere women become cruel to weaker men and having bad behavior to them. Somewhere if some child lost his parents and have to take responsibility to bring up that orphan in that time women become bad and starting torturing him in coolie Gujri doing the same thing with her nephew munoo.

> "Munoo ohe Munoo oh Mundu! Shouted Gujri from the verandah of a squat, sequestered, little mud hut, thatched with straw, which stood upon the edge of a hill about a hundred yards away from the village in the valley and her eagle eyes explored the track of gold dust which worked its zigzag course through rough scrub, beyond the flat roofs of the village houses, under the relentless haze of the kangra sun. She could not see him" (*Coolie*, 1)

Again and again called him in very bitter voice sometimes says where you died? Drifted, evil star and sometimes say that you have to earn for us and your uncle will soon send you to town for earning.

She just doesn't want to see him anymore. She was just her own kid but no him. She pressure on him to earning. Some where women herself earn and make self-respect in front of others in that days women didn't allow to go out to doing any work, but now these day women trying to come forward and make dignity to herself.

> "Bhavinaben patel's winnig silver in the women's singles class 4 table tennis event at the Tokyo Paralympic games is the stuff of history. She won India's first medal at Tokyo games, and also India's first table tennis medal at Paralympics. The 34-years-old wheelchair bound athlete was of; owed by Nishad Kumar clinching another silver" (Hass, 14)

She is inspiration examples of what differently-abled people can achieve when given right opportunities.at one last, a sepoy walks by but he pays no need to the begging outcastes. Luckily for sohini and the others, shortly after the sepoy is Pandit kali Nath, one of the priests in charge of town temples. They successfully prevail upon Nath to draw for them. As he draws the water, Nath is absorbed in thoughts about the source of his constipated bowels. Therefore, when Gulabo shouts loudly that she has been waiting the longest, he is annoyed at her words all the other outcastes besides sohini claim they were first and jostle amongst each other for the best position to receive water. Sohini catches Nath's eye because of her pretty face and her refusal to join the mellee. He tells herto come closer and orders the others to back away. After Nath fills Sohini's pitcher he tells her to come clean the temple later in the day. Sohini agrees and leaves to take the water back to her family.

Here can see how that Pandit forget his all bounders wit upper caste and lower caste only in front of Sohini beauty and call her to the temple only for sexual harassment and if he can successful molest her than ok otherwise ready for blame her by using his upper caste bounds. That's why in that people get their girl marriage very soon and it's not only lower cast but upper cast too. Get their girls marry in responsible house and get relax about herdaughter or sister. If there their parents won't ready for that than theirGarand parents force them for marry.

> "Indeed, you are in your infancy. If you insult yourself, the sour fruit of sacrilege will be for Mohini eating. Listen, words wont tie the air into knot and make a groom for Mohini. Bear this in mind, night and day asleep or awake; our Mohini is of marriage age. Mohini is of marriage age. Mohini, born on the night of festive lights and herself a light. Find her the like list groom in Bengal". (*Bhattacharya*, 24-25)

Sohini back at home with water and have to face the anger of her father Lakha. Woman did whatever for make happy men but they never become happy. I don't know why? After all what they want and why they don't want to understand women. Lakha shouts at Sohini for taking so long. He calls her a daughter of a pig and commands her to call her brothers the house only Bakha comes inside, as Rakha escaped from the house earlier in the morning and went playing. Lakha fakes an illness and fells Bakha to take over his sweeping duties in the temple courtyard and on the main road of bulashah. Bakha knows his father is lying about his illness but cannot protest. The work must get done. He drinks the tea and that tea will prepare his sister for him, takes up his tools, and leaves his house in the direction of town. Everywhere women get. Torture. Whatever India became polite to women because these days other country's people praising India. There in a newspaper mention that a 24 years old participant said the Taliban tried to rout the gathering of about 100 women using tear gas rifle bults and metal clubs or tools. She said she received five stiches to close head wound after she was knocked unconscious with a blow from a metal object. Saturday's marchers had wanted to pay respect to those soldiers, who had fought for the now defunct republic, said one of the protesters a female ex-afghan army company commander. But after placing flowers at the former defense ministry we were surrounded by armed Taliban from all sides. Said he women who is being identifying only by her first name, Rukhshana, to guard against retribution "they asked us to stop the protest she said some of the Taliban beat us' 'the 45 years-old is the team leader and guides the women in handcrafting products like dolls, bags and gariands, Assa's husband was a journalist in Kabul but threats from the Taliban forced him to move his family to India.

Razia assa, a former school teacher in Afghanistan, arrived as a refugee in New Delhi with her family eight years ago, it took her a while to rebuild her life. In November 2019, she got a boost when she got a job at silaiwali, a social enterprise.in Delhi that up cycle's waste fabric from garment factories to create handcrafted products for export to the United States and Europe. Her co-worker too isafghan women refugees, most of them the sole jobholders in there, families.

Shikiba Ahmad 45, a single mother of five children, baked cookies for years before she got a salaried post at silaiwali.

> "There was no need for me to work and earn a living back home. But after the Taliban captured our petrol pump, two cars and a house and we had income are necessities. I have to take care of the rent, food and education of my children" *(Agarwal,* 5)

A busy street lay before the brother and sister when they emerged from the temple. Bakha looked out to it vaguely. He could not concentrate on the riot of variety that was displayed in it. He had no patience to see anything or to hear anything, and he didn't want to speak, Bakha become very angry to himself and can'ts carified himself after kali Nath bad behavior with her sister sohini. He just thought why he didn't kill that hypocrite. He cried out silently. He afraid that everyone will know about it.

> "my poor sister! How can she show her face to the world after this? But why didn't she let me go and kill that man? Why was she born a girl in our house, to bring disgrace upon us? So beautiful! So beautiful and so accursed! I wish she had been the ugliest women in the world, and then no one would have teased her! But he couldn't bear the thought of her being ugly. His pride in her beauty seemed to be hurt. And he just wished; oh, god, why was she born, why was she born; then, however, he saw her bending and wiping her eyes with her apron with a sudden burst of tenderness and humility he gripped her arm close and dragged her along, writing with the conflicts in his soul". (*Untouchable*, 74)

Only because of this type of treatment decent people never want a beautiful girl to their house. Only because of the bad behavior of others. I have ability to keep my daughter, sister mother safely at home but who will take responsibility after home. No one, outer people will say there all fault of that girl. What could girl do? She does her best in all field and throw her love to others but people reflecting abusing.

> "She says you did, and you believe it now. Because I love you. Because when you are away from me, I want you because I insist on being with you, being allowed to touch you and know you. You can't bear it. Can you? No you are afraid. You might-perish" (Desai, 52)

Anand just want to explore the condition of women in his both novels. Somewhere women show her power but some where she has to face a big deal. Here women husband or brother could not do anything. In his 1st novel untouchable, sohini have to face abusing, rape, here women torture to women like Gulabo call her prostitute. And in other Pandit kali Nath called him for harass her' she totally helpless. And in coolie upper cast pressed to lower caste wives or daughters have to send to upper posted person and Gujri in other torture to Munoo.

In both novels, we across abusive linguistic expressions associated with illicit relations. The study shows that in almost all the case the addressees are the low caste/ class people. The abuses are prostitute, rape-sister. It is also observed that lower caste people abuse comparatively still lower caste people. Such as, Sohini. Bakha's sister is abused by Gulabo, the address is a person from lowest caste. It is interesting to note that there is caste discrimination within the lower castes. The abuse intends to show that sohini is a loose character and can allow any male member to have sexual relations with her. Her little social status is reduced to the no social status of prostitutes. Similarly in 'coolie' there are abusive unsex of language indicating illicit relations. Here also the addressers are the persons from the higher stranger of society and the addresses are the persons from the lower class of society, the abusive linguistic expressions, seducer of your daughter ohe lover of your mother, seducer of your sister point out the immoral sexual relations. All these expressions show the prevent sexuality and indicate male superiority over female. The above speech acts do no convey the literal meaning is conveyed by the above utterances. However the intention of the speaker is to harm the feelings of the hearer. In other words, there is no feeling of good will and understanding between the speaker and the hearer in their relationship.

Works Cited

Anand, Mulk Raj. *Untouchable.* Arnold Publishers India, 1935.

.... *Coolie.* Penguin Group, 1936.

Agarwal, Priyangi. *The Times of India.* Monday, August 30, 2021.

Bhattacharya, Bhabani. *Music for Mohini.* Orient Paperbacks, 1952.

Desai, Anita. *Cry, the Peacock.* United States Press, 1991.

Hass, Richar. *The times of India.* Monday, August 30, 2021.

CHAPTER 13

Perceptible Hopes: Dreams to Survive in Bharati Mukherjee's *Jasmine*

Ritu Priyadharshini V.

Abstract

Immigration and dislocation form the nucleus of modern women writings. It is a fact that migration, change and transition from one place to another form an integral part of all women's lives. When the immigrants reach the host country, they have a distorted psyche. For a diasporic person, identity is neither static nor fixed, but keeps on changing with time. Such person is aware of his or her past and the present life. So, women feel rejected and distorted physically as well as emotionally. As Shashi Deshpande states in *Women in the novels of Shashi Deshpande*, "There comes a time when stop take stock.... there is a critical moment In one's life when you come to a particular crisis in your life, you try to stand there and look back, but most of the time you just go on with your life. Only when you confront your past, you can go to the future". (148)

The self, dislocated from its roots has a yearning to return to its home country. The immigrants carry with them a profound sense of attachment of their home country and hence are not able to adapt themselves to the social milieu. Their minds are always in a state of reminiscence of their culture and language. Thus, their souls wander and are found to be divided; in other words, they are neither there nor here fully. The physical displacement act as a catalyst to the pre-existing notion of loneliness and despair which paves way to search of oneself amidst other souls.

Keywords: Traditional and modern world, despair, dominant social roles, a new gender identity

Introduction

Sense of identity is deep-rooted in the culture in which one lives and hence, alienation from one's culture leads to the loss of one's socio-cultural identity. The urge to identify with the present stimulates one in the quest for identity, which operates at public and private levels. It is this urge to discover a rationale in the transitivity of the objects around us that leads the alienated self in its quest for identity. The plight of longingness and belongingness involves the twin process of migration and relocation. Some immigrants learn to live lonely even in a strange atmosphere which is remarkable thing.

Creativity is an important medium through which the immigrant writer tries to reconstruct and recreate fragmental thought in a liminal space. It is more so in the case of women as the facts and fantasies of the new setting are to be manuevered into existing repertories of knowledge. Their literature establishes a complex dialectic of struggle, endurance and creativity.

Bharati Mukherjee, through her novel *Jasmine* fictionalises the process of dislocation and relocation by tracing a young Indian woman's experiences of trauma and triumph in her attempt to forge a new identity for herself. Martin Heidegger in *Indian Journal of Postcolonial Literature* puts it: "A boundary is not that at which something begins its presencing" (91). Thus, the novel is characterised by a tendency in which the feeling of being displaced is overcome, by a desire to settle down and fine a new home.

The nostalgia for the past is balanced by a desire to capture the present; the loss of identity caused through the process of displacement is mended by gaining a new one. Bharati Mukherjee's *Jasmine* can be divided into three parts. In the first part, the focus is on narrating the situation of an immigrant who is in the process of settling down and the second part the heroines are in the process of providing their identity. In the third part, the protagonist achieves a proper identity and balance between tradition and modernity. In the end, Jasmine achieves transmutation.

Jasmine takes its start with a conversation between an old astrologer and the protagonist Jyoti when she was very young. He prophesied her widowhood and exile in advance. Jyoti, born in Punjab, the fifth daughter and seventh of nine children, is a survivor of her mother's attempt of female infanticide. Named by her grandmother, Jyoti had the meaning of 'light'. She resembled the light of her family. Jyoti "was a pretty lady with delicate taste" (J72). She excelled in her studies and had a good command over English language. She wanted to become a doctor, but it was ignored by her father saying she has become mad. Sandra Ponzanesi in *Studies in Indian Writing in English* remarks that, "Jasmine is particularly beautiful, with inborn aristocratic traits, intelligent and capable of learning the tricks of survival" (J92). Later she is attracted to Prakash with whom she elopes. At the age of fourteen, she gets married and both move to Amritsar.

Prakash wanted to change the Jyoti of Hasnapur and make her a modern woman. He makes her to read his manuals and try to keep up her command over English language. He plays as the modern enlightened man. Their wedding was not a religious one: no dowry was exchanged. He acts as a mentor as he turns her away from the traditional role of a Hindu wife. Prakash gave her courage and taught her to be independent in her views. It was the first training she received in order to be a new woman. "He wanted to break down the Jyoti's I'd been in Hasnapur and make me a new kind of city woman. To break off the past, he gave me a new name: Jasmine" (J77). But all the more Jyoti felt dislocated between her Indian traditions of subtle woman and Prakash's view of modern enlightened woman: "But I felt suspended between worlds" (J76). She feels as if she is in between two worlds. In India, Jyoti feels hovering between the traditional and modern world offered by Prakash.

Both Jyoti and Prakash dreams of starting their own business, even naming it as Vijh & Wife shop and move to US. On the eve of their department to US, Prakash is killed in an attack by the Sikh terrorists. Being widowed, she could only find direction in her old Indian dutifulness. She decides to go to America to commit Sati, burning herself along with her husband's suit at the site where he decides to pursue his studies.

Fate had a few surprises for Jasmine as she went to America with a forged passport. On her arrival in Florida, she undergoes traumatic experiences when Half-face, the deformed captain of their ship, puts up a face of a protector: "There's some bad fellows up yonder. Best you and me keep us a little company" (J108). However, Jasmine ends up being the prey of her own assumed saviour. Half-face drives her to a motel, a perfect place for an American crime. He rapes her even after her claim that she was a widow. The transformation of identity starts from the moment she realises herself as a mere sexual being. She transforms herself into Kali and kills the demon who slaughters her. Jasmine contemplates her suicide, but the shower makes her to drift away from it.

No one to call to, no one to disturb us. Just me and the man who had raped me, the man I had murdered. The room looked like a slaughterhouse. Blood had congealed on my hands, my chin, and my breasts. What a monstrous thing, what an infinitesimal thing, is the taking of a human's life; for the second time in three months, I was in a room with a *slain* man, my body bloodied. I was walking death. Death incarnate. This time, my response was calm. I went back to the shower and purified myself once again. (J19)

Her sense of shame and awe is triggered when she is raped. She decides to purify herself in both body and mind and then takes a shower. In the shower, she decides to avenge the man who abused her. She bites her tongue to draw blood, and then stabs and stamps upon her molester till his blood splatters the walls and he huddles lifeless at her feet. Her transformation to the vengeful Kali is a symbol of her transformation to a new woman. Kali is the mother – goddesses of the universe, creator of time and devourer of time. Possessed and transformed by a range of the Goddesses Kali Jasmine undergoes a quick shift of identity. From a dutiful traditional widow she is now a free murderess in search of multiple reincarnations.

The incident shows the various dimensions of man-woman relationship, gender specific power equations, the inevitability and hegemonic hold patriarchal indoctrinations which consider women as a mere object, are difficult to cast off easily for it is deeply entrenched in phallocentric society.

Experience moulds a person such are evident in the case of Jasmine. The rape incident brings out a drastic change in her psyche. Thus, she is a woman who is aware of her potential and at the same time a rebel against the compulsion of conformity. It strengthened her to continue her living. There was a destruction of her old self and a creation of new psyche. When pushed from one another, she emerges not as a tragic character but as one who is determined to change her destiny and explores her identity. It paves the death of her existing or prevailing self and a new bold woman is born.

Jasmine later moves to Manhattan as a paid nanny in Hayes' family. Taylor and Wylie Hayes are a glamorous and emancipated couple with an adopted daughter Duff. Slowly she became a part of their small loving family. The acquisition of her next identity starts there. She becomes 'Jase' to Taylor. There is a transformation from the submissive widow, Jyoti to the vengeful Kali and ultimately to Jase. Jase was a caregiver and was metaphorically a mother to Duff whom she cared and loved.

Jasmine's calm acceptance of both the change in her own scale of values and love for Taylor above racial and cultural, barriers is worth nothing. She becomes herself with Taylor.

Taylor didn't want to change me. He didn't want to scour and sanitise the foreignness.. . I changed because I wanted to. To bunker oneself inside nostalgia, to sheathe the heart in a bulletproof vest, was to be a coward. On Claremont Avenue, in the Hayeses' big, clean, brightly lit apartment, I bloomed from a different alien with forged documents into adventurous Jase. (J185)

The narrative is structurally and thematically significant for, it highlights a specific goal the re-emergence and quest for meaning in life.

This idyllic life comes to a sudden halt when her accidental sighting of Sukhwinder, the terrorist who killed her husband makes her flee from that place Her main reason for running away is the fear that her presence in their household may hinder the safety of Taylor and Duff. She decides to go Iowa, far away from Sukhi. In Iowa, she meets Bud Ripplemeyer, the banker. Bud was fifty three years old and a traditionalist. He and Karin had adopted Du, a Vietnamese boy who came from refugee camp. Du, like Jasmine was dislocated in Iowa. He had seen the terrible faces of the world and suffered like hell in the refugee camp. After a shootout, Bud was in wheelchair and it was Jasmine who took care of him. Bud divorced Karin as he loved Jasmine. He gave her a new 'Jane'.

Jane was happy with Bud who cares for her and plans to marry her before their baby comes out. Her tradition uproots her as she becomes a caregiver for Bud. She cooks, cleans, feels and is found sexually attractive by relaxing sexual favours to Bud. She has learned to adjust to a new set of values but she has not shed all her values altogether. Her analysis of her relationship with Bud shows that there is clear distinction in her mind between livings with someone separated from his wife and deliberately breaking up a home. She was a catalyst for Bud to leave Karin, not a cause.

A resemblance could be traced out in the lives of Jane and Du, the Vietnamese boy. Du was only a year younger than Jasmine and adopted son of Bud and Jane. Jane could identify herself with Du. Just like her; he had two lives, one in Saigon and another in the refugee camp. In Saigon he had lived in a house with large family. In the refugee camp, he had suffered a lot-his mother cut hair, his older brother raised fighting fish, and his sister brought live crabs and worms for him to eat when he was starving to death. His mother and brother were hacked to death in the fields by a madman.

Du's doing well because he has always trained with live ammo, without a net, with no multiple choice. No guesswork: only certain knowledge or silence. Once upon a time, like me, he was someone else. We've survived hideous times. (J214). My transformation has been genetic, Du's was hyphenated. (J222)

When Du left home to seek his only sister, Jane felt abandoned. She always associated herself with Du. She knew Du was right in his decisions but she felt alienated. Abandonment, guilt, betrayal was in his eyes. If Bud was not crippled, he would have got a good father. But he felt Bud never wanted him especially when he got his own kid coming. He stepped into his future. Du could never be a total American as he would always be attached to his experience. Unlike Jane, he tried to develop his contacts with the other Vietnamase in Baden.

The transmutation of identity of Jyoti is seen throughout the novel. She transforms from one to another, assigning each identity with different names. She is born as Jyoti of Hasnapur, becomes Jasmine to Prakash, Kali to Half-face, Jazzy to Lillian, Jase to Taylor and Jane to Bud. She is described as a rebel, an adaptor, and also a survivor and her transformations reveal her identity process. The transformation is quite fast as she is unwilling to abandon ride she is on.

Lata Mishra opines in her essay in *Indian Journal of Postcolonial Literature,*

> It is Jasmine's idea of disconnected history that admits her to subdue the restraining structures of memory in her endeavour at re-inventing herself. In her self-structuring, Jasmine does not destroy or dispose of the past, but puts it to a process of excision: a simultaneous negation and preservation of the past. The past is counter balanced in terms of its power of constraint and paralysis but well-kept as a means of re-creating identity within the framework of an in-subordinated reasoning. The obvious non-existence of any sign of bereavement, wistfulness or pensiveness in *Jasmine* is quite noteworthy. (94)

Jasmine is a courageous woman. It could be ascertained in her childhood when she argues with the astrologer: "You're a crazy old man. You don't know what my future holds" (J3). Her boldness is visible through her words. With the same courage, she decides to go to America to pursue her husband's dream of her being a modern woman. She flies to America with a forged passport to complete his mission, to perform Sati in the college which Prakash dreamt of going.

Jyoti was totally changed when she transformed herself to Kali, who killed the Man who slaughtered her. As a Kali, she was strong and a destroyer and was not submissive to accept all that life offers her instead powerfully adapts herself according to the new situation. She is an instance to prove that the Indian society consists of courageous women like Jasmine who can accommodate themselves comfortable in the entire difficult situation. She protests against culture, tradition, patriarchal society in Indian soli and isolation, starvation, physical and psychological pain in American soil.

The novel *Jasmine* deconstructs dominant social roles of womanhood and marriage where passivity and marital fidelity even in widowhood is appreciated. Thus, by the exercise of free will and free choice she emancipates herself of the fetters of cultural stereotyping. The protagonist, Jasmine is then constructed as an instrument of destruction of normative value system.

Jasmine is remoulded as a lover when she is linked with Taylor and Bud. As a lover, she was happy and contends. She was satisfied and located herself one with their family. She was always reminded of Taylor because of the love she had for him. To Bud, she has acted like an Indian wife who exults in her loyalty towards her husband. She has identified all her dreams and wishes with Bud's. She thinks that even the memory of the past life amounts to a kind of disloyalty to Bud since he feels frightened by her stories of Hasnapur. She plays the temptress at his behest and hangs up all decency to yield to the sexual passion of a crippled person.

Jasmine becomes a dutiful mother to Du during her revolution as Jane. She identifies herself with Du, the Vietnamese refugee. Both of them had overcome from many trials and tribulations in their lives. Jane considers Du as the son of her and Prakash. Du, like Prakash loves to invent things. She cares him as a mother and fulfils her duties of a mother. Her changes as a wife, a Kali, a lover and a dutiful mother are seen in the novel. Dr. Deepkumar. J. Trivedi in Indian Diasporic Literature quotes:

> From the 'Sati-goddess' Jyoti to the Kali-Jasmine to 'adventurous Jase' to plain Jane has been an eventful, uneven odyssey; the protagonist's name

> changes as well as her shifts in places of residence become metaphors for an immigrant woman's process of uprooting and re-rooting. (84)

Thus, from destruction of her own self, Jyoti is recreated into a new psyche. Her destruction and recreation of self is through various experiences she was exposed to. Nirmala, remains as a typical traditional wife as she has not undergone experiences as Jyoti. If she had also to endure such events, she might also transform into a bold and courageous woman.

Thus, the protagonist, Jasmine undergoes multiple identity transformations in her quest for happiness. She is an embodiment of dutifulness, ever conscious of her relationship with Prakash. Whenever she is pushed to a tragedy, she rises from the ashes like a phoenix. She never emerges as a tragic character but as one who is determined to explore and change her identity. Different locations assign her difficult roles as a daughter, wife, and caretaker, beloved. In all the roles she partakes with full dedication and love. She never goes back to her nostalgic feelings but tries to explore the new culture, people and be a part of them.

At every stage, she is conscious to achieve an identity of her own, along with her consciousness of her being an Indian woman. Pulling herself out from the native culture is painful but at the same time exhilarating as she feels it is cowardly to "bunker oneself inside nostalgia" (185). To change a different personality is not an easy process. She has undergone difficult situation like rapes, and murders.

Conclusion

Jasmine survived all those hideous times and is not sentimental about her Indian identity. She does not suffer from nostalgic yearning either. Instead, she has used all her strength and resolve to forge new alliances of the adopted homeland. It indicates the progression in attitude. Jasmine emerges as a complex individual sustaining herself by her own efforts in a foreign land. As she grows confident in her powers to shape a new identity for herself, she is able to express her sexual desires more honestly. This culminates in her decision to reject her earlier intention of staying with the crippled Bud, and to live with Taylor, grasping at another chance of happiness. She asserts that she is not merely choosing between men; she is propounding her right to try and reposition the stars instead of accepting her fate.

Thus, the novel, *Jasmine* emancipates and evolves a viable new image a role model perceiving the irrelevance of the old stereotypes, their stultification, at the same time the transgression creating actual and symbolic independence. She indicates the progression in attitude. Jasmine emerges as a complete individual sustaining herself by her own efforts in a foreign land. Hence, through Jasmine, Bharati Mukherjee continues to explore the intimate aspects of the lives of her women characters in various stereotyped roles and thereby not only deconstructs but also affirms that the self-accommodates herself in the value system and blooms with a new gender identity for themselves.

Work Cited

Chrisna Jose "An Analysis of Identity in Bharati Mukherjee"s *Jasmine*" (Quest Journals) *Journal of Research in Humanities and Social Science* 6.9 (2018): 69-70

Mukherjee, Bharati. 1989. Jasmine. New York: Ballantine Books.

Mishra, R.K. "Indian Women's Assertion of Individuality and Identity in the Social and Familial Life: a Thematic Study of the Novels of Manju Kapoor." *The Atlantic Literary Review Quarterly* vol. 14 no. 2, Apr-Jun, pp. 111-118.

William Grimes. "Bharati Mukherjee, Writer of Immigrant Life, Dies at 76." *New York Times*. February 1, 2017. 4/6/20.

CHAPTER 14

A Reflection of the Inner Woman: A Feminist and Psychoanalytic Reading of *Jane Eyre*

Nayana George

Abstract

The images of women in literature model the way we see women and it is important to recognise and to question these images since these go on to form role model prototypes and influence the society as a whole. This paper seeks to explore Charlotte Brontë's *Jane Eyre* (1847) from a Psychoanalytic and Feminist perspective while putting forth the idea that the novel is more than just an object upon which critical perspectives and frameworks can be applied. The evolution of the 19th century novel and Brontë's own life are looked into as significant influences on this particular novel, and the same is explored and elucidated, while also venturing on a tangent as to why this particular novel should not be pigeonholed into any critical perspectives that may cause its narrative to be ignored.

Keywords: Charlotte Brontë, critical theory, feminism, women in literature

Introduction

Due to its status of being the first country to be industrialised, England faced a definitive learning curve in the 19th century. The rapid and unregulated industrialisation brought with it a host of social and economic problems that the previously agrarian nation was not equipped with prior experience to deal with. Although, lady luck did favour them soon enough, and their fortunes turned for the better. A head start compared to the other modern countries ensured that they had an earlier grasp on the world market. Through perseverance and effort and through widespread colonisation, England became the world's banker from 1870s. "By the end of the century England was the world's foremost imperial power" (Robson and Christ 1018). Thomas Babington Macaulay relished the superior qualities of the English people as he called them "the greatest and most highly civilised people that ever the world saw" (qtd. in Robson and Christ 1018).

Charlotte Brontë's *Jane Eyre* was written and set in 19th century England. This spatial and temporal location has an immense role to play in the way the novel is perceived and understood.

In 1884 Friedrich Engels observed the following: "England is unquestionably the freest – that is the least unfree – country in the world" (qtd. in Robson and Christ 1031). While this sentiment is true in certain respects, this generalisation could not be applied in the case of women. Even with the feminist movement flourishing and thriving, women were still considered inferior to men. This was seen in the way they were disallowed from handling property and money, they had limited opportunities to acquire an education, and they were not allowed to voice out their choices and opinions in governance.

The 19th Century Novel

There is a marked difference between the 19th century novel and the Victorian novel. The social and economic conditions were particularly favourable for the print industry of the 19th century. The reading public increased, and many people began earning a supplementary remuneration through a side-career in writing. While more lucrative than it was before, a career in writing was not enough to sustain a livelihood (Horseman 2-3). An aspect of interest is definitely the adjective 'Victorian.' "Queen Victoria herself encouraged her own identification with the qualities we associate with the adjective – earnestness, moral responsibility and domestic propriety" (Robson and Christ 1019). While not every 19th century novel can be categorised as a Victorian novel, Charlotte Brontë's *Jane Eyre* certainly is one that falls in the middle of the partitions.

Social conditions were slowly beginning to change in the 19th century and the novel of that time reflects these radical turnovers. A considerable shift began to be seen in the public and private discourses of the time. Women writers began entering the public discourse of a representative space of the novel, although most hidden under the veil of masculine or androgynous pseudonyms to conceal the gender aspect of their identity, something that later sparks off further feminist talks and debates. Charlotte Brontë herself wrote under the alias of Currer Bell, and so did the other Brontë sisters – Emily as Ellis and Anne as Acton Bell. Some remarkable female protagonists began to be observed in the space of the novel. Writers such as George Eliot, Jane Austen, and many others seemed to be attempting to empower the domestic space. Class identity, wealth, and determination, which were earlier seen as domains of men, began to permeate in the feminine sentiments, which was a direct result of the prevalent feminist theory and criticism discourses.

As a result of the social conditions and stigma, the only occupation that an unmarried middle-class woman could earn a living by and maintain some claim to dignity and gentility was that of a governess. But this particular occupation was also plagued with perils; there was no security of employment, only minimum wages were offered, and the status that they attained was quite ambiguous – not exactly a servant, but not considered a family member either, for they were isolated in the household. As such, the genre of governess novels became extremely popular. A famous example is *Jane Eyre*, through which the precariousness of the unmarried middle-class woman in Victorian England could be seen and experienced (Robson and Christ 1033).

Charlotte Brontë – the Person and the Writer

It is a general understanding that the genius and the neurotic are two sides of the same coin – eccentric manifestations of an abnormally developed personality. There is a lot to be said, and has been said about the Brontë siblings, in particular, Charlotte and Emily. The Brontë siblings lived in quite an isolated setting where they were the creators of a fantasy world where they ruled as the gods. However, this fantasy universe turned into an obsession, and Charlotte formally recognised her need to get away from this over-heated fantasy (Horseman 161). This shock coupled with, as Lucy Dooley puts it in her essay "Psychoanalysis of Charlotte Brontë, as a Type of the Woman of Genius," the "infantile fixation" (231) upon her father – a result of the Freudian concept of the "Electra complex" (263) – were determining influences on her art and imagination:

> The rival wife, much older than the heroine, of course, is reduced practically to the level of an animal, an inferior creature to whom no real consideration is due. The house is burned, the mad wife perishes in the flames (and we have a right to recall the significance of fire as a symbol of sexual passion) the husband is thus-freed, but at the same time is blinded. He cannot see, therefore, who it is that comes to him, to take the place of wife. His blindness satisfies the "resistance" to the fulfillment of

> the wish (in the language of the dream interpretation of Freud). The story did not demand that Rochester be made blind, but conflicting forces of the author's unconsciousness required it. The story of Rochester and Jane dramatized her own love for the forbidden man-first for her father, a love wholly unconscious, second for the teacher, a love partly conscious, and the writer had to make some concession to the fundamental obstacle to wish-fulfillment. (268)

On closer inspection, many parallels can be drawn between the author and the protagonist, and one could even venture as far as to say that Charlotte Brontë created Jane Eyre in her image. "I am poor, obscure, plain, and little… I have as much soul…and full as much heart" says Jane (Brontë 216).

> "Her smallness, her shyness, her quaint dependence and quainter independence, her quick impulses, followed by quick retreats, her piteous lack of self-confidence in company, contrasted with her certainty of the rightness of her conceptions in the world of creative imagination, all these and many more traits clearly revealed the child in her" is a very detailed description of Charlotte Brontë. (Dooley 232).

Brontë taught at a girls' boarding school – Roe Head – and then became a governess for the Sidgewick family, paralleling Jane's teaching position at Lowood and her governess position at Thornfield. Brontë disliked her governess positions and dreamed of establishing her own school; she lives this dream by having Jane operate the village school for girls, which is set up by St. John Rivers.

Jane Eyre and Bertha Mason – Reflections

Much of the critical canon around *Jane Eyre* focuses either on religion or mental illness, that too primarily upon the women in the novel. One of the most notable analyses comes from Sandra Gilbert and Susan Gubar, whose main argument is that the only way Jane can find peace and be with Edward Fairfax Rochester in the end of the novel is to become sexually comfortable in her own skin:

> For while the mythologising of repressed sexuality, it is repressed rage may parallel the mythologising of repressed sexuality, it is far more dangerous to the order of society. The occasional woman who has a weakness for black-browed Byronic heroes can be accommodated in novels and even in some drawing rooms; and patriarchal mansions obviously cannot. And Jane Eyre…was such a woman. (338)

An influential idea that Gilbert and Gubar propagate, and one that has been widely accepted by many readers and critics is the notion of Bertha being Jane's double, and even as the manifestation of Jane's inner, repressed self. There is a Post-colonial angle that comes into play here; that the darker-skinned Creole who neither fits in with the whites nor the blacks is metaphorically also seen as the *darker* side to Jane. Bertha's racial ambiguity renders her without a sense of belonging, precisely how a woman's sexuality is perceived as in the Victorian society that is fuelled by the studies and teaching of many influential analysts from various fields, including Sigmund Freud, the renowned psychoanalyst.

Furthermore, Gilbert and Gubar also hypothesise about the strains that a woman, particularly Brontë's Jane Eyre, has to overcome to rise above the patriarchal society:

> Every woman in a patriarchal society must meet and overcome: oppression (at Gateshead), starvation (at Lowood), madness (at Thornfield), and coldness (at Marsh End). Most important, her confrontation, not with Rochester but with Rochester's mad wife Bertha, is the book's central confrontation, an encounter…not with her own sexuality but with her own imprisoned "hunger, rebellion, and rage," a secret dialogue of self and soul on whose outcome, as we shall see, the novel's plot, Rochester's fate, and Jane's coming-of-age all depend. (339)

In her book *The Female Malady,* Elaine Showalter writes that Charlotte Brontë's "work shows an evolution from Romantic stereotypes of female insanity to a brilliant interrogation of the meaning of madness in women's daily lives" (66).

Bertha is Jane's alter ego; her passionate and darker side. Jane is the practical counterpart to her Dionysian other. On observing the other female characters, we see Brontë embodies two kinds of women that dominated that time, wherein the Victorian sentiments would pigeonhole a woman into one of the two extremes – the prude or the harlot. Helen Burns is a perfect fit for the glorified "Angel in the House", the Madonna-image of the time (Lundén and Srigley, 147). At the same time, Bertha serves to be the classic opposition of sadism and unleashed sexual hunger to the meekness, masochism, and self-sacrifice personified in the other.

It is an important point to note that it is only Bertha's absence and ultimate destruction that leads to Jane and Rochester's union. The understanding that this line of thought leads to is that Jane has to let go of her repressed desires, rage, and sexuality so that she can find her seemingly proper place in Victorian society as a married woman.

Other Pro-Feminist Qualities Exhibited in Jane

A conventional Feminist reading of the novel will be quick to grasp the ideals of independence and equality that Jane strives to achieve before she enters the domesticity, or as some would prefer to say, the golden cage of matrimony. *Jane Eyre* is a *Bildungsroman*; it is a novel that narrates the story of the protagonist's growth and internal development on her search for a meaningful existence in society. Here, the fact that Brontë chose a female protagonist with strong ideals and beliefs in such a time is highly remarkable and deserves accolades. Jane is a protagonist who is inherently class-conscious and is aware of her limitations and shortcomings. Yet, her desire and wish to be a social equal to her husband, thereby clinging onto the notion that it was her own merit or her own fortune, in this case, that led to her coming into money and not her dependence on her future husband. Also, her steadfast attempt to uphold her dignity and self-respect and not succumb to the fall from grace that she would have encountered had she agreed to Rochester's proposal of being his mistress is praiseworthy.

Her unwavering decision to not marry St. John even though her matrimonial future looked bleak at that moment is another quality in Jane that many Feminist critics approve. This step showed her willingness to brave a world that was harsh on spinsters and that she wanted to dedicate her life to a service that she yearned to do added more lustre to her image.

The Red Room

Neither a Psychoanalytic nor a Feminist reading of the novel will be complete without paying considerable due attention to the Red Room. There are various perspectives through which this spatial configuration can be seen. It can be viewed as the paradigm of the female inner space. Through such a lens, it brings forth the gush of repressed passions and emotions from behind the emotional wall, the flood of such intense emotions becoming too much for Jane to handle. The fear of madness is sometimes much greater than the fear of death, and this is exactly what Jane fears. "Unjust, unjust" (Brontë 11) are Jane's words regarding the sentence of imprisonment in the Red Room without a fair hearing and without having the opportunity to defend herself.

Oddly enough, in the Red Room Jane transforms overnight from a child to a more mature person. The imprisonment in the Red Room can be interpreted as a voyage into the unconscious. When Jane looks into the mirror, she sees herself looking like "a real spirit," which makes her think of one of the characters, "tiny phantoms, half fairy, half imp", in Bessie's ghost stories (Brontë 9). Jane realises that she is considered different and identified as the "the other" by the household at Gateshead Hall, similar to the lonely characters of the moor in Bessie's stories. This madness that she manages to suppress is later encountered in Bertha at Thornfield (Andersson 7-12).

The Red Room, the attic where Bertha is confined; all these are literal representations of the "attic." and Jane and Bertha are, respectively, the "madwomen in the attic(s)" that Gilbert and Gubar talk about. Jane and Bertha's vehement protestations against their confinement in these rooms could be seen as mere outbursts of their disapproval of their bodies and thoughts being confined and oppressed.

The Limitations of Critical Perspectives

It is imperative that we keep in mind that this novel is more than just a vessel for various theoretical and critical perspectives and frameworks that are rather limiting in thought. The narrative does not deserve to be ignored. As a character and as a person, Jane is not meant to be pigeonholed into the mould of only a feminist, or rather, any other narrow roles. The problem with a largely feminist reading of this novel is that they end up being disappointed in the protagonist and see her as complacent and adhering to the dictates of patriarchy. It is crucial to understand that she is merely an individual who is working out the figurative kinks and roadblocks in her life while residing in and facing the social order. Never once does she explicitly challenge patriarchy or any other such institution. She is far from being an idealist, and her sense of justice is limited to her own being. Rather than fighting injustice at a higher level, she is much more concerned about what happens with her, in the time and space that she occupies. Immediacy is key here in the resolution to her problems. She doesn't claim to be a paragon of virtue either. She is highly pragmatic and her ultimate goal is to survive, like any other human being.

The only view that might come close to doing the novel and the author proper justice is that of social realism. The novel is highly realistic and pragmatic in the portrayal of the protagonist and Jane as a character is highly disapproving of any kind of idealism, both of her by other people and in her own beliefs.

Conclusion

Through the death of Helen and Bertha, Jane is freed from the male ideal of female identity; the angel-in-the-house and the demon. She finds her good relatives at Marsh and overcomes the injustices by the evil relatives at Gateshead. Jane finds a stable ground and overcomes the rage repressed in her unconscious (Andersson 14).

To free herself in the patriarchal society and to come to peace with her inner self, Jane meets and overcomes: oppression by the Reed family and Mr. Brocklehurst, starvation at Lowood and during her wandering before reaching Marsh End, madness in the Red Room and at Thornfield and coldness by being lonely and by the way St. John treated her (Gilbert and Gubar 339). Even though she longs for love she does not let Rochester or St. John exploit her, and in the end, she finds the equal relationship she longed for.

Also, we see that although *Jane Eyre* provides us with a canvas to apply various theoretical and critical perspectives, we realise that there is a unique pleasure in seeing the text for what it is, and that is where the true beauty of Brontë's craft lies.

Works Cited

Andersson, Angela. *Identity and Independence in Jane Eyre.* Thesis. Mid Sweden University, 2011, https://www.diva-portal.org/smash/record.jsf?pid=diva2%3A463653&dswid=-1578. Accessed 2 July 2021.

Brontë, Charlotte. *Jane Eyre*, 1847. Wordsworth Classics, 1999.

Dooley, Lucile. "Psychoanalysis of Charlotte Brontë, as a Type of the Woman of Genius." *The American Journal of Psychology,* vol. 31, no. 3, 1920, pp. 221-272.

Horseman, Alan. *The Oxford History of English Literature.* OUP, 1990.

Lundén, Rolf, and Michael Srigley, eds. *Ideas and Identities; British and American Culture 1500-1945*, Studentlitterature, 1992.

Gilbert, Sandra M., and Susan Gubar. "A Dialogue of Self and Soul: Plain Jane's Progress." *The Madwoman in the Attic: The Woman Writer and the Nineteenth-century Literary Imagination.* Yale UP, 1979, pp. 336-371.

Robson, Catherine, and Carol T. Christ. *The Norton Anthology of English Literature: Volume E, The Victorian Age.* 9th ed. W.W.Norton & Company, 2006.

Showalter, Elaine. *The Female Malady: Women, Madness, and English Culture, 1830-1980.* Penguin, 1987.

CHAPTER 15

Amrita's Self-Conception in Jhabvala's *To Whom She Will*

Saranya Devi P. and Keerthi G.

Abstract

The family – a microcosm of the clan – is viewed as a functional structure in which each part is assigned a role in accordance with conventional norms. When one part, a young woman, becomes conscious of the limitations of her personal freedom due to these inhibiting norms, a struggle ensues between her and the guardians of the structure. The collective identity is threatened and the generation is alienated. Jhabvala sees it, the Indian family succeeds in resuming its collective identity by stretching its norms, on the one hand, and by including assimilation through the power of wealth and the weight of an established tradition, on the other.

Key words: family, struggle, identity, tradition

Jhabvala's early years in India were very different from those an English woman would normally have expected. She met few Europeans and lived a reasonably typical middle-class Indian life. Her early impressions, then, were full of sensuous beauty she saw all around her in the country she described as a paradise on earth. During her stay in India, she assimilated all the Indian experiences in terms of Indian customs, Indian cultures, Indian languages, Indian food habits, Indian joint family system, Indian dresses and Indian dishes.

Ruth Prawer Jhabvala has been established as an Anglo-Indian novelist by the modern critics. She has a unique place among the Anglo-Indian novelists of Post-Independence era. Ruth Prawer Jhabvala left England in 1951 to encounter an India engaged in the mighty experiment of bringing its four hundred million people into the mainstream of modern life. Such a phenomenon had transformed the face of the West two centuries ago. It was now changing the face of India. The impetus to this transformation came from the political break with the West through Indian Independence and the more meaningful East-West coming together that was a sequel to India's taking up her position on a basis of equality with the rest of the world.

The clash between the old and young generations once again forms an important theme of the novel. Her primary objective is to depict the bridging of the generation gap in a changing world, there is evident, a broadening of perspective. She was enchanted and obsessed by the Indian people, their dress, food social customs and ways of life. A new generation of Westerners, drawn by Indian spiritualism, started coming into India. Unlike their predecessors, they came not to conquer but to be conquered. How this multiple ingress was affecting the social and intellectual climate of Delhi and by implication the whole of India forms the basis of Ruth Jhabvala's exploration of India in her novels and stories.

To Whom She Will depicts about the younger generation people who wanted to be westernised and fall in love with the person outside their community and D.C. Agarwal in one of his articles analysing the situation writes:

> The traditionalists achieve much by hypothecating their individuality and freedom. They achieve a sense of security and belonging. The non-traditionalists, on the contrary have to pay the price for their identity and 'Lassaizfaire', even so it is questionable whether they will succeed in the bargain.[1]

The central figure of the novel is an apparently tragic figure called Amrita who is in her last teens, a very suitable marriageable age for girls in modern India. A fatherless child, she is the only granddaughter, on her mother's side, of an aristocratic barrister, Rai Bahadur Tara Chand. Amrita has been portrayed as a strong character when compared to Hari. Hari, Amrita's own choice of a lover belongs to a typical traditional family and who cannot be expected to have even, the seriousness of loving independently for fear of his family ties. Though ultimately she gives into the wishes of her mother and agrees to marry Krishna, their paying guest, yet she fights for her love more bravely. She not only faces the opposition of her mother Radha, who all along disapproves Hari, but also her grand-father, Pandit Ram Bahadur Chand. He is not quite averse to her marrying outside the community and is opposed to match with Hari on grounds, which are primarily social and cultural. He feels that Hari as a match for Amrita is total misfit in everyway. Hari appears to him as a king of 'autodidact' having an untutored mind, and so he opposes the proposal and tells Amrita:

> ……In your case, the margin of discrepancy between the two families, the young man's and yours: is too wide. It is a gulf which I cannot find it in many conscience to allow you to bridge.[2]

> And later declares:

> I have told her that she cannot marry this boy. She must regard that as final.[3]

However Amrita does not take this as the final word. She still thinks of the ways in which she can fulfill her love. As against Hari's feeble protests Amrita's strong and open protest is clearly portrayed. She goes to Hari and tells him:

> …..But I do not care about what grandfather says: believe me. Hari, I do not care what any of them say. Please believe me. Please. What does my family matter? You know I would give up everyone and everything for you.[4]

This reveals Amrita's character and ironically presents a sharp contrast to the character of Hari. Amrita is strong and ready to give up her family, money and status for the sake of her love. She then even goes to the extent of asking help from Tarla'a husband Vazir Dayal. She plans to marry Hari in England where there would be no one to oppose them. She is so enthusiastic about their plans for going to England that she sends Krishna to Hari, to tell him of her plans. But Hari's response is against her hopes. He turns out to be weak character. V.A.Shahane puts it:

> He did not sound certain of himself, is the key not only of Hari's character and personality, but of the entire narrative and thematic structure of the novel itself. The uncertainty, the instability, and the waywardness of Hari's emotional responses form the crux of the problem Amrita is confronted with.[5]

Amrita is, quite understandably, repelled by the attitudinising, selfishness and malevolence she sees around her and mistakenly believes them to be the products of Western sophistication. Motivation for revolt comes with romantic love for a member of a community she believes to be composed of simple unostentatious people who, to her innocent trusting mind, represent the soul of India. Yasmine Gooneratne interestingly relates Amrita's rebellion to Ruth Jhabvala's own recoil from her Europeanness at this stage of her life.

Ruth Jhabvala was enraptured by a post-independence Delhi in which, with the withdrawal of the British Raj, traditional Indian courtesies were being revived and deliberately cultivated, and so Amrita, the young heroine of her first novel *To Whom She Will* (1955) recoils from the Westernised values of her wealthy and well-bred family to seek identity with an "Indianness" that she imagines is to be found only in simple, true, and unostentatious folk unspoiled by Western ways.[6]

However, here too Amrita finds herself at a loss. Her affection for Hari is based on an idealised concept of the Indianness she supposes him to present. That her idealism is misconceived is perceptible from the way her quest for the simple and the natural leads her the people whose dividing lines are just as uncompromising as her grandfather's, and whose rejection of her is as total as the Rai Bahadur's rejection of Hari. It is the Indianness and imagined simplicity that attracts the romantic side of Amrita and endears Hari to her and it is clearly portrayed when they two have lunch in the radio station canteen:

> …..he ate with such relish and with such unselfconscious enjoyment. He handled knife and fork rather awkwardly, which was another thing she found charming about him. He was simple and unspoilt, and his way the traditional, truly Indian ways which had been lost in her family. She now rather despised her family's sophisticated, highly westernised way of living and thought of it as being false and unreal and quite unsuitable……... Once, also, she had asked Hari, why he did not always with his hands when he was with her, as he was accustomed to do; but this too had not been a success. Hari had been shocked and rather hurt; to him it had seemed as if she were suggesting h did not know how a gentleman would behave.[7]

It clearly emphasises the gaps between the way Amrita and Hari think and the fundamental differences that exist between the two, differences their families are aware from the beginning of the novel. Jhabvala repeatedly shows Amrita loving in Hari the things he tries to hide from her, and Hari loving in Amrita the things she is ashamed in herself. In effect, each is ashamed of his or her class before the other. It is perhaps not so much Hari that Amrita is in love with the Indianness. She thinks she admires in him – an element she sees as vital and full of life-and, of course, in her romantic way she idealises the very idea of being in love.

Modern fiction in English is peculiarly conscious of its technique and tools. The technique of presenting problems, the nature and the kinds of problems, have been beyond the scope of their studies. It is planned to make a critical study and bring to lime light another important facet of her art as an Indo-English novelist. One of such Indo-English writers is Ruth Prawer Jhabvala who has presented east-west perspective in her novels. She, in her wider socio-economic and political perspectives is therefore, fully reflected in her works in a big country like India which is generally regarded as not one country but many countries containing not one people. Jhabavala established herself as a great personality of India in the field of fiction. Although she has left India many years ago, she shines bright on the surface of Indian fiction. Jhabvala's characters in her novels defines that, predetermined by birth and heritage and share a common conviction that only disruption and unhappiness can result from a violation.

Work Cited

1. Agarwal, D.C. *To Whom She Will: Exploration in Modern Indo-English Fiction*: in R.K.Dhawan, Common Wealth Fiction, New Delhi: Bahri Publication Pvt. Ltd., 1982, p.215.
2. Jhabvala, Ruth Prawer. *To Whom She Will*, London: Penguin Books, 1985, p. 35
3. Jhabvala, Ruth Prawer. *To Whom She Wil*, London: Penguin Books, 1985, p. 75
4. Jhabvala, Ruth Prawer. *To Whom She Will*, London: Penguin Books, 1985, p. 29
5. Shahane V.A. *Ruth Prawer Jhabvala*, p.40
6. Gooneratne, Yasmine. Contemporary India in the Writing of Ruth Prawer Jhabvala, Westerly, Dec. 1983, p.75.
7. Jhabvala, Ruth Prawer. *To Whom She Will*, London: Penguin Books, 1985, p. 23

CHAPTER 16

The Changing Image of Indian Womanhood in R. K. Narayan's *The Painter of Signs*

Bharati Sukalal Khairnar

Abstract

The over changing reality of life is reflected in contemporary literature. The position of women in society is one of the facts. The status of women throughout the world has been undergoing a rapid change during the recent times. In Indo Anglian literature, especially in the writings of Mulk Raj Anand, R. K. Narayan, Anita Desai, Kamala Markandaya, Bhabani Bhattacharya, Ruth P. Jhabwala and others one gets a true and realistic picture of the position, behaviour, and personality of women in Indian society. The feminist perspective offers a fresh look at the narratives dealing with women in modern society. The novel under study The Painter of Signs raises a number of pertinent issues regarding Indian womanhood. It also reflects fast approaching feminist trends. Daisy, the heroine is an image of social revolt. She believes in the independence of spirit. The novel explores through the example of Daisy as to how women in India can work for their emancipation. In literature the personality of the traditional woman and the woman with the modern outlook has been presented in an exclusively male – oriented culture. The traditional woman has been left with no personality of her own. She even glorified the suffering that was inflicted upon her by the wanton male whereas women with modern outlook endeavour to come out of the suppression and begin to view her independent existence.

Keywords: Image, Womanhood, Narayan, Modernity. Conflict, Culture

In literature, the personality of the traditional woman and the woman with the modern outlook has been presented in an exclusively male – oriented culture. The traditional woman has been left with no personality of her own. She even glorified the suffering that was inflicted upon her by the wanton male whereas woman with modern outlook endeavour to come out of the suppression and begin to view her independent existence.

The over changing reality of life reflects itself in contemporary literature. The position of women in society is no exception to this fact. The status of women throughout the world has been undergoing a rapid change during recent times. In Indo Anglian literature, especially in the writings of Mulk Raj Anand, R. K. Narayan, Anita Desai, Kamala Markandaya, Bhabani Bhattacharya, Ruth P. Jhabwala and others one gets a true and realistic picture of the position, behaviour and personality of women in Indian society. The feminist perspective offers a fresh look at the narratives dealing with women in modern society.

Often women are shown to be defied as the centre of culture but in reality they are still imprisoned within the walls of their family and shackled by tradition. Indian novelists from time to time have conceived a new image of woman in their narratives. She is manipulated by the novelist as a symbol of romantic sensibility amidst simultaneous idealisation or as an agent in the author's quest for psychological insight and awareness. She is also shown as capable of resolving the age-old conflict between tradition and modernity. Now woman is no longer a paragon of virtue and chastity to be extolled by poets and philosophers but as a vibrant and confident protagonist which gives Indian fiction and Indian womanhood a role model to emulate. The changing role of Indian woman in modern society has been a favourite theme with writers like Mulk Raj Anand, R.K.Narayan, Anita Desai and others.

The novel selected for the study is R.K. Narayan's *The Painter of Signs.* Narayan is regarded as one of the greatest Indian writer in English. He has dealt with a panoply of themes and motifs in his writings. His major concerns in his novels are the place of women in society, the disruptive influence of modernity, the adjustment of Indian women in different roles and relevance of Hindu culture in religious concepts. *The Painter of Signs* is a novel teeming with clashes between tradition and modernity and highlights the change in human outlook about some of the cherished ideals, established institutions and accepted values. Raman, the hero is a graduate but he is not affected by modern trends, beliefs and practices. Raman is depicted in the third person, the world is shown as he sees it, and his vision is limited. He is very characteristic of the figures who populate Narayan's novels: full of small men, small schemes, big talks, and limited means. Raman is the "painter of signs" of the title. He paints signs for small businesses in the fictional town of Malgudi. He is an artist, a craftsman who believes in the importance of his work, and takes it seriously. Raman falls in love with a newcomer of a town – Daisy.

Daisy is an unusual western name for an Indian woman-the heroine of the novel. She is independent and is working on a government scheme promoting birth control. To go with her Indian name, Daisy is also very disciplined, independent, strong –willed, businesslike and unattached. In a strongly patriarchal society, a young woman, on her own, looking after herself unaided and unintimated, was something of a rarity. She employs Raman to paint various signs for her campaign, and soon, he finds himself accompanying her on tours around various remote villages, as she speaks to massed assemblies of strangers on the intimate details of birth control with unembarrassed and business like frankness.

Raman is attracted to her, fantasises about her and imagines Daisy as someone dependent on him. This is because he is grown up in a society where woman is supposed to be a weak, and man being stronger, protects woman. The very notion of the strong-willed and determined Daisy being dependent upon a milksoap like Raman is, of course, absurd. Until one night the fantasy of Daisy being dependent upon him slips over into a fantasy of Daisy being dominated by him, and he tries to rape her. She, alert to the situation, gives him the slip. Raman almost immediately regrets his attempt. When he meets her again, he is shamefaced, but unaware of Daisy as an autonomous being. According to Syd Harrex,

> "R.K. Narayan draws his creative sustenance from his cultural past. His novel *The Painter of Signs* contains the issues of sexual politics,romantic love, marriage, family planning, and women's liberation," (Harrex; 69).

The female protagonist in *The Painter of Signs* is Daisy who presents a newer role model for Indian women.

Raman is proud of his calligraphy, and he makes his living by painting signboards. Raman becomes sex obsessed and indulges in flights of fancy. Raman could not digest Daisy's idea of family planning though he was educated and knew the gravity of population problem. The conversation between them created conflict. Daisy told him,

> "I am going on a tour of the surrounding villages for an initial survey, and to look out for places where we can write our messages on the walls permanently. The headquarters want a picture of a family – a couple with

> two children, with the message 'We are two, lets ours be two: limit your family' – in all the local languages."[2] (POS: 55)

They decide to perform Gandharv type of marriage but Daisy does not want to become a mere housewife or a cook. She is a new woman. Raman wants to see her in the modality of a traditional Indian housewife but she transcends her limited social and family role and rejects her partner. She states;

> "When a man says I love you – it sounds mechanical and unconvincing. Perhaps credible in western society but sounds silly in ours. People really in love would be struck dumb, I imagine."(POS:125-126).

She walks away in her pursuit of duty. She is in contrast to the traditional Raman.

Daisy spoke of her past and childhood in some village home where her father owned fields, gardens and orchards; theirs was a large joint family consisting of numerous brothers, sisters, uncles, sister-in-law, grand aunts, and cousins. Of this population fifteen were children.

> "I sometimes wished I could be alone; there was no time or place to consider what one should do or think. Practically no privacy……. but I did not like so much common living."(POS: 128).

Narayan has not placed the female protagonist, as is conventionally done, as the guardian of the tradition and culture in this novel. Still, Daisy in the traditional saree embodies the postcolonial tussle between modernity and tradition. The western attitude to work and social changes is emphasised in Daisy's character. Her longing for privacy and the concept of a nuclear family was the result of her western education. Unlike many Indian women, Daisy is adventurous, courageous, determined, and industrious. She is willing to take risks and confronts dangers. That she has the tenacity of will is evident in the resistance she brings to bear on the Christian missionary organisation to foil its attempt to convert her. In return for the help she received from it she agreed to change her name to Daisy.

The novel *The Painter of Signs* was first serialised in the Illustrated Weekly in 1970s.It raises a number of pertinent issues regarding Indian womanhood. It also reflects fast approaching feminist trends. In the novel, Daisy paves the way for the active feminine principle. There is a gradual shift in the authorial stance from a passive to an active feminine principle. Daisy is also an image of social revolt. She doesn't succumb to any pressure. She believes in the independence of the spirit.

To quote Tejinder Kaur; In an interview by S. Krishnan when asked how Narayan gave such "an orthodox cast of mind to his heroine Daisy," Narayan himself explained that;

> "In *The Dark Room* I was concerned with showing the utter dependence of women on man in our society. I supposed I have moved along with the times. This girl in my new novel is quite different. Not only she is not dependent on men, she actually has no use for them as an integral part of her life."(Kaur: 18).

Narayan seems to dread the fate of the male in the new social order based on rejections-Raman's aunt rejects the new, liberated woman and opts for freedom to pursue her God: Raman rejects his aunt's God in his quest for a rational approach to life: and finally there is Daisy rejecting everything for her freedom as an individual. The issues of sexual politics, romantic love, marriage, family planning and women's liberation are sign-posted within a design of ironic humour in this novel.

Narayan's new woman like Daisy is bold, self-reliant and assertive. She struggles for freedom, asserts equality and searches for identity. In the process, she empowers not only herself but also her man. Narayan's new woman is involved in bringing positive changes not only in her man but also in society. Daisy claims to have little time for love, even though she seems to need it as much as Raman, and eventually drops Raman after agreeing to marry him. The novel ends with Raman trying to feel relieved, trying to recover his old life of idleness in Malgudi. This is romantic irony or irony of self-betrayal in the novel. Raman finds that he has lost his beloved aunt but not gained a wife to replace her.

R. K. Narayan has given a realistic picture of the inevitable struggle of women against the degradation of the female by male chauvinists. It not only voices a strong protest against the ill-treatment of women but also explores through the example of Daisy as to how women in India can work for their emancipation.

Works Cited

1. Narayan R.K. *The Painter of Signs*, Chennai, Indian Thought Publications, Reprint 2006.
2. Harrex Syd, R. K.. Narayan: *An Anthology of Recent Criticism*. Ed. C. N. Srinath, New Delhi, Pencraft International, 2000, P.69-88.
3. Kaur Tejinder, "Feminist concerns in The Three Novels of R.K Narayan: The Dark Room, The Guide, and The Painter of Signs." *The Quest* 8.2, Dec. 1994, P. 12-20.

CHAPTER 17

The Mantle of the Land and Amma in Ismat Chughtai's "Roots" ("Jadein")

Satarupa Sengupta

Abstract

The princely state of Marwar (Jodhpur), which joined the Indian Union two years after Partition, and even considered joining Pakistan, is positioned in Chughtai's short story "Roots" ("Jadein", 1952) as a "special" area where ties between Muslims and Hindus are "so intermingled" that it is not possible to segregate them. This "intermingling" is threatened only by reports of violent riots between Hindus and Muslims in India and Pakistan, the arrival of refugees in Marwar following Partition and also by the anxieties in the minority Muslim community about its future. Amma remains in Marwar while her family migrates to Pakistan. She herself seems to be cocooned and enveloped in the land whose patriarchal labels might have changed but which has wrapped her in its embrace along with the network of ties that the land seems to encourage in the people who are rooted in it. The identity of the land runs through the network of ties like her own blood which runs through her children's veins. Chughtai's text presents a feminist argument about the power of a community to enable the feminine capacity of the land to overcome the violence of the patriarchies that alter its labels and to prevent the displacement of those rooted in it, as Roopchandji and Amma succeed in bringing her children back to their land.

Keywords: Partition literature, Feminism, Ismat Chughtai, Refugees.

It could be argued that the violence following the partition of India was the consequence of the resistance to transition from minority rule (by the English and before that the Mughals) to (Hindu) majority rule with measures to protect the security and liberty of minorities, and from a feudal aristocratic society to democratic capitalism with its need for popular government. In the 1930s and 1940s, the Muslim League had demanded the formation of Pakistan, a new nation-state comprising the Muslim-majority provinces of British India when India gained Independence. A question that could be asked is why there existed in the two decades preceding Indian Independence apprehension and trepidation about assuming the label of "minority" in what was to be a democratic secular state under the Indian Constitution. The minority in a feudal aristocratic society would have been subject to governance by a ruler(s) who was/were not himself/themselves feudal subjects of the ruler. The idea of being governed by a majority that would not merely dominate the composition of the government but also call itself the governed seems to have generated intolerable anxiety in the pre-Independence period. Once the need for the existence of representative government that is selected by the masses who comprise the population of the nation-state and government not by heredity or the "merit" of violent force is accepted, whether those classified as the minority group hope to find representation in government and in laws might depend on the strength of their effect in social interaction and public action.

One of the arguments used by the Muslim League while demanding the formation of Pakistan following the independence-to-come of India was related to their definition of differences between the Indian nation and the Muslim nation. Muhammad Ali Jinnah said in his presidential address to the Muslim League in 1940 in Lahore that "it is a dream that the Hindus and Muslims can ever evolve a common nationality; and this misconception of one Indian nation has gone far beyond the limits". He thought that "Hindus and Muslims belong to two different religious philosophies, social customs and literature[s] … [and] derive their inspiration from different sources of history". Such an argument made before the writing of the Indian Constitution and determining the process of electing representatives of the masses in independent India was decided indicates that Muslim leaders such as Muhammad Ali Jinnah did not think that the government of the future Indian state would represent the objectives of the minority as well as the majority even before the government had been formed. This also implies that he and other leaders such as him did not think that Muslims were able to interact socially and act publicly as they wished. It could be argued that Ismat Chughtai's short story "Roots" ("Jadein", 1952) looks at the ways in which social interaction and public action may obliterate tensions about the extent to which government and laws may represent the goals of minority communities, and in the context of the Partition, it could be examined whether it is suggested by

Chughtai's story that feminist methods may reverse decisions about migration and prevent violence and whether women such as the narrator's Amma have a role to play in relation to such methods.

Scholars such as Gyanendra Pandey have examined the ways in which Partition-related violence is erased from the "historical" accounts of local communities or blamed on "criminals", "outsiders" and "madmen" (199). In the princely state of Marwar (Jodhpur), which joined the Indian Union only on 7 April 1949, two years after Partition, and even considered joining Pakistan, the problem of the transition for Muslims to the status of minority in a democratic state such as India would perhaps not have occurred immediately at the time of Indian Independence. Marwar is also positioned in Chughtai's story as a "special" area where ties between Muslims and Hindus are "so intermingled" that it is not possible to segregate them. The reader is informed that the "Hindus and Muslims had much in common and could not be distinguished from one another by their names, features or attire" (127). The Muslims "who came from outside Marwar" are represented as those who were migrating to Pakistan at the arrival of Indian independence whereas the "old inhabitants" (127) seem to have been partitioned off from the Partition-related problems generated by the inauguration of the states of India and Pakistan.

The story opens with a description of Partition-related violence in a South Asian city – it could be any city. It also appears to be Jodhpur in the kingdom of Marwar, which was protected by British armed forces, and had a "Civil Lines" or "residency" section which is "quiet" (126). Since accession to either India or Pakistan was a possibility and since Hindu refugees from the Partition-related violence in other South Asian locations were arriving in Marwar and Muslim refugees from other Indian regions stopping there briefly on their way to Pakistan, and also since the Muslims of Marwar too were considering migrating to the Muslim-majority state of Pakistan, the "intermingled" Muslims of Marwar are described as a "minority" after the decision is made to "throw [them] out" (127) in "Roots". Whereas the role of bad governance and problems such as penury, the pressure of rapid population growth and lack of knowledge in encouraging communal violence are alluded to in the story, the text seems to accentuate the negation and cancellation of the decision of the Muslim narrator's family to migrate to Pakistan as a victim of Partition-related violence and threats of violence through social interaction and public action by Hindus such as Roopchandji and Muslim women such as Amma who can no longer deny the violence taking place even in "intermingled" Marwar.

Amma, the elderly mother of the Muslim narrator and the widow of the family which is a friend of Roopchandji's family, seems to have been silenced by the naming of "foreign" national identities and the imposition of flags on spaces to which she had formerly belonged. Her family members decide to migrate to Pakistan. Considering the implication of her family members' statement that one's home country – "a land of our own" – may be chosen and may not be that in which one is born, and that Indian "kafirs" (presumably Hindus) had "tortured innocents", the narrator wishes that her mother had said: "This is the place where one was born, one grew up in body and mind. If this cannot be one's own land, then how can the place where one simply goes and settles down for a couple of days be one's own?" (133-35). The narrator also wishes that her mother had argued that one's home country was not "a pair of shoes – if it gets a little tight, throw it away and get a new one" (135). The real silence of the mother – apart from the anger she expresses against plans made by her family to send her to Sindh, Dhaka and Rawalpindi – highlights the fact that one's homeland might not be chosen in freedom.

The fact that Partition refugees who arrived in India had only the "option" of accepting their displacement due to violence from their homes across the border and had to also accept that this sole "option" could be also described as the alternative of the "safer" state "chosen" by them is related to the significance of their position as citizens in Independent India. Refugees were sometimes also asked by resentful citizens who had not been displaced by Partition and were worried about the distribution of national resources the reason why refugees had not agreed to the demands of the majority community in their country of "origin". For members of the refugee majority community that had to cope with the permanent label of "refugee" remaining more important than their identity as citizens of Independent India, this also meant having to tackle the expectation that the space of the past and its memories would always remain more important than happy memories of life after Partition and Independence, should they exist. For members of the minority community who did not migrate even under threats to life during the Partition riots, this meant having to cope with the permanent label of "anti-refugee" in their own land as they were considered reproductions of the "foreign" majority community that had forced refugees into the country or killed them during the process of displacement. In the story "Roots", such members of the minority community turn against their decision to seek refuge in Pakistan through the social interaction and public action of Hindus such as Roopchandji and Muslims such as Amma. The anxieties associated with minority status in a Marwar that was trying to determine whether it should join India or Pakistan are represented by analysing the lives of the narrator's family and Roopchandji's family in the story.

Partition scholars such as Ritu Menon and Kamala Bhasin have noted that Indians who visited Pakistan to interact with refugees and Indian refugees from Pakistan have recollected the separate lives of Hindus and Muslims in pre-Independence and pre-Partition India and the prejudices that shaped social interaction and public action pertaining to them (75-76). For instance, some individuals have recollected that many Hindus treated Muslims as "untouchables" because of their religious and dietary differences (for instance, Muslims ate beef and Hindus did not). In the case of the narrator's and Roopchandji's families in Marwar, there seems to be "intermingling" which is threatened only by reports of violent riots between Hindus and Muslims in the independent states of India and Pakistan, the arrival of refugees in Marwar and also by the anxieties in the minority Muslim community about its future in secular, democratic, Hindu-majority India (it should be noted that the constitution of the Indian republic was approved on 26 November 1949 and came into force on 26 January 1950).

The narrator recalls that her family and Roopchandji's family "were so close to each other over three generations that no one had the slightest suspicion that the country's partition would rupture their relationship" (129). Their political differences – some members of the narrator's family and Roopchand's family are supporters of the Muslim League, others are Congresswalas and the rest of them are supporters of the Hindu Mahasabha and the communist and socialist parties – do not dispatch their "mutual affection and friendship" (129). The women of the two families are reportedly "untouched by politics" and "talk of spices like coriander and turmeric and their daughters' dowries" (130). They perhaps represent the feminized land that has to accept the labels associated with the new states of the Muslim and Hindu patriarchies. When the narrator's father passes away in the period before Partition and Independence, Roopchandji, who is also a doctor and treats all the illnesses of her family, takes on the role played by the Muslim patriarch and plays a supervisory role with respect to the education of the children and intermarriage between the narrator's family and Roopchandji's family. School fees are waived and the Hindu family does not accept dowry from the narrator's family when Munni marries Gyan Chand's son Lallu (132). Terms such as "kafir" (black) used by conservative Muslims for Hindus and the "shuddhi" (purification) rituals performed by conservative Hindus when they come into contact with non-Hindus do not seem to be a significant part of the narrator's pre-Independence memories with respect to the two families. But with Independence and Partition, even the children of the two families become embroiled in the conflict between Hindus and Muslims with the grandchildren of the narrator's family writing "Pakistan Zindabad" on the school wall and Roopchandji's grandchildren "Akhand Hindustan" (130). Even Roopchandji (whose *bhabhi-devar* relationship with Amma cuts across religious barriers) does not offer free medical care to the members of the narrator's family any more as Sheela bhabi (his daughter-in-law and assistant/midwife) does not listen to their requests (133).

When the narrator's family, apart from Amma, unbinds or unfastens all links with their land and Roopchandji's family to migrate to Pakistan, the doctor looks at the "vacant house [of the narrator's family] like a thief" as though he has stolen the narrator's family's home from them (136). The attachment between members of a community – in this case the diverse community in Marwar of the narrator's locality – and between that community and the land are compared with that of a tree that roots itself immovably in soil. Amma remembers the burial of the umbilical cords of her children in the soil of the courtyard of her house and the death of her husband whose body had been "laid near the door" (136-37). These biological connections with the soil are also mirrored in Roopchandji's attempt "at wrenching out the things that were deeply entrenched in his very existence, like roots" (137). It is perhaps possible to argue that the majority and the minority communities as a whole are gendered as male and female in a princely state that was to become a part of Independent India. Amma's womb could also be represented as a land in which the roots of her children's identities are enfolded and swaddled. Amma herself seems to be cocooned and enveloped in the land whose patriarchal labels might have changed but which has wrapped her in its embrace along with the network of ties that the land seems to encourage in the people who are rooted in it. The network of ties could be seen as "feminine" and subordinate to the violence of the patriarchies that created India and Pakistan. The identity of the land runs through the network of ties like her own blood which runs through her children's veins.

Amma is absorbed in thoughts of her children after she chooses to remain in Marwar while her children migrate to Pakistan – "She had nursed the crop with her heart's blood through fifty years, and that day it had been exiled from its own land to find a new land" (138). She is overwrought that the "new soil" will not protect her "saplings" and that they might return as refugees to their "old" land and is uncertain whether the "old" land will allow them "the opportunity to develop their roots again" (138). But her "tearful" eyes also note Roopchandji's family's "eyes behind the door and chiks, eyes that were brimming over with tears" when her family departs for Pakistan (136). Roopchandji's wife brings "two trays of food" to Amma's house but the trays "remain untouched". The reader is informed: "When two women indulge in backbiting, their tongues run like scissors; but when they are overwhelmed with emotion, their lips get sealed" (138). Scholars such as Partha Chatterjee have said that the home was seen as a matriarchal space of religious training against the patriarchal Westernised world of business and the public sphere in pre-Independence India (622-33). It is also a space where one becomes cognizant of ties with others who are rooted in the land in Chughtai's story. The task of the nationalist woman was to ensure that her children became cognizant of such ties. The silence of the mother and the statements of the narrator who aims to speak for her mother seem to raise the question of assignment of blame – is Amma to blame for the decision made by her children to uproot themselves from the land? Is Roopchandji's wife also to blame for her children's hostility towards the narrator and her family following Partition?

It is possible to conclude that Chughtai's text presents a feminist argument about the power of a community to enable the feminine capacity of the land to overcome the violence of the patriarchies that alter its labels and to prevent the displacement of those rooted in it. Gendering in Chughtai's story does not seem to represent the phallic male (Roopchandji, for instance) as impermeable to the networks of ties and the identity of the land running through them that break through the surfaces of the bodies of the diverse population that host them and live in them, diminishing tensions through social interaction and public action not linked only to political representation. The value of the minority community to Roopchandji must be performed for the future state of India (a republic) that Marwar would join to seem harmonious towards minorities in all space-times of citizenship – he brings back the "good-for-nothing children [some of them were adults] from Loni junction" to Amma and calls them absconders who "were not ready to trust even the police superintendent" (139-40). The minority family may not return without the action of local "non-communal" communities. The action of "recovery" or rescue perhaps reminds the reader of the abducted women and children who were designated nationalities after Partition regardless of whether their families really wanted them back if they had been "polluted" (raped or forced into marriage with the abductor) or of whether they themselves wished to return to their original families and communities, as scholars such as Urvashi Butalia have said (95-96). In Chughtai's story, the children are welcomed back by both Amma and Roopchandji, who have prevented their uprooting and transplantation outside the blanket of the "old" land.

Works Cited

Butalia, Urvashi. "Abducted and Widowed Women: Questions of Sexuality and Citizenship during Partition". *Embodiment: Essays on Gender and Identity*, edited by Meenakshi Thapan, Oxford University Press, 1997, pp. 90-106.

Chatterjee, Partha. "Colonialism, Nationalism, and Colonialized Women: The Contest in India". *American Ethnologist*, Vol. 16, No. 4, 1989, pp. 622-33.

Chughtai, Ismat. "Roots". 1952. *The Quilt: Stories*, translated by M. Asaduddin, Penguin Books, 2011, pp. 126-40.

Jinnah, Muhammad Ali. *Presidential Address to the Muslim League* in 1940 in Lahore.

http://www.columbia.edu/itc/mealac/pritchett/00islamlinks/txt_jinnah_lahore_1940.html. Accessed 28 November 2021.

Menon, Ritu, and Kamla Bhasin. *Borders and Boundaries: Women in India's Partition*. Rutgers University Press, 1998.

Pandey, Gyanendra. *Remembering Partition: Violence, Nationalism and History in India*. Cambridge University Press, 2001.

CHAPTER 18

Depiction of Women in Ishiguro's 'A Pale View of Hills' and 'The Remains of the Day'

Sagar Vyas

Abstract

Kazuo Ishiguro is a British novelist, screenwriter, and traditional Japanese songwriter who won the Nobel Prize for Literature in 2017. Among his many accolades and honours are the Booker Prize (1985), the Order of the British Empire (1898), and the Order of the Rising Sun (2018). The female characters in Kazuo Ishiguro's novels exhibit a wide range of emotions. Some characters are put under extreme but manageable stress, while others go insane. As a result, these characters can only be adequately comprehended if they are taught in a feminist context. Feminism is the concept of equality for women in social, political, and economic realms. Feminism divides opinions on the challenges women encounter as a result of gender prejudice in the political and social spheres. Furthermore, all efforts and struggles aimed at improving the lives of women were grouped together as "women's issues." It can be classified into three groups. The first wave of women's rights occurred in the nineteenth and early twentieth centuries, followed by the second wave in the 1960s and 1970s, and the third wave in the 1990s. This research paper explores some of Ishiguro's prominent female characters from his novels *A Pale View of Hills* and *The Remains of the Day*.

Keywords: Oppression, Feminist, Human Psyche, Feminism.

Feminism is the concept of equality for women in social, political, and economic realms. Feminism divides opinions on the challenges women encounter as a result of gender prejudice in the political and social spheres. Furthermore, all efforts and struggles aimed at improving the lives of women were grouped together as "women's issues." Its focus moved throughout time to various facets of the era. As a result, it can be classified into three groups. The first wave of women's rights occurred in the nineteenth and early twentieth centuries, followed by the second wave in the 1960s and 1970s, and the third wave in the 1990s. Feminist theory was born as a result of these women's organisations. It can be found in a variety of subjects, including the women's world, women's history, and women's literature criticism. Feminism has shifted dominant viewpoints in many aspects of Western civilisation, including culture and legislation. Women's rights activists have advocated for women's legal rights, such as contract rights, property rights, and voting rights; women's rights to physical integrity and independence; abortion rights; and reproductive rights, including access to contraception and quality prenatal care; protection for women and girls from domestic violence, sexual assault, and rape; and employment rights, such as maternity leave and wage equity. For the most part, white middle-class women in Western Europe and North America were supporters of women's ideology and movements. Other ethnic women, on the other hand, have supported other feminist beliefs. As the Human Rights movement gained traction in the United States and European colonialism in the Caribbean islands, Latin America, and Africa began to fade, these women's new ideas and beliefs grew in popularity.

A Pale View of Hills was later published as his first novel in 1982. It tells the narrative of Etsuko, a middle-aged Japanese woman living alone in England, and begins with a talk between Etsuko and her young daughter, Niki, about Etsuko's eldest daughter, Keiko, who recently committed suicide. The reader learns that Keiko was Etsuko's daughter from her first marriage, and Niki was born from her second marriage to English as the novel unfolds. After remarrying, Etsuko went to England with her husband and two daughters. But, unlike Niki, who was half-English, Keiko was entirely Japanese and hence unable to communicate in English. This made him feel increasingly isolated in his life, finally leading to his suicide. Etsuko is haunted by the guilt of causing Keiko's death. By excusing himself from the story, Etsuko seeks to redeem himself as a narrator.

The primary character, Stevens, is a long-serving supporter at Darlington Hall, a lovely home near Oxford, England, in Kazuo Ishiguro's novel *The Remains of the Day*, published in 1989. Stevens is a remarkable Englishman who is all work and no play. In 1956, he went on a journey. Her major purpose was to track down a former housekeeper in the hall and convince her to return to work. He narrates occurrences from the 1920s and 1930s from his travels. Stevens acknowledges his doubts and regrets throughout his journey, occasionally excusing his actions. At the end of the journey, he recognises the foolishness of his condition and decides to change his ways in order to live a more fulfilling life.

Never Let Me Go is a 2005 science fiction novel by Kazuo Ishiguro. The novel was set in a dystopian version of England in the late 1990s, where regular civilian lives were extended by a government-sponsored initiative that brought people together. Clones are raised at schools, which are separate from the public, and are treated as pupils there. They begin donating internal organs to regular individuals in need as they reach adolescence. All "donors" are looked after by "caregivers," partners who haven't started the donation process yet. Clones keep donating organs until they "complete," which is a euphemism for death after three or four organ donations. Kathy, Ruth, and Tommy are three clones who are crucial to the story. They were classmates at Hailsham, a clone school. They have ups and downs in their friendships and relationships.

Depiction of Women

It is worth noting that many of the female characters in Ishiguro's books mirror stereotypes of "Japanese women." To begin with, the major protagonists, Etsuko and Keiko, as well as minor characters Sachiko and Hanada's wife, are excessively reliant on others in the novel *A Pale View of Hills*. These supporting structures, aside from Keiko's story, are the men in their lives. Etsuko and Jiro's marriage was not ideal, even if it was not unhappy. After her marriage fell apart, she sought safety in the affections of a British man, whom she married soon after.

One of the goals of this marriage is to make Keiko feel better, but that hasn't worked well. There was, in fact, a negative reaction on Keiko's part. His family had been separated from him. His low self-esteem was confirmed, and he committed suicide, which is another essential aspect of Japanese society. As a form of competition, the Japanese have traditionally praised suicide and seen it as a way to reclaim their dignity. This belief is represented in the novel's news article on his suicide. Etsuko was taken aback when she learned that the English considered the Japanese to be genocide. Keiko, unlike Niki, was a faithful Japanese woman, and this was noted in more than one publication. This is understandable given that they are both typical Japanese women. Sachiko is portrayed as a widow who yearns for a husband following her first husband's death. Her motivation is identical to Etsuko's: to provide a better life for her daughter. Despite her American partner, Frank's many betrayals; she wants to be able to move to the United States with her. Her loyalty has long been a symbol of Japanese women's submissiveness to their husbands.

The episode in Canada, where his wife voted for different candidates, is an example of a Japanese woman's typical expectations. Many people believe women should not have their own opinions. Their viewpoints should be similar to those of their husbands. "If they choose to go against her husband's decision, she will be harshly retaliated against. Is that really true? "Asks Ogata-San". He hasn't spoken since I came back for tea". The other three stopped laughing, and a man with a pale face looked at Ogata-San in surprise.

Miss. Kenton, who appears to be in love with Stevens, refuses to accept it since he believes it is unseemly for a woman to propose marriage to a man. He holds his breath, waiting for Stevens to say it first. When she discovers that Stevens is not interested in marrying her, she sets out to find another man. She was unhappy with her life and planned to divorce her, but when she learned that her daughter was getting married and that her grandchildren were on the way, she changed her mind. He claims that he has come to love her. This is a symbol of purity and humility.

Ruth's motivations were zealous and self-serving. Tommy is the person he loves because he needs a companion, not because he really loves him. She even broke up with him at one point. However, he later discovers that Tommy is drawn to Kathy and that Kathy reciprocates his feelings. He makes the decision to join them. Finally, in his final days, he makes up for his error. However, it would never be enough to make up for lost time. "You should have been two. I don't think I ever saw that. I really did, from the back, as I remember. But I separated you. I'm not asking you to forgive me for that. That's not what I want now. What I want is for you to get it right. Fix what I messed up." (NLMG)

Sachiko's stress was brought on by her decision to stay with Frank, an alcoholic. He is working extremely hard in order to save enough money to relocate to the United States. Frank, on the other hand, spends it all on drinks. Mark's actions are equally troubling. Sachiko, desperate for a better life in the United States, does not kick Frank and sees him as his ticket to a better life in the United States. On the other hand, Frank, on the other hand, is unlikely to be able to transport Sachiko and Mariko to America. Despite this, you live with

Frank and are constantly in pain. Her pressure stems from her wish for a better future for her child, which parallels Banks' mother's narrative. The strain on Canadian wives is felt all over the world, as women all over the world seem to be losing their rights to speak up for their spouses and make decisions for them. Even his right to vote was violated in this case. When he refused to vote for Canada's preferred party, he was threatened with violence. When other people hear the storey, they are surprised not that he will hit her if she votes for a party other than the one she supports, but that he will hit her if she votes for his wife to vote for a party other than the one she supports.

Conclusion

Finally, it may be claimed that Ishiguro has done an excellent job of representing female characters. However, the majority of these ladies represent the qualities and characteristics of the Japanese stereotype woman, and the natural tale of the mother portrayed by them has a worldwide appeal. They are frequently willing to endure for the sake of their children. In addition, Ishiguro's grasp of women's status around the world is mirrored in the home and social remedies that these women conduct. He depicted the struggle of women and their mental abilities, demonstrating how they carry and conquer suffering.

Works Cited

Ishiguro, Kazuo. *A Pale View of Hills*. London: Faber and Faber, 1982. Print.

.... *The Remains of the Day*. Boston: Faber and Faber, 1989. Print

.... *Never Let Me Go*. London: Faber and Faber, 2005. Print.

Shaffer, Brian W. *Understanding Kazuo Ishiguro*. Columbia, S.C.: University of South Carolina P, 1998. Print.

https://www.jetir.org/papers/JETIR1908593

CHAPTER 19

Depiction of Women in Literature: A Reading of Indian Literary Texts under Gender Theory

Suparna Roy

Abstract

Within this complex spectrum of 'culture' Indian Literature has represented accurate sufferings of numerous characters. Identity and our skirmish in finding its appropriate nature, has often pressurised the psychic nature of humans, particularly women. To be precise the struggling of marginalised identities is more toilsome in comparison to the 'centered' identities. In this phallocentric Indian society, the 'white-cis-phallus' is the centre and the remaining becomes the 'other'. Marginalisation can be considered as a chain of events taking place in a society to create certain restrictions for few and power for the rest. Gender, class and caste are further divided into layers, creating a stratified structure where power dynamics moulds and produces identities, not for recognition but for marginalisation, oppression. Within this marginalised 'remaining' the identity of women and their effort to break the imposed roles of Woman/Wife/Mother is somewhere trapped between the supposed links between 'sex' and 'gender' which then is to be inherently related and 'culturally' bound. Therefore my paper would focus on politicised children's literature – *Brave Rajputs* by Anant Pai, and presentation of Tilo in Chitra Banerjee Devakaruni's *The Mistress of Spices*, gender-power dynamics in Mahasweta Devi's *Breast Stories*, Jhumpa Lahiri's *Lowland*, and Khaleid Hosseni's *A Thousand Splendid Suns*.

Keywords: Women, literature, identity politics, gender

Introduction

The History of Feminism has drawn three prominent waves which further included many fragmented definitions and political standpoint(s), like when initially the black women protested saying that their journey can be partially or no where similar to the journey or the struggles of 'white-women'; hence, the world was presented with Black-Feminism. Feminism assisted in diagnosing the pathologies of culture which if described as a complex social apparatus dices the norms and regulations and is a stratified concept with hues that light up the disillusionment and dissent. Multiculturalism indeed has appreciated the difference in cultures but has also made avenues accessible to analyse it from queer perspectives. Over the first, second and third wave of Feminism, few crucial comprehensions of 'deconstruction and post-structuralism' enhanced the understanding of 'identity and politics' in simultaneity. As the plurality of Feminism was now utilised based on required privileges, and the advantage of a particular group of people resulted in overlooking the disadvantageous position of the remaining.

It therefore becomes immensely necessary to adopt the lens of gender theory while studying and visualising both literary and socio-political framework of any culture and important to apply the same in everyday life and not just limit to educational sphere, because then only we can sensitise people that gender is performance rather than essentialisation, and how within the mainstream literature application of Gender studies assists in understanding the 're-presentation' of the marginalised identities, where presentation just remains an illusion. Politically, Gender is molded as a device to regulate and control bodies/identities, to conveniently maintain the "nude-makeup" like social structure of our society. Both Diasporic and Dalit Literature has enhanced and elevated the presentation of heterogenous cultures dwelling in Indian geographic dimension. In these stated literary domains, the subject 'women' has been juxtaposed with fragmented cultural subjugation threaded intricately with norms and regulations. Within this complex spectrum of 'culture' Diasporic Literature has represented accurate sufferings of numerous characters. Identity and our skirmish in finding its appropriate nature, has often pressurised the psychic nature of humans, particularly women. Considering Dalit Literature, which again depicts the subjugation of voices within a completely separate yet interlinked area of power operation on bodies? The term 'Dalit' literary refers to the "untouchables"; within India Caste is immensely a branch of identity politics and device of suppression; it is the power to 'reclaim' the culture; while simultaneously a boxed category of the four Varna Systems in our Culture, where the lowest and "filthiest professions" and designations are bestowed to them.

Women and Literary Spheres

Sara Raasch in her work *Snow Like Ashes* (2014) said – "That's why Literature is so fascinating. It's always up for interpretation, and could be a hundred different things to hundred different people. It's never the same thing twice" (Raasch, 2014, 10). Literary theory and its interestingly fluid usage in literary texts even till date has made the field of Literature intersectional, reflective, interpretative and hence a spectrum, a sequence of thoughts, a journey through which the reader are able to make the 'illusive' world associated with reality. Gender and sexuality are the two more complex terms, culturally constructed and ambiguously related, in the spectrum of feminism which considers "sex" an operational term to theorise its perspectives on cultural deconstruction. In accordance to Stevie Jackson and Jackie Jones article – *Contemporary Feminist Theory*, which can be related here, states that, "The concepts of gender and sexuality as a highly ambiguous term, as a point of reference" (Jackson, 1998, 131). Helene Cixous notes in "Laugh of Medusa" that men and women, as identities and bodies, enter the symbolic order during a different way and therefore the subject position hospitable either sex is different. Cixious's understanding that the centre of the symbolic order is 'phallus' and every-body surrounding it stands within the periphery making women (without intersectionality), the victim of this phallocentric society. To thin, 'gender and sexuality' as an inherently, unquestionable connection, then it only results in constructive understanding that henceforth becomes an oppressive tool of marginalisation, that keeps getting filtered as per geo-locations; the dichotomy of 'penis/vagina' over years has linked itself to male/female understanding of bodies. The complexities created on and around 'a body' get an immediate deconstruction when Judith Butler said in her book *Gender Trouble* (1990), 'body is just a word', and that it is strategically used under artificial rules for the convenience of 'power' to work, which in turn has become a "norm" to attach one's sexuality with their Gender and establish that as "naturally built". The natural and the inherent link that has been associated with the body of a women from the archaic to present times, where the 'pens' have narrated the identities of women keeping in association with theses "natural links" has brought about a crisis, as to 'what a woman is'!

Children Literature – Brave Rajputs

The reason of selecting children's book lies in the fact that they are most politicised ones! Amidst the fun, moral lessons, structured, "normal" projection of human society, deconstructive studies revealed with various hermeneutical devices that these children's book are indeed at times product of our patriarchal culture! For instance, *The Jungle Book* by Rudyard Kipling or even the most thrilling, amazing favorites of many – *Harry Potter* by J.K Rowling can be viewed as books which are heteronormative, where 'phallus' is the 'centre' and every other character revolves around it! Similarly the book I selected to present the family relations is *Brave Rajputs* by Anant Pai – a children's textbook but it reveals many unsaid hues. This book is completely perfect to present how relations are 'marketed', because it sexists in return of something which is the same in the case of Gauri's. From the given five stories in this book, I would focus and analyse the story of Rani Durgavati. First I would like to start with the cover picture which is very heteronormative, the 'compulsory' link of a female and male. To move onto the second fact of the book is that only one 'her-story' – Rani Durgavati, is presented among the four 'histories'. Now focusing on the relations of these Rajput royalties after clearly depicting the tribal family and kinship ties, we see majority of Rajputs married their daughters in return of alliance as was Durgavati. The relationships were merely engrossed with and desired for the need of power and security. Marriage can be seen as a necessary evil in any culture for which humans named as women are treated in almost every possible derogatory ways. In this book the story of Rani Durgavati as a 'brave Rajputani' who fought for her honour and sacrificed her life maybe is just for the kids to know. A deep reading only reflects how relationships are 'marketed'! She only survived to fulfill her role as a daughter, wife and a mother and when it came to herself, her individuality which should have been separated while analysing the rest roles she performed as a 'Rani', she stabbed herself to protect her honour as a "true" Rajputani. As the 'self' always remained in conflict with the 'other' created by the society, we sacrifice the 'self' to maintain the 'other', particularly women!!! A culture – *'sabhyata'*, as we regard is something to be respected and followed regardless of any obstruction, but from the spectrum of theories what gets highlighted is –'flaws', 'fractures'! Somewhere in this field of multiculturalism that veils India, each and every subculture remains ruthlessly in competition with each other, as all of them are similar in their disinheritance and dispossession.

Power and Women in *The Mistress of Spices*

Divakaruni's novel *The Mistress of Spices* is an exuberant novel where Divakaruni builds an enchanting story upon the fault line in American identity that lies between the self and community, Tilo's arrogance of her own precocious ability of knowledge regarding the magical properties of spices and her understanding that she has to live for others and not herself, that she must not pursue love, perhaps, which eventually takes place! Despite the fact, that Devakaruni focused on immigrant experience and tried to negotiate between the needs of each under the earth moving stress of desire, what's highlighted in her narration is Tilo's realisation of abandoning her own desires to maintain the magical powers she possesses on 'spices' through which she aids others who visits her shop in Oakland. Devakaruni did not presented Tilo as a strong human here just by giving her the magical powers, rather she made her a cramped character like our social definition of what a woman should be! Even with powers Tilo is powerless when it comes to desire and love. The woman should select to live for others, which Tilo did from her childhood and became the source of income for her parents. As she has to live for others, Tilo's character is given power, which will only remain if she abandons her desire, which eventually she does until she breaks through all the chains of magic and makes love. But the interesting fact is why a woman has to choose; her character could both have power and desire. Gita Rajan in her article – "The Mistress of Spices: Deploying Mystical Realism" considers the "transitional apace a subject occupies when shifting from a "solid" to "liquid modernity" and therefore she refuses to flee to an "earthly paradise" (Rajan, 2002, 336) with Raven at the end. She insists, instead, on returning to earthquake-ravaged Oakland" (Rajan, 2002, 226). The attempt of writers trying to portray women as 'superhuman' reflects how women are considered from a sub-human perspective. That is why Tilo wants to re-build her apprentice again in the destructed area to reflect her great humanity, principles and ethics. With all superhuman powers somewhere the basic requirements of a woman to be happy is obliterated from the social definition of what a woman should, hence Divakaruni's simple plot that she tried to shoot in an extraordinary manner fumbles at patriarchal threshold.

Gender and Diasporic Literature in Lahiri's Lowland

From the perspective of multiculturalism and Diaspora, Gauri's journey can be visualised. Liberty is when we have "A Room of Ours Own", when we treat humans beyond categorised identitics and stop expecting them to respond in accordance to the expected or demanded social roles! The journey of one's identity, particularly a

Woman's is somewhere static and is not enjoyed by the surroundings if it grows and undoubtedly Gauri grew in 'migrating' from Kolkata to America beyond the roles of a wife, a mother, and only desired to become a human whose life and identity can be a beautiful journey of 'delicate chaos'! The eventual and gradual experiences of her in America, did not make her feel disoriented from her inner self, rather was an avenue to leave the imposed roles on her body and become someone she wants to be. Her desire to not become what her newly married husband/ prior brother-in-law wanted her to become again, gets mirrored when she compares her 'pregnant' body with other "women's" body in her surrounding, while taking her classes in the University campus – "...She put on her winter coat over her sari...She saw students going in and out...women n in dark tights and short wool coats..." (Lahiri, 157). Shubhash, married Gauri to give the child of his dead brother (Udayan) a name – "I'll make it mine, I've promised you that" (Lahiri, 164), to give a proper shelter and "freed" atmosphere to Gauri in comparison to Kolkata. But amidst, all such providing mentality Shubhash expected Gauri to become and play those roles of which she was somewhat weary of; therefore, when Gauri did not effectuate those roles, Shubhash was disappointed even when she tried to adopt a new physical appearance –

> A few minutes later he heard her key in the lock...hair hung bluntly along her jaw bone dramatically altering her face...The clothes covered her skin but they accentuated the contours of her breasts, the firm swell of her stomach...exposed...He watched as she went into the bedroom, not apologising for the spectacular mess she has made, just putting away the new clothes she'd bought, then throwing the old things into garbage bags (Lahiri, 169).

Shubhash was aware that he has "inherited his brother's wife" (Lahiri, 169), but somewhere hoped that after the birth of the child (Udayan's) the unconscious difference between them will become less. Eventually, after the child's birth both of them made love, slept together, caressed the child together, but along with it stood an uninterrupted silence; Shubhash's questioning that whether he did the right thing in marrying Gauri; Gauri's innate feelings of responsibility towards her child Bela (the father of who, is no longer alive) made her experience a sense of separateness from that little body; moreover, her complex feelings of perceiving Shubhash as his dead husband's brother and then her present husband also made her semblance that – "an act intended to express love could have nothing to do with it. That her heart and her body were different things" (Lahiri, 194). Here, a comparison can be drawn between Chitra Banerjee Divakaruni's works *The Vine of Desire* (2002), a sequel to *Sister of My Heart* (1999). In the sequel, Sudha's making love with Sunil (her sister's husband) also made Sudha felt the same detachments of heart and body while being under Sunil (Who desired her from the moment he saw her). We can see how the woman characters in all these literary texts are always presented as the 'object' of desire, the object to the gaze, and not the subjects who can control their anatomies. Literature has possibly been that arena where hypothetical realities are spaciously celebrated. The character of woman is never separated from the identity of motherhood; it keeps surrounding woman as the ultimate destination. In comparing these two texts, we can very clearly see, both Gauri and Sudha were with children; the fond men has is towards the anatomies who are associated with the 'eternal concept of motherhood'; whereas, Anju (anjali), a woman who has been presented as straightforwardly path-breaking was not admired neither loved, for Sudha always had the admirers t her back. In presenting the life stories of women through literary narratives, which also try to depicts the cultures, histories, politics of a particular time somewhere veils the identity of woman and motherhood as inseparable, and men admiring the same as adequately "ideal" and appreciable.

Shubhash surmised that having a child with him may make Gauri feel a little less separate from these individuals who surrounded her – Bela and Shubhash. But Gauri did not wanted to become a mother/wife again. The sense of 'uncanny' where among the close ones; an 'unhomely' feeling evolves and separates the individual from the rest. Gauri faced the same excitability and again a comparison can be drawn between Nora of *A Doll's House* (1879) by Henrik Ibsen, where the 'mistrust of her husband whom she bore three children made her think of what she is, her identity was questioned, her place and treatment as a "doll" by her husband was reflected and hence she left the marriage to explore [her] self. Quite similar is Gauri's experience as she was shocked by Udayan's betrayal, realised how she was just used by him for his own activities, how she does not deserves the pain and loneliness, he forced her into, and how Bela and her marriage with Shubhash only reminds her the layers that stripped her carefree self under burden of darkness where she is unknown and is submerging in the hues of 'undeserving' from which she needs to save herself. This instantaneous realisation and thinking of which over years with them made her decide to leave for better. This silent and distanced skirmish of Gauri with time resulted in her leaving both Bela and Shubhash to survive and exist as her own self, a self which no longer desires to repeat the same husband-wife game of Kolkata in America – "I have not made this decision in haste…Tell her whatever you think will be least painful for her to hear…My address is uncertain…Good luck, Shubhash, and good-bye. In exchange for all you have done for me, I leave Bela to you" (Lahiri, 257). Gauri's abandoning of her constructed identity assisted her to explore a newer self where she met different shades; different experiences grew her into a person who was now open to the surprises of life.

Devis' portrayal of Reverse Discourse through a Dalit and Brahmin Woman

Cultural construction of identities and designations are perilous to combat with, as culture acts as 'destiny in excuse'! In Mahasweta Devi's narration of the life-story of Jashodha in Breast Stories, few crucial concepts that Breasts could possibly depict as the 'giver' – motherhood as profession, body and breast as the universal shelter – The Milking Cow, "auspicious faithful woman", and breast as objects signifying reverse power discourse. The presentation of Jashodha here can be linked or related to the Hindu mythological character – Yashodhara, who was profoundly known as Yashodha Maa, who was a famous Hindu figure of chastity and purity recognised as the Mother of Krishna.. This identity of women as mothers is emphasised to such an extent that without the function of motherhood and ability to become a mother, one is considered as a woman. This political analogy of presenting and intermingling these two identities – women and mothers, is somewhere to regulate the very fact that 'sex' as an act of pleasure is ignoble; while if that act is procreative and produces products (of capitalism, as Michel Foucault regarded in *History of Sexuality,* 1976), then the act is "pure" and in this process the chastity and femininity and the "ultimate" identity of women is sustained, a reason for which heterosexuality became a benchmark! In the presentation of Jashodha as the Milk Mother of the Haldar house, she recurs and succumbs to the very historical reality of how the identity of woman is culturally constructed – "Such is the power of the Indian soil that all women turn into mothers here and all men remain immersed in the spirit of holy childhood. Each man the Holy Child and each woman the Divine Mother" (Devi, 42). The creation of woman as mother was implemented and conditioned in Jashodha when she was ready to become a professional mother agreeing to feed and allow the children of Haldar House suckle her nipples as the rule of the house was any man of the house can "bring a second wife only of the first wife completes producing twenty children" (Devi, 49), but all the wives stopped after twelve or thirteen, and the mistress of the house was worried that since-

> Daughter-in-laws will be mothers. When they are mothers, they will suckle their children. Since they will be mothers as long as it's possible-progressive suckling will ruin their shape. Then if the sons look outside, or harass the maidservants, she won't have a voice to object. Going out because they can't get it at home – this is just (Devi, 45).

Hence, they hired the 'suckling-mothers' for the infants of Haldar House, and eventually became the Mother of the World! Jashodha accepted as she wanted to serve her husband who lost his legs and had no other work and her own children (which by her age of fifty-five was twenty in number), so considering her breasts as the "most precious objects" (Devi, 45), Jashodha was ready to become a professional mother. This entire practice reflects how by elevating woman to the position of 'divinity' they were sexually exploited as baby producing machines. Simone De Beauvoir's stated the binary constructed – mind/body binary, where men is the mind and women the body, is getting clearly reflected for the girls/wives/mothers in the situation of Bengal as presented by Devi. The wives are nothing but objects of attraction where their beauty and body is the only thing in demand for "use"; hence their shapes are important to keep the phalluses (husbands) attached to them, and so Jashodha was the only option. Eventually in this profession of being a mother Jashodha was formulated by the only duty her body is able to perform, and at the end she suffered from breast cancer in her process of maintaining the ultimate identity of a woman-Mother.

The story concludes with a reverbant notion that Jashodha's death was the death of God, because she was treated god that saved bodies and lives, and all because of her breast; however, the identity of 'mother' gets a question mark here because her husband who abandoned her when she 'lost her glory', said that the idea of a mother is "hair in a huge topknot, blindingly white clothes, a strong personality. The person lying in the hospital is someone else, not Mother" (Devi, 67). This statement from a man clearly shows how the cration of identity is done based on the needs and conveniences of a phallus in this phallogocentric society. This statement proves Jashoda's entire life and struggles as a lie, for the person who is lying on the bed has been the Mother to numerous lips and minds, and she dies being a mother only, but the comment of Kangalicharan (her husband) is a crucial word-play and ambiguously syntactical construction of the creation and regulation of the identity – women. The modulation of the identity of a woman with supposed natural links and inheritance (which are fixed by social practices) thus marginalises a body in stratified layers, where the personal only objectified to patriarchal consumption.

Mariam and Gender Struggles in *A Thousand Splendid Suns*

Khaled Hoseini

Hosseini's work clearly presents the deplorable and cramped culture of the Muslim community specifically Afghans! The suffering of women is clearly portrayed in his work. Though in *A Thousand Splendid Suns*, Hosseini amalgamated the crucial war time and family suffering and made a breathtaking story set against the volatile events of Afghanistan's last thirty years – from the Soviet invasion to the reign of the Taliban to post-Taliban rebuilding – that puts the violence, fear, hope, and faith of this country in intimate, human terms yet what gets highlighted is the objectification of women, "unconsensual" sex, marital rape and physical abuse. It is a tale of two generations of characters brought jarringly together by the tragic sweep of war, where personal lives – the struggle to survive, raise a family, find happiness – are inextricable from the history playing out around them, perhaps which only reflects the incomplete fact of the novel. Although Hosseini tried to create the unflagging hope, strength and toughness of human spirit, the tragic character of Mariam gets more focused. In hope to reunite with her father, she losses her mother at an early age, her father being a coward never accepts her and then she realises what her mother said that she has no one in the world except her mother and that her' illicit' father tell her lies. When she realises this fact, it's too late, for she is then married off to an aged man – Rasheed, who turns out to be a despicable brute, tormenting and torturing her as she was not able to give birth to a boy. Even the fact that she was not ready to have 'sex' did not matter to him. Then she saw her husband marrying another woman – Laila, who loses everything due to the attack of Talibans and the bomb blast, except her unborn child and to save whom she agrees to marry Rasheed, who then torments Laila immensely because she was losing her "beauty" as Rasheed said that he married a "pari" and Laila now has turned to "old-corpse". Mariam kills Rasheed, one night to stop him from killing Laila. The 'sexual objectification' of women, oppression, betrayal and tremendous psychological tormentation shows how important it is to view any situation from 'queer' perspectives and not just with 'cultural' ideations. Within the complex fabricated network of multiculturalism, it is important to make culture liberal so that humans get the deserved respect. Queer studies has somewhat helped us to borrow a lens through which the objectification of women only as sexual objects can be magnificently presented to the hypocrite world.

Conclusion

Majorly, in literary spheres we can demonstrate plethora of presentations and re-presentations, productions and reproductions of identities. It is very difficult for people to believe that Literature is true, just as it is simple to make the heads believe history is the truth; however, literary depictions of lives are not fictitious; they are very much the realistic re-reading of identities with the educational and political framework of narrative and power discourse. Thus the texts selected here ranges from children literature to multi-cultural phenomena; from subaltern discourse to Afghan's war struggles and reality. Therefore, gender theory and its application along with post-stucturalist feminism has ensured to showcase the layered oppressive domains of Women in each cultural context and how they are thus identified as the 'objective subjects' voicing for themselves.

Works Cited

Butler, Judith. *Gender Trouble*. New York and London: Routledge, 1990.

Cixous, Helene. "The Laugh of the Medusa." *Journal of Women in Culture and Society*, 1976, pp. 875-895.

Devakaruni, Chitra Banerjee. *Sister of My Heart*. United States: Black Swan, 1999.

Devakaruni, Chitra Banerjee. *The Vine of Desire*. United States: Doubleday, 2002.

Devi, Mahasweta. *Breast Stories*. Indian: Seagull, 1997.

Foucault, Michel. *History of Sexuality*. France: Penguin, 1976.

Hosseini, Khalid. *A Thousand Splendid Sun*. Bloomsbury, 2013.

Jackson, Stevi and Jackie Jones. "Contemporary Feminist Theories." *Edinburgh University Press*, 1998, pp. 280. *JSTOR*, www.jstor.org/stable/10.3366.

Lahiri, Jhumpa. *Lowland*. United States: Random House, 2013.

McIntosh, Mary. "Gender Trouble: Feminism and Subversion of Identity." *Feminist Review*, 1991. *SAGE journals*, https://journals.sagepub.com/doi/10.1057.

Menon, Nivedita. *Seeing Like A Feminist*. UK: Penguin, 2012.

Pai, Anant. *Brave Rajputs*. India: Amar Chitra Katha,1999.

Rajan, Gita. "The Mistress of Spices: Deploying Mystical Realism." *Meridians,* Vol. 2, No. 2(2002), pp.2015-236. *JSTOR*, www.jstor.org/stable/40338518.

Raasch, Sara. *Snow Like Ashes*. New York: Harper Collins, 2014.

CHAPTER 20

Moving beyond Materialism: The Feminism of Female Travels of Hollywood

Namitha Nandan

Abstract

The representation of women in popular culture and especially in Hollywood has for time immemorial been coloured by the hues of materialism. Women were for ages seen as superficial and physical beings who crave for wealth or jewels or dresses. From women who ensnared wealthy men for material benefits to women who harried stores to fill up their inner void, the portrayal of women as well as their coping mechanisms at times of distress have all been predominantly consumeristic. Even in the postmodern era of 'woke' individuals, popular genres like comedies or remedies with female leads, aka chick flicks, have also served the same "woman as just a body" concept through their "empowering" makeover scenes. In such a situation where the identity of a female is almost inseparable from the body, it's appearance and an insatiable greed for material comforts, the need to have a tool to view women as thinking, feeling and living individuals is a necessity of the era. This paper tries to see how the female travels of Hollywood breaks the age-old stereotypes related to female gender to truly empower women. The paper will trace the various hues and nuances of representation of women in Hollywood over the years and will look into how travel movies, especially the solo travel movies, help in rectifying the wrongs and shortcomings of the previous representations.

Keywords: Representation, Hollywood, materialism, chick flicks, women empowerment, travel movies

Introduction

American literature and the Hollywood as a whole has usually portrayed women as materialistic beings. Their love for shopping, the obsession with clothes and jewellery and the need to satiate a deep yearning for acceptance by dolling themselves up are all tropes that have been used and reused in American literature, especially in

Hollywood. From the perfect homemakers of the early days to the carefree modern woman who sets off on the quest for the perfect Prada handbag, most of the female characters in Hollywood throughout its history have been almost indiscernible from their materialistic desires.

Materialism in general and the materialism of women in particular are subjects that have received harsh criticism in the recent times (Pollay, 32). Starting from the films of the pre-feminist era to the rather ironical chick-flicks of the woke twenty-first century, women characters have been in one way or another, been tied to materialism. From 'gold-diggers' like Meredith Blake from *The Parent Trap,* to shopaholics like Rebecca Bloomwood (*Confessions of a Shopaholic) or* Carrie and her friends from *Sex and the City,* and the countless teen queens whose lives and dreams get a boost post a makeover, women have for time immemorial been reduced to nothing but a body that craves for nothing more than a few commodities. A known or unknown submission to the yearning of the patriarchal male gaze is well evident in all of these instances. To quote Eileen Fischer and Stephen Arnold, "Women have been assigned the "private realm" role of consumers, and simultaneously devalued for being so concerned with the materialistic activities of consumption" (185).

From the moment a woman is born she is forced or compelled to circumscribe her dreams and desires to the walls of conformities and expectations set forth by the society. The typical characteristics of femininity as prescribed by patriarchal norms do emerge as a hindrance in the women's quest to conquer her dreams. In the book *The Mass Psychology of Fascism*, William Reich makes the case that psychic repression depends on social oppression, and as a result, the modern conception of the fascist state has been taken up not by sinister external forces but internally, by the masses themselves. The pressure to act out the role of someone who the male gaze finds beautiful or attractive, clips the wings of their dreams, goals and desire and women are compelled to live a life where their libidinal energy is robbed of its freedom. All these pressures result in bitterness, contempt, confusion and anger and alas takes a toll on the female psyche. American literature and Hollywood has for ages have taught women to treat this ailment or void with shoes and bags. However, recent trends in Hollywood, especially in the travel genre has indeed come up with a better alternative, one that acknowledges women as beings with depth and genuine emotional and mental needs.

The exploration of the travel genre, to show women as something more than just pretty faces or greedy consumers is quite a positive turn in Hollywood. Women leaving behind riches, the need to satiate the needs of men and their gaze and abandoning any label or restriction that circumscribes their freedom is what we get to see in 21st century Hollywood. Consider films like *Eat, Pray, Love* or *Wild* or the Oscar winning *Nomadland,* travel here presents with a freedom to move beyond all restrictions, both societal and psycho-physical to treat themselves and create a new subjectivity. Travel therefore emerges as a tool for overcoming the materialistic restrictions in the representation of women, in these travel movies. This paper tries to trace the history and hues of female representation in Hollywood and how the travel genre has helped female characters emerge as human beings with thoughts, dreams, emotions, goals and not just owners of pretty faces.

The Gold-diggers and Makeovers

Back in the time of Jane Austen, to marry into wealth was indeed a necessity for a woman, as she had no other way to survive in a world that prevented her from having an inheritance or a decent job. But in the later decades of the twentieth century things were quite different, with the second wave of feminism really putting down a firm foot. Ranging from damsels in distress to gold-diggers and shopaholics, the stereotypical representations of women in Hollywood can be seen as nothing short of an atrocity.

A quick peek into popular culture and Hollywood in the 1980s would have greeted you with "a group of lusty, independent females determined to have fun, to succeed and to develop a healthy bank account, while masquerading behind a girlish demeanor" (Radner 21). What is evident here is the overdose of materialism and consumerism that governed the representation of a female on the silver screen, with the body and its pleasures taking centre stage. On one side the gold-digger trope that Hollywood had used and reused since *That Certain Thing* or *House of Mirth* changed from characters driven by a need for economic stability (Slavens 71) to the dumb blonde bombshell, "an outrageously stereotypical representation of gendered difference" (Poole 246). If this trend was looked upon with disgust and skepticism, the succeeding trend of the "miracle makeover" was indeed the same old materialistic tendencies, that women were so blatantly ridiculed for, served in a new bottle under the garb of "transformation, rejuvenation and alteration" for "empowerment" (Weber 80).

According to Joel Gwynne, "the reconstruction of femininity has become one of the dominant themes of popular culture in the twenty-first century, and nowhere is this more evident than in the prolificacy of makeover narratives in postfeminist media culture" (61). Be it *Clueless* or *The Princess Diaries* or *Wildchild,* from the '90s to the early 2000s, the makeover was indeed something that brought about a new vigour in the lives of women and 'the "ugly nerd" gets a makeover to claim social acceptance' trope as used in *Never Been Kissed* or *Buff* subtly hinted at the fact that no matter how intelligent or capable a woman is attraction quotient governed by the male gaze is what determines her position in the society. These makeovers can be seen as "contemporary manifestations of normalisation" or as a creation of "homogeneous bodies" (Heyes 18). Be it dolling up women as "eyecandies" or giving them a complete makeover, the bodies are "infused with the ostensibly demanded qualities such as gender conformity and heterosexual competence" (Weber 84).

If the gold-diggers stereotypical showcased the avarice of the gender, in the name of empowerment the makeover sessions of early 2000s reiterated the importance of the materialistic or bodily aspects for the gender. The ability to move beyond greed for products or just the body was circumscribed by these Hollywood representations.

The Schizoanalysis of Travel

From Herodotus to the teens of the twenty-first century, millions have been enthralled and enticed by the phenomenon known as 'travel'. For ages, people have used travel as a tool to alleviate their pains and sorrows, or as a trail to redeem themselves from all worldly sins. The travel motif in literature, quite like in real life, has always been celebrated as an essential constituent that facilitates the evolution of characters. In the female travels of Hollywood a similar output is visible. Be it the one of a kind *Thelma and Louise* or adaptations of travel memoirs such as *Eat, Pray, Love* or *Wild,* the woman is, in the truest sense of the word "empowered". Travel provides them with an opportunity to reclaim their autonomy through "altering their identity and life situation by abandoning home and travelling alone" (Tiyce 1247).

The female, "typically representing stasis, home and hearth" (Pidduck 173), enjoys a taste of freedom as she ventures out into the world, without the chains of duties or obligations or labels. Travel is not merely a leisurely activity or commodity that is consumed but is "associated with ideals of youthful freedom, personal development and fulfilment" (O'Reilly 155). The withering away of the social identity of the traveller provides women with an opportunity to explore life and themselves without any restrictions.

Travel, especially the backpacking trips in Hollywood is the one that completely frees women from the jail of consumerism or materialism. The travellers leave behind everything they own, the identity, the riches, the clothes, the house, to set out on a journey where they get to connect with themselves. Here the individual gets to interact with the bare self that is devoid of any adornments. The focus shifts from "what she owns" to "what she is". Travel therefore provides the characters with a means of self-discovery (Yang et.al. 34). In *Eat, Pray, Love* we see Liz Gilbert packing away all her belonging before she sets out her journey to find meaning in life and a word for herself. The ginormous backpack that Cheryl drags around on her Pacific Crest Trail is symbolic of how the exterior additions have been keeping women from self-realisation and exploring their inner world. When Cheryl abandons the components of her heavy backpack and moves on towards her goal with just the bare necessities, she is leaving behind the burden of "what she owns".

The next striking aspect of female travels is the independence that the process provides. The separation of the woman from her home or comfort zone, helps in bringing to light her capability as an independent individual (Swenson and Zvonkovic 546). Be it Liz from *Eat, Pray, Love* or Cheryl from *Wild,* these women are independent. They do not have a man to save them from distress or provide them with comfort and luxury. The woman does not have to please any onlooker. She is free to experience her body and make her own decisions without having to lend an ear to patriarchy saying how things are "supposed to be". In case of Liz, she learns to embrace the folds of fat that adorns her midriff and Cheryl does not feel embarrassed by the stench of sweat she sheds as she moves closer to her goal. They are also portrayed as individuals who are capable of taking care of themselves. In *Nomadland* even though Fern has lost her husband and means of livelihood, travel provides her with a chance to survive in this postmodern society without an outsider's help.

The power that travel movies, especially of the later years of the 2010s, provides female characters autonomy over their lives. Love and the material security that comes with it is a choice that these characters get to abandon. The body, as a sexual object becomes a medium of experience. The exterior is not dolled up to please the man nor is the advances of the man accepted to reiterate the sexual status of the female body. Here we get to see the notion of woman as a sex object getting shattered. While Fern swims naked and enjoys her own body she is getting to claim ownership of her own body. As James Williams observes "Orthodoxy and order are subjected to fierce critique and replaced by esoteric lines of flight, shown to be at work – for the better – at the very heart of practices, institutions and beliefs we once thought unassailable", travel shatters the supremacy of the male gaze's dominance on the perception of the female body (46).

Conclusion

The paper has tries to trace the various hues of the stereotypical representation of women in Hollywood. The regressive and sexist approach of painting women as superficial beings and mere bodies, has not yet left Hollywood. In this postmodern era, where individuals tend to scrutinize each and every aspect of life and society, the conservative thoughts of the earlier centuries do sneak into seemingly harmless films under the fake façade of empowerment. The hateful gold-diggers gave way to ugly nerds whose lives changed post a makeover, but still the dominance of materialism and the concept of body prevails in the representation of women. A close examination of the travel movies of the late 2010s have shown a dramatic change in the representation of women. The body is no longer the sole constituent of the female identity but it is just a body that gets to experience something new without social constraints or inhibitions. The female emerges as an independent individual, who has no yearning for material possessions. Nor does she require a new haircut or extra makeup to find her place in the society and in the world. These travel narratives helps us to view women as independent individuals with thoughts, dreams, goals and desires that go way beyond Prada bags or Gucci shoes.

Works Cited

Fischer, Eileen and Stephen Arnold. "Woman in a Material World: Two Interpretations of a Consumer Case Study", in *SV – Meaning, Measure, and Morality of Materialism*, eds. Floyd W. Rudmin and Marsha Richins, Provo, Association for Consumer Research: UT. 1992.Pages: 181-187.

Gwynne, Joel. "The girls of Zeta: Sororities, ideal femininity and the makeover paradigm in The House Bunny." *Postfeminism and contemporary Hollywood cinema.* Palgrave Macmillan, London, 2013. 60-77.

Heldman, Caroline, and Nicole Haggard. "Women in Hollywood: The ongoing fight for equality." *Collectif: A Space Dedicated to the Advancement of Women and Girls* (2017): 2-12.

Heyes, Cressida J. "Cosmetic surgery and the televisual makeover: A Foucauldian feminist reading." *Feminist Media Studies* 7.1 (2007): 17-32.

Murphy, Ryan. *Eat Pray Love.* Columbia Pictures, 2010.

O'Reilly, Camille C. "Tourist or traveller? Narrating backpacker identity." *Discourse, communication and tourism.* Channel View Publications, 2005. 150-170.

Penn, Sean. *Into the Wild.* Paramount Pictures, 2007

Pollay, Richard. "The Distorted Mirror: Reflections on the Unintended Consequences of Advertising," *Journal of Marketing,* 50 (April). 1986. Pages: 18-36.

Poole, Ralph J. "Blonde bombshell and homely housewife: Selling the woman in 1950s Hollywood comedies." *Almighty Dollar.* LIT, 2010. 245-265.

Radner, Hilary. *Neo-Feminist Cinema: girly films, chick flicks, and consumer culture.* Routledge, 2010.

Reich, Wilhelm. *The Mass Psychology of Fascism.* New York: Farrar, Straus & Giroux,1970. Print.

Slavens, Clarence R. "The Gold Digger as Icon: Exposing Inequity in the Great Depression." *Studies in Popular Culture,* vol. 28, no. 3, Popular Culture Association in the South, 2006, pp. 71-92, http://www.jstor.org/stable/23416172.

Swenson, A.R., Zvonkovic, A.M. *Navigating Mothering: A Feminist Analysis of Frequent Work Travel and Independence in Families.* Sex Roles 74, 543-557 (2016). https://doi.org/10.1007/s11199-015-0545-2

Tiyce, Margaret. Healing through travel: Two women's experiences of loss *and adaptation.* Southern Cross University, 2008.

Weber, Brenda R. "Makeover as takeover: Scenes of affective domination on makeover TV." *Configurations* 15.1 (2007): 77-99.

Weber, Brenda R. "Visible Subjects." *Makeover TV.* Duke University Press, 2009. 81-126.

Williams, James. *Gilles Deleuze's Logic of Sense: A Critical Introduction and Guide: A Critical Introduction and Guide.* Edinburgh University Press, 2008.

Yang, Elaine Chiao Ling, Mona Ji Hyun Yang, and Catheryn Khoo-Lattimore. "The meanings of solo travel for Asian women." *Tourism Review* (2019).

CHAPTER 21

'Husband-worship' – A Tool of Subordination of Women Depicted in Selected Hindi Songs

Ekta Laddha and Pulin Bhatt

Abstract

Indian cinema is an emphatic medium to portray society and its effects are everlasting as the common man remembers the visual effects more than the literature and thus it holds responsibility in conveying positive message. Women are generally not given the center stage and the heroes are magnified. This marginalisation is moreover accompanied by the subjugation of women and uplifting men by their grandeur. Women are considered as epitome of beauty and docility and their fate is determined by the hero's capacity to rescue heroine from the clutches of villain. It is due to the patriarchal setup that the gender stereotypes are never challenged. The submission of women to men asserted the male authority and it continued till the gender stereotypes were followed. Along with that, they know that marriage is a sacrament and made to believe that husband is the deity whom they have to worship. Some songs have communicated the idea of husband-worship and these notions are followed as ideals. In this regard, the paper attempts to discuss how Indian Cinema has depicted woman through its songs and how the audience conceives the notion of woman through. It has been observed that there are certain songs, which portray husband as the sole and supreme authority and woman or a wife as a devotee.

Keywords: Cinema, Women, Husband, Stereotype, Deity.

Feminism throws a challenge on the age-long tradition of gender differentiation. Besides, the important focus of feminism are the revisal reinterpretations of writings by men and their effects on women, representations of women in texts, texts by women and women's portrayals of men and their responses/reactions to the tradition of gender roles. The male writers have mostly represented women as inferior and weak. Gendering and some sort of misogyny are evident in the texts written by men. Similarly, the lyricists have portrayed female as inferior and male as superior, and they have composed such songs which portray female as an object and not as a subject. The movies portrayed the marginalisation of women and instilled a sense of inferiority among them and the songs that they introduced also carried a similar notion. There is something particular about Indian women and there is presupposition that they consider husband as deity and they worship him. Marriages are made in heaven and one who marries is married for seven future births. This concept makes it clear that husband and wife are united by the will of God. Marriage is considered as a sacrament and the patriarchal setup grants the man a status due to which husband is raised on a pedestal and veneration is accorded to him. They are not considered on equal footing and a wife has submit to husband's authority as she has left her natal home to reside in husband's home and she has to work in accordance with the rules of new family. There are certain fasts which a lady has to keep for the longevity of husband, well-being of a family and proper health of children. Her duty is to be docile and subservient to the family and the husband. In *Status of Women in Ancient India*, Gayatri Gupta says:

> ...even the attainment of paradise for women depended upon marriage. The religion prescribed for them was the service of the husband. Through these services women could attain heaven. Naturally husband was for a women a divine incarnation, a god, as well, to be gained only through marriage. Thus, women's education, worldly duties as well as emancipation depended upon marriage but in these conditions her status was not that of an equal partner of the husband but of a disciple and devotee.(Gupta,41)

Maria Mies in her book *Indian Women and Patriarchy: Conflicts and Dilemmas of Students and Working Women,* says, "The structure of this relationship with its principle of male dominance and female subordination is diametrically opposed to the principle of companionship." (Mies, 102) Her husband is not her companion but her household deity and her duty towards him is submission and obedience. Moreover, it is considered as a pious relationship which is fixed in heaven and therefore most Indian girls do not wish their marriage unmade and they feel content with their lot and do not dream of resistance. In marriage, husband and wife become legally a single defined unit, which is male; women surrender themselves in marriage relation. A man chooses woman for marriage and reproduction and in marriage, a man becomes the woman's food supply. It is a process of mutual dependence. Men control the economic strata and those women who become economically stable do not get trapped in the cycle of marriage.

Deborah Madsen in book *Feminist Literary Theory and Practice* says, "The married woman surrenders all her rights, including the right to control her own body, though her husband gives up nothing; she becomes an unpaid domestic drudge, robbed of her labor"… (40).Moreover, Rama Mehta in her essay "From Purdah to Modernity" says, "During her childhood itself, she was carefully nurtured into the discipline that she would have to observe in her adult life, hence the need of conditioning from the early age to the established social norms and pattern" ("From Purdah to Modernity",115).

But the duty of the wife is to worship her "master" (pati) as her first god; for only thus can she hope to make spiritual gains. Her prayers, sacrifices, fasts, ascetic exercises, and pilgrimages are all for the salvation of the husband, she must always try to please him and serve him. Above all she should in no way give even the impression of violating marital fidelity, neither during the lifetime of her husband, nor after his death. Mies says "When a woman lives like that and worships even a lecherous, cruel, unfaithful, or sick husband like a God, she is called in the classical texts a *pativrata*, one who worships her lord. She is considered as the highest ideal of womanhood in Hinduism." (44).

Gupta asserts that:

> During the period when Sutras, Dharmasutras and Epics were compiled the ideal of pativrata was firmly entrenched and this ideal was inculcated in girls from childhood. Thus, by the time the maiden had attained marriageable age, she was fully prepared psychologically for the kind of relationship that this form involves. Having been brought up to regard the husband as her ideal and almost a god, she was ready willingly to accept anything as a matter of grace and thus there could be no question of unsuccessful married life. Besides there were also the chances of growth of that love, which grows only through lasting companionship and which can seldom grow out of sheer romantic attraction. (83)

Mies in her book says, "This merger of religious and marital duties made the attitude of complete submission appear as "natural". That is why women as forced upon them did not feel it." (101).Gupta states, "She was never to waver from her loyalty and never to find fault with her husband. She must follow him in prosperity as well as in adversity. He may be well-disposed or ill-disposed towards her, wicked, libidinous, poor, or sickly he must be obeyed and loved". (106)

Clara Nubile, in *The Danger of Gender* (2003), writes about 'what it means to be woman in modern India':

> Being a women in modern India means to be entrapped into the inescapable cage of "being a woman-wife-mother"...A woman cannot exist outside the boundaries of married life and motherhood, otherwise she is perceived as useless and unworthy according to traditional Indian views...Indian women do not appear to have their independent role in society. Moreover, they must have a male-appendix in order to have a role. India women are thus linked by male-definitions sex segregation patterns. Only if a woman is a wife and a mother-both examples of male appendices-she gains a status in the outer world, although a very subordinate one... The main difference between India and Western societies is that Indian women live as a part of a community, a group, a family: first the father's family, then the husband's one and finally the joint family. Individualism is considered a western perversion and female individual space is unacceptable and inconceivable. (Nubile,22-3)

A girl is taught to look beautiful, cultivate modesty, preserve her chastity; be mild, submissive, always willing to serve; be proficient in all activities involving housekeeping; to blindly follow the dictates first of her parents, then her husband and in old age, live at the mercy of her son. It thus indicates how cultural upbringing affects the gender discrimination from the beginning and this is being inculcated how the boys are privileged than the girls. It infuses a feeling of dominance in boys who from the childhood learn how to exercise authority over girls. Girls are prepared mentally that they are to be transplanted in husband's paternal family and in the family they are to take up roles in the domestic sphere, do household work, give birth, and take care of children. There is an over-emphasis on the female's domestic role – i.e., daughter, daughter-in-law, wife, mother, mother-in-law, grandmother and other domesticated social roles.

The films earlier supported the belief that an educated wife would be portrayed as a threat to the male ego as she was not supposed to have an opinion of her own and if she had, she was not supposed to express it in front of elders, the in-laws, and strangers. Mies states:

> According to the cultural ideal of pativrata and sati, the husband was the first god for the wife. Her most important and perhaps only dharma was to obey him, to serve him, to sacrifice herself for him, to remain faithful to him up to death, according to the sati ideal even after death, and to worship him. "Husband-worship" is the technical term that paraphrases

> the totality of the virtues of a wife. Foregoing one's own desires, passivity, complete merger of the personality of the wife with that of the husband constitute the appropriate role behavior for the wife. (101)

T.N.Madan in essay "The Hindu Woman at Home" says:

> Marriage is a kind of religious, social, and emotional bonding that occurs not only between two individuals but also between two families. As a maiden crossed the threshold of virginity and stepped into the nuptial life, she was transformed into the important roles of grihni. The mantras from the marriage hymns show the significance of a woman's role as a wife. She has to take care of every relation in the household, and it is her prime duty to look after everyone and convert 'house' to 'home'. The notion that women are an almost inferior race, so acknowledged even by themselves, that they are dependent on men and must serve men, and be themselves served only afterwards, is widespread.("The Hindu Woman at Home",73)

Feminism therefore now includes the struggle against women's subordination to the male within the home; against their exploitation by the family; against their continuing low status at work, in society and in the culture and religion of the country; against their double burden in production and reproduction. In addition, feminism challenges the very notions of femininity and masculinity as mutually exclusive, biologically determined categories.

Mies says, "Every little Hindu girl knows the stories of Sita and Savitri, and through magazines, schoolbooks, religious festivals and films this pativrata-model is popularised and idealised even among the non-sensitised castes and groups, so that even now it exercises a decisive influence on the social norms of female behavior".(45)

The attributes of Sita-Sati-Savitri are adopted as the prerequisite for the depiction of any woman. It has been a recurring phenomenon that the conditioning of woman is done in such a way that they have made themselves entirely dependent on men. Woman were overshadowed by male character. The objectification and commodification of woman insinuated the minds, and they cannot defy male characters and assert their individuality, their identity is not recognised and crushed at times. Women were shown as docile and weak in films and they have to adapt the role. The songs of movies of 1950s, 1960s, 1970s and 1980s are taken into consideration to emphasise how husband-worship is inculcated through these songs.

The songs that reinforce such conventions are illustrated as follows:

The song of movie *Kathputli* (1957):

bol ri kathputli dori kaun sang bandhi
sach batla tu nache kiske liye
bol ri kathputli dori kaun sang bandhi
sach batla tu nache kiske liye
bawari kathputli dori piya sang bandhi
mai nachu apne piya ke liye

jaha jidhar sajan le jaye
sang chalu mai chhaya si
wo hai mere jadugar
main jadugar ki maya si. ("*Keep Alive Binaca Geetmala List*")

The song thus exemplifies that a wife is a toy in the hands of a husband who can run according to his wishes and she is mute as a puppet who cannot utter anything but has to follow blindly. It is remarked that the fate of a lady is being determined by the husband who will decide where she has to go and like a magician, he will make the wife move. It is being accepted by the wife that she is not an equal but subservient to the husband and this predetermination of fate is acceptance on her part. This shows that the life of a wife is like a puppet who has to dance according to the tunes of her husband, and she has to be subservient and that she is willfully doing it. It is very demeaning to be a slave of somebody, but she is suppressing her identity for the sake of her husband. Her life is reduced to nothingness if there is no husband in life.

Another song from movie *Khaandan* (1965) says:

tum hii mere mandir, tum hii merii puujaa
You are my temple, you are my prayer.
tum hii devtaa ho

You are my God.("Tum Hi Mere Mandir Lyrics and Translation: Let's Learn Urdu-Hindi")

Another song raises husband on a pedestal wherein wife considers husband as everything. Her pronouncement is an indication that she is a devotee, disciple of her husband and that she is tied through religious means. She accords highest veneration wherein she proclaims that he is the temple, worship as well as deity. It is affirmation of the fact that she is diminishing her own identity and willfully acknowledging that she is subservient to his supreme authority. It gives an upliftment to male and patriarchal system which wants the woman to be subjugated and man to be the supreme and associating the cultural ties with religious rites so that a woman devotes entirely to husband. The women have subordinated their roles to traditional pativrata or sati ideal of self-sacrificing woman. Their roles within the family as wives, daughters are re-emphasised. The image of woman is reconstructed from Hindu classical texts, The Indian ideal of womanhood is to show the higher moral and spiritual standard. The stories of Sati and Savitri are very well entrenched in the minds of ladies and they consider being pativrata as their ideology and do not wish to deviate from the path.

Another song from movie Aman (1967) is Apne piya ki prem pujarin,which states, "*Apne piya ki prem poojaran/Karke baithi sringar/O aaj aaye piya more dwar*" ("Apne Piya Ki Prem Poojaran (Aman)"), depicts willingness to do worship by being completely submissive. This song is indicating how the worship of God is done. Husband is equated with God and as the worship is done, so is the worship of husband is done. He will be offered flowers, and there will be complete devotion, and everything will be offered to husband as he is everything. She has dressed herself beautifully for the sake of husband. She is eagerly waiting for the arrival and is ecstatic on welcoming the husband. It reinforces the concept of submission, devotion, and nullification of identity in front of husband who is raised on the highest pedestal.

Another song depicts the worship of husband from Movie *Archana (1973)* saying:

Tan man tere rang rangungi
Chaya ban kar sang chalungi
Seva karungi, ang lagungi

Archana mai teri sajana, ha ("Tan Man Tere Rang Rangungi Lyrics | Tan Man Tere Rang Rangungi Archana Lyrics | Lyricsgram.com")

The song thus indicates that the wife is going to worship husband and in that regard, she will be offering all kinds of service to him. She is not asking for anything as she feels he is the fruit of his worship and she will blindly follow like a shadow. It is again minimizing oneself for the sake of oneself. It is a blind devotion in which nothing is asked in return and everything is offered for the submission. It is raising husband on a high pedestal and become a devotee to worship. It gives a sense of comfort to the male authority that the wife would be fruitfully serving like a disciple. Husband is having an upper hand who can subjugate a wife as per his needs as she will be serving entirely.

Another song from movie Naseeb Apna Apna (1986) says:

Bhala Hai Bura Hai Jaisa Bhi Hai
Mera Pati Mera Devta Hai
Bhala Hai Bura Hai Jaisa Bhi Hai
Mera Pati Mera Devta Hai

("Bhala Hai Bura Hai Jaisa Bhi Hai Lyrics in Hindi")

This shows blind devotion to husband wherein a wife considers that whether good or bad, her husband is everything. However wrong he does, she will keep worshiping. because she is considering him as husband but as a deity from which she cannot question anything. She is not rationalising the wrong or righteous deeds but focusing only on what is conditioned as a part of socio – culturally upbringing where a woman has no right to question male. It illustrates that husband has to be worshiped at any cost whether good or bad. Though she is visualising that he is deceiving her, yet her blind devotion does not allow her to consider him as a bad person. It is being inculcated that husband is everything and thus worship as God but despite knowing that he is doing wrong on her part, she is devoutly following.

It is observed that through these songs the women idealised themselves and devoted their entire life to the service of home, husband and its needs and they do not think about their own selves. It is their prime concern to remain focused only on the well-being of husband and family and they are willing to self-sacrifice in that sake as well. Moreover, these songs by female herself typify the idea that they are willing to do so but it does not represent their point of view. These are being sung so that women get enchanted and follow these cherished ideals of patriarchal setup. They are in the make-believe world that they are happier when married because husband is the ultimate source of happiness but if companionship is accorded instead of deity-worship, it would be on equal footing. To consider husband having upper-hand and wife considering herself inferior would amount to create imbalance in the minds and therefore give a false impression that she is nothing in comparison to husband.

Conclusion

It can thus be concluded that the Indian Hindi songs are a popular medium of communication and thus they should portray equality. The characteristics of husband-worship is emphasised through various fasts where a wife fast for her husband and this is being prevalent in Hindu culture. Husband and wife are like the wheels of a car and thus it depends equally on both ends to maintain the sequence of life but the pressure on one side may create dire consequence in the long run. Indian cinema has evolved, and many transitions have occurred indicating there is room being created for women where they are being centralised but this would create men on the periphery and thus it should be maintained that both shall equally contribute to the affairs of life and instead of subordination, there should be coordination. Marriage is a tie of unity and thus it should be of equality as well.

Works Cited

"Apne Piya Ki Prem Poojaran (Aman)." *The Song Pedia*, 1 Sept. 2020, thesongpedia.com/apne-piya-ki-prem-poojaran-aman/

"Bhala Hai Bura Hai Jaisa Bhi Hai Lyrics in Hindi, Naseeb Apna Apna Bhala Hai Bura Hai Jaisa Bhi Hai Song Lyrics in English Free Online on Gaana.com." *Gaana.com*, gaana.com/lyrics/bhala-hai-bura-hai-jaisa-bhi-hai.

Gupta, Gayatri. *Status of Women in Ancient India*. 1st ed., Shree Niwas Publication, 2012.

"Keep Alive Binaca Geetmala List." *Keep Alive*, www.keepaliveusa.com/binacageetmala/song/bol-ri-kathputli-dori-kaun-sang-bandhi-sad-version.

Madan,T.N."The Hindu Women at Home." *Indian women. From purdah to modernity. Ed by B.R. Nanda*, Vikas Publishing House, 1976, pp. 67-76.

Madsen, Deborah L. *Feminist Theory and Literary Practice*. Pluto P, 2000.

Mehta,Rama. "From Purdah to Modernity." *Indian women. From purdah to modernity. Ed by B.R. Nanda*, Vikas Publishing House, 1976, pp. 112-120.

Mies, Maria. *Indian Women and Patriarchy: Conflicts and Dilemmas of Students and Working Women*. 1980.

Nubile, Clara. *The Danger of Gender: Caste, Class and Gender in Contemporary Indian Women's Writing*. Sarup & Sons, 2003.

"Tan Man Tere Rang Rangungi Lyrics | Tan Man Tere Rang Rangungi Archana Lyrics | Lyricsgram.com." *Songs Lyrics | Movie Song Lyrics | Lyricsgram.com*, www.lyricsgram.com/song/tan-man-tere-rang-rangungi-3189.

"Tum Hi Mere Mandir Lyrics and Translation: Let's Learn Urdu-Hindi." *Mr. & Mrs. 55 – Classic Bollywood Revisited!*, 30 Oct. 2018, mrandmrs55.com/2018/10/30/tum-hi-mere-mandir-lyrics-and-translation-lets-learn-urdu-hindi/.

CHAPTER 22

Silenced Voices of Women Portrayed in Indian Literature and Cinema

Nisha Bhagwat Gosavi

Abstract

Since ages women have been nurtured according to the wishes of others. Their voices are dominated and controlled by others just like the puppet show where the puppets don't have their own freedom and identity, they are controlled by others. Specifically if we will talk about Indian women's image the struggle has been going on since ages. Today literature and cinema is playing a role of mirror for the world showing the reality in its bare true outlook without decorating it. Biopic, historical cinemas are few examples of reality cinemas. 2017 release *Begum Jaan* is one such film situate in the milieu of late Indian Independence period of 1948. This is a very heart touching and disturbing film takes us into the world of Begum Jaan and how she fought like a queen instead of surrendering to the unethical demands of the government officers. It is the Hindi re-erect of the critically commended Begali film *Rajkahani* (2015). There are many unheard and unsung stories and sagas of miseries of women in the Indian society where they have to search for their own self image first then the journey starts to explore the external world. The present paper attempts to give voice to such sagas of miseries portrayed in Indian literature and cinema.

Keywords: women's image, struggle, sagas of miseries, Indian cinema

The Transformation of Hindi Cinema: Journey from Silent Era to Talkies/Theatres

The world of dreams means our Bollywood, as this world takes the public into the world of dreams where people try to get relief, happiness, and inspiration. Cinema is such a world which carries the strength of changing minds of people. It was Lumiere Brothers who first shown the path of cinema to the Indians. Taking inspiration from the English movie *Life of Christ* Dadasaheb Phalke first seen the dream of creating the castle of cinema in India and he started his journey alone. The first silent Indian cinema came to dictate on the hearts of Indians was *Raja Harishchandra* released on screen in 1913. Initially directors focused on depicting the mythological and historical world through their cinemas. Under the banner of Prabhat Films many hit cinemas given by this film company to the audience. How we can forget the picture of woman playing the Trombone (Tutari) an instrument which has a close relation with Maharashtrian culture taken as the logo of Prabhat Films.

Prabhat Films contributed forty five Hindi and Marathi films to the early Indian cinema. V. Shantanram strongly believed in the ideology of film holds the power to bring revolution in the society and touch the millions of lives. Here we are not merely talking about the transformation of Hindi cinema but simultaneously the transformation-taking place in the minds of Indian society as well. Women freedom issue was raised in *Amarjyoti* 1936 release directed by V. Shantaram.

The area of expertise of V Shantaram's movies was they brought a new revolution of raising voice against the evil traditions which had been followed blindly by the society. In *Manoos* (Aadmi) V. Shantaram portrayed the thrash about of a prostitute named Kesar who breaks the malevolence surroundings within which she is destined to breathe. Though the cinema was silent but it spoke through volumes regarding such social issues. The year 1938 considered as the familiar sight year in the history of Indian cinema as the industry celebrated its silver Jubilee. This year also witnessed the Second World War which had left its impact on films also. Many films addressed to the issues related to youth. With newly formed National Studios Mehboob Khan released his three films *Aurat* (1940), *Bahen* (1941) and *Roti* (1942). After seventeen years Mehboob Khan remade *Aurat* as *Mother India* with Nargis in the lead role.

In the history of Indian Hindi cinema 1950-60's is the age known as the Golden Era of Hindi cinema. In the post independent age the themes of films shifted from mythological to Indian self-determination struggle, vice, loss of morals, humankind etc. In this era Amiya Chakravarti's *Seema* won the hearts of people, this film focused on a young girl's crushed life. 1950-60' was celebrated as the Age of innocence.

Depiction of Women in Indian Literature and Films

Since the initial phase of cinema, various directors from different angles have portrayed women. When we compare Indian cinema from its initial stage up to its present status we can observe a drastic change in it. Some changes really deserve appreciation but some changes are spreading wrong messages directly or indirectly to the public. In some movies women dominates the stage as compare to male characters these women are very bold and courageous.

There are many unheard and unsung sagas of miseries of women in the Indian society where they have to search for their own self-image first then the journey starts to explore the external world. There are very few women who got such cases are rare but more of them have to fight a huge battle to achieve freedom of living their life without wearing the masks of ideal woman image. Here one thing need to be focused is the ideal woman image's concept is determined by the society. It has been observed that in different countries and cultures women are blamed for the disintegration, failures, loss of relationships. As we all know the very popular quote/proverb good things are never remember but the single inaccuracy becomes the part of criticism in the society.

In Henrik Ibsen's *Doll's House* the central character Nora done so many sacrifices for her husband but her husband ignored her sacrifices, devotion and blamed her for her one mistake. Women has to face two kinds of struggles in their life one is internal and another is external. Internal struggle starts from the days of her upbringing and clashes with the new watercourse external struggle. Both internal and external struggle goes hand in hand till her final departure from the world. It is not just the question of equal status in the society but the main concern is women should get equal status in the minds also because today giving social status is not sufficient but we need to generate a positive thought process in the minds of people.

Kamala Das, an Indian poet in English openly discussed and raised questions on the treatment given to women in Indian Society through her poetry. The common thread of her poetry is they deal with the issue of 'free choice in women's life' is most significant aspect and Kamala Das was denied the access of freedom of choice by the Indian society right from her childhood and her personal experiences shows us the true mirror of Indian society who is having numerous cracks in it these are the cracks of imbalance, biasness, partiality, discrimination on the basis of gender, inequality inferior treatment to women, narrow-mindedness and so on. And women are forced to look themselves in the same mirror for centuries. In 2018 Malayalam director Kamal created biopic film on Kamala Das named

Aami. Before the release of this biopic there was heated debate and opposition was raised by the people and demanded to stop the release of this biopic on screen. But director Kamal had given a very accurate remark on the people's opposition on the release of this biopic. According to him films are the most trendy and discernible means reaches to every corner of the world. Director Kamal tried to portray Kamala Das's lifespan from childhood to conversion to Islam in this film.

Whenever any author and director tried to give voice to the problems and injustice done to women in the Indian society such as discrimination, ill treatment and childhood marriages these authors had to face harsh criticism from the society another such example is of Katherine Mayo's *Mother India* (1927) book where the treatment given to women in Indian society, the untouchables, animals etc. criticized was by the author. Many Indian print media announced this book as 'scurrilous libel' against Hindus and Hinduism.

This work has given nativity to new moderate Indian feminism and changed the perspectives of women looking at their existence. After taking inspiration from this work the bollywood director Mehboob Khan taken the same title for his Hindi movie as *Mother India* released in 1957. This movie proved as an Indian epic drama film starring, Sunil Dutt, Rajendra Kumar, and Raaj Kumar. This movie was the remake of Khan's earlier film named *Aurat* released in 1940. It is an inspiring story of a woman struggling with poverty and unending efforts to survive in all difficult phases of life and her life's journey hardly she witnesses' happy moments. Immediately after few happy married life days her husband leaves home without informing.

Works Cited

Raj, A. *Hero: the Silent Era to Dilip Kumar.* New Delhi: Hay House Publishers Pvt. Ltd, 2010.

Sarri, A. *Indian Cinema: the faces behind the masks.* New Delhi: Oxford University Press, 2011.

<https://herso.org/issue-1-vol-3-oct-2014-index-1/>

<https://www.cinemaazi.com/feature/neend-hamaari-khwaab-tumhare-prabhat-film-company>

<https://indianexpress.com/article/entertainment/malayalam/aami-kamal-kamala-das-5056993/>

<https://en.wikipedia.org/wiki/Begum_Jaan>

CHAPTER 23

The Predicament of the Subdued: A Panoramic view of Psychoanalysis in Preeti Shenoy's *Life is what you make it*

I. Jancy and M. Beulah Hemalatha

Abstract

Preethi Shenoy, is a name full of energy and life which sprinkles positive thought on the youth through her works. The novel *Life is what you make it* is a story of courage, determination, destiny and emergent hypothesis. It is also about how life can take a turn from what is planned, and yet how one makes success out of it. Preethi Shenoy is a contemporary author who portrays the life of the common man. The paper examines the relation between Psychology and Literature and hence dealt with the hidden desires and struggles of the protagonist relating with the Freudian Psychology such as Id, Ego, Super Ego, Instincts and Talk Therapy. The inner conflict and the bipolar disorder of the protagonist reveal Freudian influence on the society, people and culture. The paper also displays the struggle of the protagonist not only with her inner conflict but also with the conventional society where a girl has to follow certain norms.

Keywords: Talk Therapy, Bipolar Disorder, Hypothesis, Instincts

The term 'Psychoanalysis' is propounded by Austrian Psychologist Sigmund Freud during the late 19th and early 20th century. Psychological criticism uses the theory of Psychoanalysis of Sigmund Freud to analyse the conflict of Psyche. It expresses the hidden meaning in a text by interpreting the dream, conscious, unconscious mind and the repressed feeling of the mind that is exhibited by the author. During the late 19th century and early 20th century Freud's Psychoanalysis was born out of the self-analysis from Freud in 1897. He first started treating the patients with therapy and thereon had general ideas about conscious and unconscious mind. His reading of the plays of William Shakespeare too has brought out the understanding of human psychology.

After Freud, many critics related the theory in order to interpret the text by means of incidents that shows the characters Psyche. The people started to use Psychoanalytic criticism to elucidate the text, as it always proceeds to form a set of Principles that paved the way to describe the life of characters. It also pacts with Id, Ego and Super Ego in which Psychoanalysis is the process of applying of what people know to three parts of human personality and to discover how a person behave. In this way, the literary critics analyse and organise the work of art by means of personality structures of Freud's dreams, repressed desires and structures of mind.

Preeti Shenoy is a contemporary writer who influences a lot of people by producing an optimistic wave through her works. She is known for her simplicity in conveying her thought. Her contact with different cultures and language made her to write on various life pedestals. In this novel, *Life is what you make it* she brings out the fact that "Destiny does not exist but created". By reading her work *Life is what you make it*, the readers can gain the ray of hope, love and determination. She also nicely brings out her determination can even overcome destiny. The text can be associated with Freudian theory of Psychoanalytic criticism. In which the protagonist's personality can be studied according to Freudian perception. The novel narrates the story of Ankita Sharma who lived with her parents in Delhi. She had her higher education in Delhi where she had friendship with Vaibhav which later turned into love. Due to her father's transfer they moved to Cochin. Then Ankita had her degree in St.Agnes whereas Vaibhav had his IIT in Delhi. Ankita was a young girl enjoying life with bloomed exquisiteness. "No more school uniform. No more strict rules. No more being treated as a kid. I would be 18 on my next birthday and officially an adult. I feel excited as legally it meant I was eligible to marry and vote" (68).

During the Inter-College competition, she met Abishek, the General Secretary of Mahavir College where love bloomed slowly. Later, Ankita passed in the entrance exam of BBA and went to Bombay leaving Abi which leads to his death. "I would begin studying the books I had borrowed from the Institute Library. It was like a whole new door had opened and there was so much to discover" (156).

Finally, she developed Bipolar disorder and got admitted in mental hospital and got recovered with the help of the doctors and parents and gave a Rebirth to her soul and Life. Through which the title is justified. Life is what you make it. The author wanted the readers to believe that they can make their life by their wants whatever the quandary may be there will be an end. So, she wanted to should think positively and move on from the problem by thinking in a positive way. Thus, according to the writer life depends on our thoughts and erection.

The Fredian classification of Human Psyche such as Id, Ego and Super Ego can be seen incorporated in the main character Ankita Sharma. Id which is also known as Pleasure Principle is found in the unconscious mind. It is the basic need and wants of people. As Ankita Sharma belongs to the traditional Indian Society, she is restricted by her parents to talk with boys but she is a modern young girl who wanted to be free. So, we can see the Id, which outburst into desires and makes her to hide from her parents the letter written by her to Vaibhav and then to Abi. She also talks over phone when her parents were out for a morning walk. Thus, the Id performs its duty by satisfying its basic wants.

Superego which is also known as the Morality Principle, argues the desire of Id whether it is morally right or wrong. This is exhibited when Ankita came to know about the suicide committed by Abishek. She got totally lost and developed Bipolar disorder. The act of morality is seen where she is not able to accept the truth and was really guilt-ridden.

Ego which is the balance between the desires and happenings is located in the conscious mind. It brings out desires in a socially accepted way. It is also related with the reality principle. It has to demand itself to the external world. This can be related to the novel when the protagonist came back from Mumbai. She was questioned by her parents for the letters with the boys. Her mother shouted "How many guys will you trap with your witty charms you stupid litter tramp" (84) and also she called her as "Shameless whore" (85). On hearing these words, she was totally broken but she doesn't know why they were angry on her. She didn't understand and doesn't know how to react. So, she kept quiet and moved. Thus she tried to balance between her desires and the guilt. Thus, the protagonist had an internal tussle lead her to commit suicide twice which Freud calls as Death Instinct (Thanatos).

According to Freud, "Goal of life is death". The death instinct also drives the person towards self-destruction. The acts of Ankita trying to fall off from the building and trying to push herself into the railway track prove it. Therefore, after admitting in National Mental Health Institute, Ankita Sharma was diagnosed of having Bipolar disorder which is the beginning scene of the novel. She is in grief, gloom and anxiety when she was admitted. Such a young spirited girl with all the success bloomed have never imagined of being in a mental hospital. Thus, destiny played a crucial role in Ankita's life. But Dr.Madhusudhan was a kind hearted psychiatrist who he helped her to emerge out of her problem. He soothed her by saying "Creativity is closely related with Bipolar Disorder" (35). Thus, the Psychiatrist plays a prominent role in bringing her back to normal.

Talk therapy, which is imbibed in Psychoanalytic Criticism, involves treating mental disorders by delving into a person's uncounscious mind. In this novel, Dr.Madhusudhan helped Ankita a lot even though she had many friends over there. She spent her time by talking with them which means talking therapy. Thus finally, she fought her battle in a dauntless way and came out of the battle field in a heroic look and stepped into her normal life. The next dimension of Ankita's life can be seen in the sequel of Preeti Shenoy's *Wake up Life is Calling.*

Works Cited

Shenoy, Preeti. *Life is What You Make it.* Srishti Publisher and Distributor. New Delhi. 2011

Seema, Suneel. *Man-Woman Relationship in Indian Fiction.* New Delhi: Prestige Books,1995.

blog.preetishenoy.com

CHAPTER 24

Women's Representation in Indian English Fiction: A Glimpse

Geeta V. Waghmare

Abstract

The subject and context of Indian writing in English have captivated the literary world. Despite the fact that outstanding literary works written in English were discovered over a century ago, the present trend in Indian literature in English is unparalleled. Many authors have gained national and international recognition. Indian women novelists have portrayed women in a variety of ways. Recently, India's most accomplished postcolonial women writers have exhibited a remarkable breadth of abilities. The portrayal of a woman as a strong, independent fighter against patriarchal oppression and the presentation of gender issues that upset women are just a few of the many themes explored. Many Indian women writers have referred to these fundamental factors in their writing. The present research paper entitled "Women's Representation in Indian English Fiction: A Glimpse" have shown different natures of women and gave voice for emancipation of women through the writings of Indian women Novelists like Anita Desai, Nayan Tara Sahgal, Arundhati Roy, Shobha De, Kiran Desai, Jhumpa Lahiri, Manju Kapur etc.

Keywords: Role of Woman, Novelists in India, Social and Psychological perspective, Subjugation, Emancipation.

Introduction

Tradition and traditional family and societal norms are the silent victims of women's representation in Indian English fiction. As seen by literature, women's roles have evolved over time. In many ways, the role of women authors in India, particularly the role of Indian women novelists, is crucial. So many Indian women literary figures have demonstrated their dominance and grasp since the commencement of Indian English literature. Their significance has been recognised in all areas. In the sphere of novel writing, there are several female authors whose contributions are so outstanding, eye-catching, and authoritative that they herald the start of a new age in Indian English literature. Only a few female writers were aware of their presence in the literacy in the past, but since independence, we have seen the rise of a huge number of female writers who are interested in writing books every year. Sarojini Naidu expresses wonderfully the importance of women's participation in the growth and development of society in the following words:

> "Other national questions come and go, they are result of the time changing sprit: but one question that had never changed since the beginning of the time itself, and life itself, is the duty of womanhood, the influence of womanhood, the sanctity of womanhood, this simple womanhood as the divinity of God on earth, the responsibility of womanhood in shaping the divinity into daily life." (Kher: 58)

Prominent Indian Woman Novelists in English

After 1980, Indian woman novelists have demonstrated a remarkable consistency and stamina in placing them in various perspectives. Amrita Pritam, Kamala Markandaya, Anita Desai, Nayan Tara Sahgal, Shobha De, Arundhati Roy, Kiran Desai, Jhumpa Lahiri, Manju Kapur, and others have all made a name for themselves in the world of writing.

Anita Desai is a well-known early Indian woman English author, and her works such as *Cry the Peacock, Voices in the City, Where Shall We Go This Summer, Fire on the Mountain, Bye Bye-Blackbird,* and others explore the female voice from many social and psychological perspectives. She speaks out on the various challenges and complexities that women face on a regular basis. She is the true representative of the female voice. In her works, she presents a distinct Indian feminine consciousness. Anna Lorre, a critic, correctly observes her significance in the present generation:

> "Anita Desai is in Vanguard of a new generation of Indian writers who are experimenting with themes of inner consciousness……. . she gives her readers valuable insights into the feminine consciousness through her memorable protagonist." (Weir: 124)

Nayan Tara Sahgal is another well-known Indian author. *This Time of Morning, Storm in Chandigarh, The Day in Shadow,* and *Plan for Departure* are some of her novels. She has depicted the clash between her female characters and Society in her works. Her protagonists, particularly the female protagonists, are fighting for independence from society. Her heroines in books are aristocratic society's wives, who are sensitive and curious about their personal freedom. Her characters are steeped in Indian culture, and they yearn for independence and self-determination. In her work *The Day in Shadow*, one of her characters says:

> "I hate this country except for the freedom it brought for countries and people, especially for woman. But it is Barbaric, otherwise, full of rotten, elastic standards and the worship of money. I hate the whole mass of women affair." (Sahgal: 35)

We witnessed the development of a big number of female novelists writing novels in India and overseas in the 1990s and subsequent years. Arundhati Roy, Manju Kapur, Jhumpa Lahiri, Shobha De, Kiran Desai, and others have drawn a great number of readers due to their phenomenal creative literary success. They are inspired by the words of Toni Morrison, a brilliant American woman author who believes that only a woman can tell a woman's true tale. Only women can fight for women's rights. She may be practically correct, but her assertion must be considered because it has been noted that female writers are more authentic and vociferous in advancing the status of women in male-dominated societies.

Even in Kerala, which has the greatest level of literacy, Arundhati Roy, who won the Man Booker Prize for *The God of Small Things*, underlines the issues of women in a male-dominated society. She occasionally has the opportunity to expose the lives of neglected and aimless children, as well as shattered houses and sexual abuse of women. The thematic implication of *The God of Small Things* in a feminine perspective, as Vimaljeet Soni correctly points out, is as follows:

> "In *The God of things Things*, Arundhati Roy implicitly presses for greater social reform in the rigid positioning of woman and the intolerable fight of the deprived class. She narrates and pain and misery of a lonesome mother in an indifferent world perceived through the eyes of her seven year old child – a world where the age of old subjugation of woman and the indescribable humiliation of the underclass still persist."

Shobha De's significance to the realm of English-language women writers cannot be overstated. She is a modern-day life critic. She is unafraid to express her emotions and passions in a male-dominated society that forbids women from going beyond and crossing the line. Shobha De's fictional and non-fictional works, such as *Socialite Evenings, Starry Nights, Sisters, Strange Obsession, Sultry Days, Snapshots, Second Thoughts, Small Betrayals, Shooting from the Hip, Speedpost, Selective Memory*, and others, portray the true tale of the current generation. In her writings, she criticizes man's dictatorial mindset and preaches vehemently for the empowerment of women. She speaks out against male-dominated values that marginalise women's roles in society. Her works' core themes revolve around women, their roles, uniqueness, and likes and dislikes.

By writing from a feminist standpoint in the twenty-first century, Kiran Desai, Jhumpa Lahiri and Manju Kapur reached a new zenith. Despite the fact that they were living in another country, they worked to better the status of women in India. Kiran Desai, another female author who received the Booker Prize for '*The Inheritance of Loss*,' is an outspoken feminist. In a male-dominated environment, her female heroines are successful in revealing their identities. Desai wonderfully portrays three generations of female characters. Sai, Noni, and Lola represent the educated and urban classes, whereas Nimi (Bela) represents the rural and uneducated. *The Inheritance of Loss* portrays Indian society's subjection of women. In this work, Kiran Desai not only plays Nimi, but also a number of other female roles. Others are meek and subservient, vain and lost, while others are assertive, confident, and self-reliant. Desai has examined many elements of womanhood through numerous female characters, but Bela's subjugation and degraded standing in society is best shown.

Jhumpa Lahiri is interested in the conflicts that arise between first and second generation expatriates, as well as the communication barriers that they face on a daily basis, and the conflicts that arise between Indian parents and their half-American children, as are many other diasporic women writers. In her works and short stories, the majority of the female characters are either expatriate moms or their children who are divided between their Indian tradition/belief and modern life. In *Interpreter of Maladies, The Namesake,* and *Unaccustomed Earth,* the female characters are diasporic women who enjoy freedom of choice in America but struggle to adapt to changing conditions.

Manju Kapoor's works are particularly relevant in the first decade of the twenty-first century because her stance toward feminism differs from that of other Indian English novelists. She was named the Commonwealth Writers Prize winner for Best First Book (Eurasian section). She has received critical and commercial recognition both in India and abroad. In her portrayal of Human Relationships, especially man-woman relationships and husband-wife relationships, her feminism is well-defined. Her five novels, *Difficult Daughters, A Married Woman, Home, The Immigrant, and Custody,* all deal with normal middle-class ambitions, desires, and aspirations. But she tries to find or create a new society for women in which they can have freedom, liberty, and free expression.

Conclusion

In a nutshell, the evolution of women's characteristics may be seen throughout history in literature. Because society was governed by men, and most published writers were men until contemporary times, the portrayal of women was undoubtedly skewed. As a result, throughout history, women have been neglected and dominated. It doesn't matter if she exists, has a personality, plays a role, or is a woman. The marginalisation and subjection of women before to the mid-nineteenth century can be traced back to their minor roles in literature. The protagonist changed as women gained more equality. By observing these shifts, it becomes clear that the protagonists not only personify female identity, but also develop into the new figures that women aspire to be.

Work Cited

Singh, K.K. "*A Critical Companion to Manju Kapur's Novels*" Jaipur: Aadi Publications, Print, 2015.

Kher, B.G. "*The Pageant of Life*" Ahemadabad, 1959 p.58.

Weir, Annemarie. "The Illusions of Maya: Feminine Conciseness in Anita Desai's Cry The Peacock," *Journal of South-Asian Literature*, XVI, 2 (1981), p.124.

Soni, Vimaljeet. "*A God of Small Things: A Feminist Analysis*", Indian Writing in English (ed.) Manmohan, R.Bhatanagar, Vol.V New Delhi: Atlantic Publisher, 1991, p.171.

Sahgal, Nayantara.*The Day In Shadow* New Delhi, 1976, p.35.

Iyenger, Srinivas. *Indian Writing in English,* Sterling Publication. New Delhi. Print, 2013.

Manohar, Murali D. *Contemporary Indian Women Novelists in English.* New Delhi: Serials Publications, 2010.

CHAPTER 25

Breast as an Object: Breast Stories by Mahasweta Devi

Megha Soni

Abstract

In the society, 'Breast', always an object for male gazing, and eventually, it is also the national gaze as well. Mahasweta Devi's short stories and other literary works are particularly based on the plight of women in the society. Her narrative mainly documents the struggle of the women to overcome the oppression and violence brought by high-cast landlords, moneylenders and corrupt government officials. Her literary work exposes that the suffering of women have long been avoided and were not even considered as 'wrong' but the unusual consequence of everyday life. Devi's short stories reveal the truth of women's misery and the potential of enduring and resistance. In my paper, I am going to discuss "Mahasweta Devi's Breast Stories" to explain the 'Breast' as an object and the present paper is also an attempt to analyse highly appreciated for work of Mahasweta Devi which is exploring the socio-economic and demographics, cultural – signification and commercialisation of the breast, to examine how women often employ them in their bare life struggles to combat poverty and starvation. According to Gayatri Chakravorty Spivak, the breast of a woman in these stories becomes the instrument of a vicious denunciation of patriarchy. Indeed, breast, common to all women can be constructed as the motif for violence in the short stories, 'Breast-Giver', 'Draupadi' and 'Behind the Bodice' all these three short stories are inside the Mahasweta Devi's work, 'Breast stories.'

Key words: Breast, women, exploitation, object.

Mahasweta Devi was an extraordinary writer who had been writing, working, and fighting for the marginalised tirelessly for the past six decades. She was a strange mix of an activist and a writer who had carried both duties fiercely all her life. She is famous especially for her works related to the study of rural tribal communities of West Bengal, women and Dalits. In her Bengali fiction, she often expresses the brutal oppression of tribal people and untouchables by upper caste landlords, money-lenders and government officials. Mahasweta Devi's short stories signify the position of women in the society. The world of her short stories is that of the exploited and the dehumanised. Here sexual exploitation combines with class and caste subjugation to relegate the woman to the lowest rung of the village hierarchy. She essentially reduces the hierarchical structure of Indian society into two stark and rigid categories, the dominator faceless and unchanging and the dominated-helpless, writhing and increasingly stripped of identity. In the short stories such as Rudali, Draupadi, Stanadayini (The Breast Giver), and Behind the bodice, reflect all these types of facts.

Mahasweta Devi's 'Breast Stories' consist of three short stories, namely Draupadi, Breast-Giver (Standayini) and Behind the Bodice (Choli Ke Pichhe) deal with exploitation and have the common theme the Breast. In these stories the translator Gayatri Chakravorty Spivak depicts in her introduction that the Breast is not only a symbol, but more than a symbol, like an object or commodity for male gazing in these stories. In Draupadi, it is transformed into a commodity and in Behind the Bodice, 'an object' which is supposed 'normality' of sexuality as male violence. The 'Breast Stories', is also constantly overlooked account where women are stripped of their honor and humanity. Mahasweta Devi's literary works expose the violence, means, how women have been victims of the discrimination, exploitation, brutality, physical, emotional, and psychological rape and so many social evils. We see in Breast-Giver, how Jashoda has been exploited and degraded for many years and also in other two stories, Draupadi and Behind the Bodice, the protagonist Dopdi and Gangor also face the same things. In these stories the Breast become the object of attention of male gaze. Gayatri Chakravorty Spivak, the translator of these three stories stated in the introduction to the Breast Stories.

> "The breast is not a symbol in all her stories. In 'Draupadi', what is represented is an erotic object transformed into an object of torture and revenge where the line between (hetero) sexuality and gender violence begins to waver. In 'Breast-Giver', it is a survival object transformed into a commodity, making visible the indeterminacy between filial piety and gender violence, between house and temple, between domination and exploitation. Devi's mature fiction never romanticises the socio-libidinal relationship between the sexes.. . ." (Book Introduction vii)

> "'Breast-Giver' is the story that builds itself on the cruel ironies of caste, class, patriarchy. Devi keeps Jashodha's name unchanged from the

> Sanskrit scriptural form. Although the orthodox Hindu middle class nominally reveres the brahmin, the prerogatives of economic class are in fact much more real for it. The underclass 'Hindu female' (Breast-Giver), as long as she credits Hindu maternalism and family value, is unable to save herself. Even in her lonely death, she remains 'Jashodha Devi' – literally, the Goddess Jashodha, honorary goddess by caste." (Book Introduction viii)

The first story of 'Breast Stories' is 'Draupadi', a story of a tribal women being tortured and rape by police officials. The story is very powerful among the three 'Breast Stories'. In Draupadi, the victim's body is brutally abused with unutterable ugliness. In the story, the protagonist treated as an object of torture and revenge where the line between heterosexuality and gender violence conjures. Draupadi was published in Mahasweta Devi's work 'Agni Garbha' in 1978 and translated by Gayatri Chakravorty Spivak in her collection, whose title is 'Breast Stories' in 1997. It is the story of a woman who herself is the result of exploitation of female servants. In the story, Draupadi pronounced Dopdi who along with her husband Dulna, also most wanted criminals in the West Bengal. The story is not only based on violence but also a resistance by a poor, illiterate tribal women who suffers denial to cloth herself. The story points out the misery of a woman.

> "Shaming her, a tear trickles out of the corner of her eye. In the muddy moonlight she lowers her lightless eye, sees her breasts, and understands that, indeed, she's made up right. Her breasts are bitten raw, the nipples torn. How many? Four-five-six-seven–then Draupadi has passed out.........." (31)

> "The commotion is as if the alarm had sounded in a prison. Senanayak walks out surprised and sees Draupadi, naked, walking toward him in the bright sunlight with her head high. The nervous guards trail behind.
>
> What is this? He is about to cry, but stops.
>
> Draupadi stops before him, naked. Thigh and pubic hair matted with dry blood. Two breasts, two wounds.
>
> What is this? He is about to bark.
>
> Draupadi comes closer. Stands with her hand on her hip, laughs and says, the object of your search, Dopdi Mejhen. You asked them to make me up, don't you want to see how they made me?. ...." (32-33)

> "Draupadi pushes Senanayak with her two mangled breasts, and for the first time Senanayak is afraid to stand before an unarmed target, terribly afraid." (33)

These lines have been taken from the text, which represent the objectification of women. She always has seen, as an object of desire. In these lines, we can see that the Dopadi denial to put on clothes. They all were trying to cover her with clothe but Draupadi refused. It shows the hypocritical nature of men and society. She sees her own breasts, they are bitten raw and the nipples of breasts torn, because not only one but four-five-six and so on raped her, even during that time when her body was bleeding. They continuously did the rape, just like hungry dogs. As a counter-offense, when she makes herself naked and displaying her crushed body, the Senanayak walks out surprised and got nervous. He shouted and about to cry, "What is this"?, but naked Dopdi come closer and she stands with her hand on her hip and says that it's Dopdi Mejhen, the object of your search. In the last, Dopdi pushes Senanayak with her two mangled breasts. In this story, Mahasweta Devi gives the voice to voiceless. Dopdi take her revenge in her own way. She raised her voice even after being brutally gang raped.

In Mahasweta Devi's second story "Breast-Giver", she talks about the story of a subaltern and women Jashoda, a poor Brahmin woman, who had taken Motherhood as her profession to support her family. After the accident of her husband Kangalicharan, she has been appointed as a professional mother of "Haldar family". She started breastfeeding to all grandchildren of Haldar family to earn money, for the survival of her own family. She had to breed annually for the production of milk. In the Breast-Giver, the story reveals the totally different dimension of motherhood.

"The Mistress was out of her mind trying to feed the boy. As if relieved to see Jashoda she said, You come like a god! Give her some milk, dear, I beg you. His mother's sick – such a brat, he won't touch of bottle. Jashoda immediately suckled the boy and pacified him. At the Mistress's special request Jashoda stayed in the house till 9 p.m. and suckled the Mistress's grandson again and again. The cook filled a big bowl with rice and curry for her own household………..." (43)

"If Jashoda becomes the Infants' suckling-mother, her daily meals, clothes on feast days and some monthly pay will be enough………." (45)

"Jashoda received a portfolio when she heard her proposal. She thought of her breasts as most precious objects………..." (45)

"Jashoda wiped her eyes and said in a heavy voice, I've carried so many, I was the regular milk-mother at the Master's house. You know everything. I've never left the straight and narrow." (55)

These lines as quoted from the text represent the breasts as an object. In the story, the protagonist Jashoda do the work of wet nurse, she is just like a production machine of milk to feed her husband and children. Actually Jashoda received a proposal, according to proposal, if Jashoda becomes the infants' suckling –

mother, then she will be provided well prepared rice and curry every day. Here, breasts are just a commodity which is helping Jashoda to feed her family. She also thought of her breasts as most precious objects. Jashoda fed 50 children of hers and her Master's, for this, she had constantly conceived to keep them filled with milk. After feeding 50 children, she contracts breast cancer and her breast milk has dried up. Now, she is useless for Haldar's family. It is very hard for her to sleep without a child at the breast. For her, motherhood is a great addiction which does not break even when the milk is dry. She had never thought that she wouldn't have a child's mouth at her nipple, because her breasts feel empty, now her usefulness ended. She spent her whole life for her Master's family and her own family but in return she got nothing. Even at the time of her dying situation nobody come from Haldar family. She treated as a milk production machine. Her breasts are just an object which was useful and useless both. Jashoda took up Motherhood as a profession, she has many children during the time of feeding but at the time of her cremated no children was there. She was cremated by an untouchable.

'Behind the Bodice' is the last story in the series of 'Breast Stories'. It is a story of a Dalit migrant labour Ggangor's annoyance and resistance against her exploiters. In the story, Mahasweta Devi explores how natural aboriginal breasts become an object of study and attraction for media and anthropologists. There is an another character in this story, Upin Puri, an ace – photographer. He sells his pictures for newspapers and magazines at high price. Upin married to Shital, a famous Himalayan climber. One day when Gangor was feeding her baby, Upin click several pictures of her breast and sold them for publication to newspaper without acknowledging about the result of it. He just wants to click some natural photos of Gangor's breasts but he has no idea that he is going to ruin her life because of his one mistake. He has made a mistake that Gangor's breasts, is only an object of photography and nothing else, so knowingly or unknowingly he becomes the cause of her victimisation.

> "Yes, the picture of a banner. Written on it in English, 'The half-naked ample-breasted female figures of Orissa are about to be raped. Save them! Save the breast!' ...." (123)

> "A high – breasted rural woman sits slack with her breast shoved into infant's mouth. The breast is covered with the end of her cloth. The same girl is walking with many girls carrying water on her head. Breasts overflowing like full pitchers..............." (124)

> "And then he'd said, God those breasts are statuesque! Did you see the mammal projections?......." (125)
>
> "Train passing, Gangor's crowd looking at it. Her breasts like the cave paintings of Ajanta, against the back-drop of the sky. Dirty choli. Dirty red cloth, hair full of lice, filth.....filth........." (126)
>
> "Shital looked at the pictures with care. Chest, breasts. What is the breast? Fat tissue, this that, a lot of bother.
>
> Why was Upin so worried?
>
> Ujan was leaving, he left. Shital closed the door and put her hand on her liquid silicone implanted front. Behind Shital's choli is a silicone chest. Upin had said, This is all artificial, Shital?
>
> How would Upin know their secret – these breasts remain aggressive forever. Like plastic flowers, Shital? Upin would say.........." (130)

All these lines which have taken from the text are clearly showing the plight of Gangor and the breasts which are natural not manufactured or an object. But how and why did Upin first think they were the object of Photography? In this story there is not only one character who suffered due to breasts but also one another, Shital, Upin's wife. She has liquid silicone breasts. One day Upin said to Shital when she was looking her breast that her breasts are artificial. Not only gangor but Shital also suffered. Upin's one mistake put Gangor inside the marsh, where she faced rape, gang rape, biting and tearing gang rape, police abuse, court case, gang rape in the lockup etc. So, Gangor was demolished by numerous men. The men who ruined her were police man, a worker contractor and other men. She was manhandled and exploited and later in the end, she becomes a whore and an alcoholic.

Conclusion

Mahasweta Devi's stories are totally based on the exploitation of the female body as well as forming a resistance factor of the female body. After analysing these stories, I have come to conclusion that these weaker, marginal, downtrodden women are always treated as an object. These women are gradually excluded from the society and even their primary rights to live are also snatch. In the society the tribal and lower caste women are keep outside. They have no power and rights to live their own life according to themselves. Women are not treated as human being but always be playthings, sensuous, an object and flesh piece etc. Mahasweta Devi's stories document the tortured of human body. In these stories the socio-economic, cultural significance and commercialisation of breast can be seen, how women struggle to survive their life? How do they feed themselves? How do they feed their family? Etc. In all these stories women employed their breast to reek out a subsistence living to provide enough food to feed their family. In 'Breast Giver', Jasoda worked as a wet nurse to feed her family. Mahasweta Devi' stories always articulate the misery of women, their power of enduring and resistance.

Work Cited

Devi, Mahasweta. *Breast Stories.* Trans. Gayatri Chakravorty Spivak. New York: Seagull Books, 2018. Print.

Walia, Gaganpreet. "The Theme of Gendered Subaltern in the Works of Mahasweta Devi." *Research Scholar-An International Refereed e-Journal of Literary Explorations.* Vol 3. Issue I, (2015): 346-352.

Uppar, Sachin. "Mahasweta Devi's Draupadi: A Feministic and Gender Perspective Analysis." *Epitom Journal – International Journal of Multidisciplinary Research.* Vol 2.Issue 7 (2016): 30-33.

Priyadarshini, Sahana. "Women in Mahasweta Devi's Breast-Giver, and Dhouli." *International Journal of Creative Research Thoughts.* Vol 7. Issue 3 (2019): 447-451.

CHAPTER 26

The Reciprocal of Rhetoric and Apishness in Anita Desai's *Where Shall We Go This Summer?*

S. Sandhya

Abstract

Desai's heroines are for positive act. She creates a balance between inner self and the outer world, individual self and the societal consciousness. Her characters are simple but historically powerful. They enkindle a sense of immurement and isolation like burrow, net, gossamer, trap and cage. Her images are neither paranormal nor mis-related. Its imagery is mainly pre-eminent, pre-figurative or epideictic in nature and its pattern are singularised. In the novel, Desai shows the disconnections between Sita and her family. The novel is seen as the inability of human beings. The isolation is overlapped as lyrical and rhythmic splendour of her novel. Desai brings out that self-adjustment in the only solution to all the problems and troubles of self-alienation for which one is responsible. All of her women characters are bitter in the beginning of their journey but the journey of self-adjustment makes everyone to feel comfortable at the end of the novel.

Keywords: Alienation, human relationship, love, apishness, isolation.

Introduction

The rhetoric of the narrative brings an ability to lift the moments of aesthetic experience of the protagonist of Desai's works that appear to have reached a wholeness of her characters recognising the positive streak in all of her characters to see a growth potential in their efforts. And the apishness of the novel explores the work of self-alienating, denoting the pathological proportions and the change of attitude to and from. In an interview, with Atma Ram, Desai says that suicide is too melodramatic and alternative for the middle-aged woman that the heroine is.

Reciprocal of the Rhetoric and Apishness

The novel denotes the stress between an erogenous wife, Sita and the logical, practical and worldly temporal Raman. Husband-wife strife deficiency of their mutual level relationship and estrangement are the major themes of the novel. The love and affection between Sita and Raman but it is stopped due to misconstrue, lack of patience. The estrangement continues primarily from their disposition.

Sita is very sensitive, sharp-eyed, poetic and inventive. If Raman is extravert Sita is introvert. If Raman looks for immediate present, Sita has higher feeling about life than an ordinary woman. Sita lives with her four children and is loath to beget or to abort the fifth one. She likes to keep it in her womb but she is very afraid of bringing out the child in this violent world. She is fed up with the city life in Bombay. She wants to go to the magic island, Manori, in the hope of forbidding the delivery with miracles. But her miracles have failed instead of peace, she has become alienated. She understands and goes back home to start her passive life. Sita realises the difference between the wish and the need. She thinks that what a man likes and what he is forced to do. Her willingness is to bear the child and hand over to Raman.

The story is told with past events as flashbacks. It is separated with many events. The first part of the play depicts the arrival of Sita to the 'Magic Island' with her daughter Menaka and the son, Karan. The second part speaks about the life of Sita at Manori for twenty years. The next part says about her choice of the future. Desai espouses the pattern of monsoon to express the uproar in the mind of Sita. This enables the inner life of her protagonist who is the central figure of the novel.

Sita's father is a well-known freedom fighter who follows the principles of Gandhiji and has taken care of his disciplines as the second Gandhiji. His life is gone in jail so she has no mother to take care of her. She has refused to accept the regular life of a normal child. She lives an abnormal life. She likes to spend her days out of her home. She likes to go to a different place. She does not go to any attend any school to learn discipline because her father is not free to give her education in a proper manner.

> "She belonged, if to anyone, to this whole society that existed at the particular point in history – like a lamb does to its flock and saw no reason why she should belong to one family." (25)

After independence, Sita's father has planned to settle in a small island called Manori with his family and his disciplines. He has named his house as 'Jeevan Ashram'. It means the '*home of Soul.*' He brings his social theories into practice. He has practised many social welfare activities for the villagers. He has suggested several opinions to the villagers to bring agriculture. He himself digs a well for the villagers. Many changes have been brought on this island. He voluntarily does all things to the people. They start to believe him for his magical things. One of the villagers calls him as magician and all start to repeat it. In a quarter of time, he has made to be a legend. Sita spends her time with her brother Jeevan and sister Rekha. In course of time, her father's miracles grow large in number by his supernatural activity.

According to Sita, her father is an enigma. She has doubt that her father cures people by magic or by medicine. She is upset to hear the bad news of that her mother has run away. She feels that she does not have mother. The figure of her mother makes and turns her into a roamer. She decides to an unrealistic attitude towards her life. She questions herself, why does her mother leave her husband who has lived as second Gandhi. After the demise of her father, she has been brought to Bombay by Raman Deedar who is a friend of her father. Raman sets up funeral ceremony for her father. She is sent to college by Raman. Later, he is charmed by her beauty and falls in love with her and marries her "Out of pity, out of lust, out of sudden will for adventure, and because it was inevitable." (99)

Being a businessman, Raman is not able to spend his time with his affectionate wife, Sita. He is so busy with doing his work and has his own lifestyle to follow. His mind is fully occupied with business deals not the love of his wife. He believes the welfare of the society not the sprite of his wife. He lives to fill the mind of the people of the society not to satisfy his wife. He has good relationship with every one of the society except his wife. Because he does not find time to spend with her. But he wants to control her on his needfulness. Sita feels that her life is made to be dull, ordinary and with full of lamentations. Sita expresses her husband to be the life-lover. She loves to share her life him with full of care and satisfaction. She tries to prove her value to him. She respects him as her mother and father.

Sita believes that marriage is travesty, and all human relationships are true to the absence of love. She feels terribly sorrowful with her husband and even with the concern of her in-laws. Her life is choked with revolting and painful in Bombay. She understands that people in cities are artificial, bored, spiritually dispelled and with idiotic lives. Beside this, Sita scrutinises that people in Bombay are just for machin life. The people of Bombay are "nothing-nothing but appetite and sex. Only food, sex and money matter animals." (47)

Sita once asserts to Raman that she is happy only in her 'Hanging Gardens' where she meets a Muslim woman who plays her head in the lap of an old man. He seems down at her and rubs her tenderly. Sita has never stumble upon like these gentle moments in her life. Sita has never got such kind of sentimental and love with Raman which feels for the first time in her life. Sita is rebellious together with her husband and kids because of her affective reactions within the society. She does not like force or violence in nature. To her sturdy feelings, she discovers it as everlasting.

Desai's chief anxiety is human relationship. Her central theme is that the existential plight of an individual whom she ventures through mismatched couples, sensitive wives, and ill-matched husbands. Desai is a silent observer perceiving everything minutely and precisely. Whenever she creates a distinctive situation, she provides it an ideal poetic treatment to each detail. Though her characters are self-conscious of the relative around them, they carry with them a sense of loneliness, isolation, and cynicism. She deals with the displacement of traditional life, wildness of behavior and morbidity of personality, maladjustments with familial life of contradictions.

Desai dives deeply and tries to figure out the discrepancies and dichotomies of the virgin territories of contemporary lifestyle. She affixes a new dimension turning hidden into the realities of life and throws into the deep depths of the human psyche to score out its mysteries, confusion and chaos within the mind of her characters. It is imperative on our part to converse her techniques of articulating such practices of inner and outer realities. It appears that the imagination of the writer is disgusted by emptiness of modern life, a sense of insecurity surrounds the milieu of her novel as is the case with Saul Bellow or Margaret Atwood. Thus, she spotlights the complexities of human nature, misrepresentation of personality and an infinite multiplicity of individuals; we must find out reality of life in such people.

Desai within the light of her characters, we discover in her writing a shot to find, underline and express the significance of things through imagery and symbols. Sometimes, she completes and sometimes she incompletes that she recognises. For truth and reality, the inner and outer life of every individual is anticipated in this chapter. As a talented artist, Desai knows to select from the vast amount of material and presents it extensively as if she has the psycho-analytical approach to the predicaments of modern life. With the help of flashback technique and interior monologues Desai captures the inner qualities of life for her fiction which covers a large area of subject matter for discussion.

The rhetoric falls in each part of the novel to maintain the form and structure. Raja becomes selfish, Tara becomes ordinary, Baba becomes abnormal and Bim becomes the heroine who is capable of heroine of being courageous and independent. Thus, the narrative corroborates the conclusion. However, the apishness runs parallel to the rhetoric and supports for a clear picture of Bim's assume, her awkward and difficulty. Bim is affected by her psychological problems, and she moves everything in deep which makes her to be stress of self-alienation.

Being a woman novelist, more intensely her heroines are very trustworthy, and she studies the heroes too. She does not have any relevance for feminist movement as she builds it clear that her concern as an artist is with individual men and women. But she is chiefly interested in bang of psychic depths of her characters. Most of who respond adjacent to the absurdity of life or the existentialist problems. She focuses on characters rather than social milieu. She never produces common characters but expresses the extremity of despondency to her characters who are essentially existentialists. Symbolism is a device to give meaning and significance to a work of art. It is associated with definite objects to characterise the incidents, characters, words, and phrases. Desai is very much broadminded in the use of symbols either consciously or unconsciously. Her use of symbols beautifies the narration of stories and presents life to the situation of character. And in few cases that reimburses for other disabilities in conversations.

Desai is more interested in the interior mind of a person than in social and political realities. She is concerned exclusively with the personal turmoil of individuals. Hardly interested in social conditions, political events and the mundane habitual of the characters; she explores the interior layers of her character's psyche and brings to the surface, by the repression of nonessentials, various shades of human mind. The apishness runs parallel to the rhetoric and supports for a clear picture through her characters. Her protagonists are the persons for whom loneliness alone is the treasure and most of them are female characters. They are all fragile introverts. Desai's handling of the emotional life of the characters ranks her among the distinguished humanistic writers of the modern age.

Conclusion

Desai is a minstrel of the human heart, an artist shaping the outline of her inner world. She brushes aside inconsequential things of an individual and gives us fleeting thoughts with razor like sharp awareness of the futility of individual's existence. Thus, most of her characters are overcast by shadows and half-shadows, half-revealed and half concealed. Thus, the image of isolation divulges the dusky passions and confused emotions of the one soul pining away in self-alienation shining for self-identification.

Works Cited

Anand, T.S. Where Shall We Go This Summer? Anita Desai's Stance against Negativism. *The Fiction of Anita Desai.* Ed. R. K. Dhawan, New Delhi: Bahri Publications, 1980. Print.

Desai, Anita. *Where Shall We Go This Summer*? New Delhi: Vikas publishers, 1975. Print.

Kalpana. H Destiny of Women in the novels of Anita Desai, *Contemporary Indian Literature in English; A Humanistic perspective.* ed, Mithilesh, K Pandy, Ludhiana, Kalyani publications, 1993. Print.

Khanna, Shashi. *Human Relationships in Anita Desai's Novels.* New Delhi: Sarup & Sons, 1995. Print.

Krishna, Sivaram. M. From Alienation to Mythic Acceptance: The Ordeal of Consciousness in Anita Desai's Fiction. *Indo-English Writers Series,* 1985. Print.

Rao, Vimla. Where Shall We Go This Summer? An Analytical Study, *Indian women Novelist.* Set I-III, ed. R.K. Dhawan, New Delhi, Prestige Books. 1991. Print.

Sudipta. B. *Alienation: A symphony in Time.* Jaipur, Indian scholar publications, 1993. Print.

CHAPTER 27

Sufferings of a Transgender Woman in Ajay K. Pandey's *An Unexpected Gift*

R. Devendiran and B. Kathiresan

Abstract

This paper focuses on the condition of transgender community in Indian society and also brings out the struggles and discriminations faced by the transgender individuals in employment and housing and also in their daily life. The present article also examines how the author had portrayed the transgender woman through the character named 'Sheetal'. It also brings out the struggles faced by a widowed man named Abhay who has to take care of his toddler child and the problems that he faces in bringing him up.

Keywords: Transgender, Discrimination, inequality, Sufferings, Indian society.

Introduction

Transgender people are facing problems like discriminations and inequalities in the society we live in since before the 1800s. Ajay K. Pandey's "*An Unexpected Gift*" is about the feelings, pains and also the problems faced by the transgender community in the society, especially when they start to interact and mingle with the society as both men and women do. The transgender people do dance on the streets and mislead their lives only because of the way the society treats them. If they were respected and given an equal status among the society they won't mislead their lives and even do not indulge in menial activities.

An Unexpected Gift

The story revolves around a widowed father named 'Abhay' who works in an IT company. He had lost his wife named 'Kanika' to brain tumour after giving birth to a baby boy 'Ayush'. Soon after the death of his wife, Abhay found it very difficult to take care of his child and his performance in his office also lowered. One day his boss introduced him to a woman called 'Sheetal' who is a transgender woman, which Abhay comes to know later. First the job assigned to Sheetal was to take care of his child Ayush. Sheetal was doing well in taking care of the child but later when Abhay came to know that Sheetal was a transgender woman, Abhay sacks her from his house. Then one day Abhay realised his mistake and the injustice that the society had made to transgender people. He at once went to Sheetal's house and asked her to re-join the job to take care his child from the next day. The secretary of the apartment where Abhay staying was Mr. Ashok Kumar who is an old man of his father's age and Abhay approached him to seek advice regarding the transgender woman, Sheetal in allowing her to work in that place. Ashok Kumar was both religious and a modern man. He often uses Ramayana and Mahabharata to teach life lessons to people whenever any lost soul came to him. He then narrated a story from Mahabharata, where 'Shikhandi' is a transgender man, whom the people accepted him as a king. Also he questions why the present society fails to accept the transgender people as humans.

Ashok kumar's advice has made Abhay to realise the injustice or the torture that had been given to the transgender people, for a course of time. Then everything was going good until a call from the Day Care centre where Abhay had put Ayush during the day time. The principal of the Day Care centre said to Abhay that his son's growth is not much equal to that of his peers and as a motherless child you should take full responsibility over him and the problem was Ayush cannot speak or communicate as a child of his age. Abhay felt that his son should not feel different when all of his friends talk about their mothers. So he requested Sheetal to make Ayush to call her 'Maama', but not 'Auntie'. Sheetal at once agreed to do the same with tears from her eyes. Sheetal felt happy when Ayush calls her Maama. Then Sheetal introduces 'Subhajit' To Abhay to whom she is going to get married soon and Sheetal needs Abhay to speak to Subhajit's family on behalf of her. Though Abhay tried his level best in explaining and convincing Subhajit's father he didn't gave permission to the marriage. As a conventional and conservative family man, he doesn't agree to the words of Abhay and later they planned to marry secretly without the permission of Subhajit's family. Sheetal even after getting married to Subhajit came to work regularly to take care of Ayush. She often insists that what she was doing is not a job, but it is what she had been longing for which makes her happy in her life, she said it was a gift to take care of a child.

Everyone asked was 'can a transgender woman become a real mother' only Abhay knows that she is no less than her love Kanika. Then days passed Abhay came to know the struggle been faced by Sheetal for a long time in his apartment from security guards, next door neighbours and everyone who knows that she is a transgender woman. This made Abhay to feel bad and he arranged a job in the IT field for Subhajit in Pune. When Sheetal came to know this she started to cry and later because of Abhay's compulsion she agreed to leave Ayush. It was on Sheetal's Birthday that she and Subhajit were about to leave the city to Pune. She cried and asked Abhay not to let Ayush to forget her and never allow him to know that he had been brought up by a transgender woman. Abhay realised the presence of motherly quality in Sheetal and how much she meant to Ayush. That night Abhay was restless and more concerned about his son and he doesn't know what he would do after Sheetal leaves in the morning. He was wandering in his living room restlessly. Then he decided something and packed all the things of Ayush and went to the railway station and wrote a letter to Sheetal saying that he had sent his son Ayush as a birthday gift to her. Sheetal felt very happy and thanked him wholeheartedly.

Abhay and his Personal Life

Abhay is a young man who was interested in theatre and acting right from his childhood, his father was against his wish but only his mother supported him in succeeding theatre, performance and in acting. During his college days he loved a girl named Kanika, who was more supportive for his acting career, with her he managed to play theatre scenes in college events. Later they both got married and settled down. After a few months Abhay came to know that Kanika was suffering from brain tumour and later she died. Then onwards Abhay's life was filled with full of pain and suffering, as he could not take care of the child Ayush alone. As a widower he was struggling to do all the activities alone. During that time he came to meet a transgender woman Sheetal who was very much concerned towards his child and finally Abhay gifted the child to sheetal.

Transgender woman – Sheetal

Sheetal was born in a middle class family. She was brought up like a boy but when she grew up she noticed something unusual about her body. She started behaving like a girl and liked things which are meant for girls. She used to dress up like a girl and wore lipstick. Her father hated and felt ashamed of her behaviour but only her mother came forward to help her and in school everyone started to make fun of her appearance and also those people started to call her as 'eunuch' and 'hijra'. Then her mother sent sheetal to her mama-ji's house where her mama-ji was little supportive for her in the beginning but later started to accuse her like her father and everyone did. Eventually her mother died in the course of time that made sheetal to lose the contact with her family.

After that Sheetal got a friend named Subhajit who had helped immensely in bringing up sheetal and gave her moral and financial support. He even took sheetal to Noida from her uncle's house where Subhajit is about to do his higher studies. Sheetal became happy only after joining Abhay's house to take care Ayush (Abhay's toddler child). Sheetal felt something pleasant because since being a mother was her long awaited dream. It got fulfilled because of Abhay's good and kind heartedness towards a transgender person like sheetal. Sheetal finally got married to Subhajit with the help of Abhay though no one had supported the marriage between sheetal and Subhajit, but sheetal was happy on that day of her marriage. After the marriage sheetal visits Abhay's house regularly to take care of Ayush, but her happiness lasts no longer. When Abhay arranged a job for Subhajit in Pune and asked sheetal to move with Subhajit to Pune by leaving Ayush. Sheetal was heartbroken at first by hearing this and later agreed to move to Pune with the request of Abhay. It was her birthday when Sheetal is about to depart to Pune. At last towards the end sheetal got Ayush as her birthday's unexpected gift from Abhay.

Sufferings of a Widowed Father

Abhay and his own father were widowers. Abhay's father lost his wife and also Abhay lost his wife Kanika. Among the two widowers only Abhay struggled a lot, because he had a toddler son to take care of. Abhay lost his wife to brain tumour and at that time his child Ayush was just seven months old. It is unimaginable to think about a male to parent a seven months old baby without a mother. This had totally ruined the professional life of Abhay. He cannot concentrate on his career and more than that Abhay became mentally stressed and instable and he began to consume drugs and started to smoke quite often thinking only about his child's future. The only thing that was running on Abhay's mind all the time was his child Ayush and his future.

Abhay had put Ayush in a Day Care centre where Ayush would stay in the day time. One day when Abhay was in his office he got a call from the principal of the Day Care centre 'Aparna' asking Abhay to meet her in the office regarding his son. Abhay went to the Day Care centre and there the principal told him that his son's growth was not as a child of his equal age. Ayush cannot speak and communicate as a child of his equal age. By hearing this he felt too bad of not being able to bring up his child as others do. The principal also advised Abhay that as a motherless child Ayush's life was in Abhay's hands and he is the one who was solely responsible for the child's future. By hearing this Abhay felt bad on his inability in bringing up the child. At that moment he was thinking about his wife Kanika but on the contrary the first word his son uttered was 'Auntiee'. He asked his son's care taker (Sheetal – a transgender woman) to make sure that Ayush does not feel different when every one of his friends talks about their mothers. So Abhay hesitantly asked Sheetal to make Ayush call her 'Maama' but not as 'Auntie'. This incident is such a heart-breaking one when a father begs someone other than his wife to be called as mother by his child.

Finally towards the end of the novel Abhay came to know that his son loves Sheetal very much as a mother as Sheetal does. Abhay accepted his inability in bringing up his child and handed over Ayush permanently to Sheetal, concerning the future of his child. It was such a big thing to gift one's own child to someone.

Sufferings of a Transgender Woman

Right from her childhood Sheetal had been suffering a lot from her family members, society, friends and everyone she meets. When Sheetal was young her father came to know that she was a transgender, her father at once felt ashamed and started to hate her and does not show any love towards her. "I guess he had only loved his son, not me." (AUG. 53)

Her mother warned sheetal not to come out of her house, because the boys from the neighbouring houses started to call sheetal as 'eunuch' and 'hijra'. This made sheetal and her mother to feel bad. When sheetal asked her mother about that, her mother felt pity on her daughter and replied sheetal as 'you are my daughter'. "Am I also a eunuch,? Ma? I asked my mother the same night... 'No. ..who said that? You are my daughter'." (AUG. 54)

Her mother's words made her feel comfortable because hearing herself as a girl was her long awaited dream. No one likes Sheetal's including her father, her relatives and her neighbours. For that reason Sheetal was sent to her mama-ji's house where her name by birth 'Sheel' was changed to sheetal "My name at birth was Sheel, but When I reached Maama-ji's house, I had a new name----Sheetal." (AUG. 55)

This is such a worst thing to change one's name because of the society's discomfort in a person's nature. Sheetal was also not allowed to go to school after knowing she was a transgender woman. After that she lost her mother. Everyone accused that Sheetal she was responsible for her mother's death. This incident is again a kind of torture to a person accusing her to hold responsibility for one's death to whom she was in love. After her mother's death she was completely detached from her home. "After my mother's death, the fragile thread that bound us had broken". (AUG. 56)

Sheetal stood hopelessly and finally when she proposes to marry Subhajit, everyone opposed except Abhay, even their wedding was held only in the presence of Abhay and Ayush. In her workplace Sheetal was not allowed to enter into the apartment and also the society members framed certain rule against a transgender person like her. "No transgender people, eunuchs or unmarried maids are allowed to work..." *(AUG. 174)*. Thus Sheetal faced too many problems in the society to live a life as normal as human beings.

Conclusion

The reason Sheetal faced too many struggles and inequalities in life was the lack of public understanding. People fail to understand that they were also human beings living in the society; they also have the freedom to access everything that was meant for a human being on this earth. The author Ajay K. Pandey had clearly brought out the struggles and the discriminations faced by transgender people in the society and above all he had beautifully portrayed the motherliness of a transgender woman. "Yes, a transgender woman could also be a mother" (AUG. 111)

Work Cited

Pandey, Ajay.K. *An Unexpected Gift,* Westland publishers, 2019. Print.
http://en.m.wikipedia.org/wiki/transgender_inequality

CHAPTER 28

Depiction of Women and Feminism in Shashi Deshpandae's *That Long Silence*

Krishna Priya J.

Abstract

God created men and women equally, but the women's rights were limited to small. Feminism as a movement might have originated in the West, but with the deterioration in the status of women in India and the subsequent efforts made during the freedom struggle to pave the way for equal access to education and equal status, there arose a need for feminist studies. The feminist movement advocates equal rights and equal opportunities for women. Feminism was portrayed by many writers of English literature and one among them is Shashi Deshpandae (1938). This paper examines the feminist perspective of Shashi Deshpande's *That Long Silence* (1988). This novel won the Sahitya Akademi award in the year 1990. In this novel, the soul protagonist is 'Jaya', whose complete control was taken over by her husband Mohan, after their marriage. Deshpande realistically depicts the inner conflicts of Jaya and her quest for the self or identity. This novel is about gender discrimination and inequality prevalent in society.

Keywords: Feminism, Women, Identity, Indian customs

Introduction

Feminism is always meant for independence of mind, spirit, and body. Its theory is that both men and women should be equal politically, economically, and socially. Shashi Deshpande derives the title of her novel "*That long silence*" from the classic understatement by Elizabeth Robins in her speech to a world body. This novel "*That Long Silence*" comes relatively close to the real-life experience. Simon De Beauvoir says, "One is not born, but rather becomes a woman. It is civilisation as a whole that produces this creature which is described as feminine" (The Second Sex: 295).

Feminism in The Novel "*That Long Silence*"

In this novel, Deshpande deals with the burning issues regarding women's position in the family and the society. The prime character of the novel 'Jaya' is the perfect representation of the modern women of today. She can be intercepted as a present time women of indecision who waves between family and self-assertion. She is an intelligent woman with graduation in English, a writer, and a columnist who had a bright career. Unfortunately, none of these attributes would provide her a respectable position in the eyes of her husband Mohan, who had socialisation in a typical traditional environment. Jaya always recollects her days before and after marriage, and her lovable memories of childhood.

Before marriage Jaya has optimistic views on life as her father always encourages her by saying "'I named you Jaya' he said, 'Jaya means victory' "(15). But after the death of her father, 'Ai' her mother does not support her. This makes Jaya feebler and more vulnerable. Her mother always prefers her son and she even gifts their ancestral property i.e. the Dadar flat to her son rather than her daughter Jaya.

And after marriage, Jaya lives in the family life thinking about her family and her husband Mohan. On their wedding, Mohan renamed his wife Jaya as "Suhasini" as he wanted her to be 'Soft, smiling, placid, motherly woman' (16). Her period of marriage life comprises of confrontation between two phrases of her personality where the later had to be triumphant to appease her husband's ego and to save her marriage. And in the end, she comes out to be a decided and determined woman who now knows how to strike a balance between her family and her identity in the family.

Deshpande beautifully described Jaya's married life as,

> "A pair of bullock yoked together. It is more comfortable for them to move in the same direction. To go in different directions would be painful and what animals would voluntarily choose pain?" (11-12).

Without any attachment or love between them, the bullocks yoke together and share the burden between them. Likewise, the monotony, solution, and loneliness enter the marriage life where there is no love but only compromise. Whenever Mohan finds Jaya's behaviour to be odd towards him and his family, he tells, "My mother never spoke against my father, however badly he behaved to her" (83). Thus, he gradually pushes her into the traditional world and reveals his expectations from her. Jaya regretfully accepts the fact that she had accepted everything about Mohan by blinding herself to the consequences like Gandari and was also ashamed of her ignorance and inaction.

> "If Gandari who bandaged her eyes to become blind like her husband could be called an ideal wife, I had bandaged my eyes tightly. I didn't want to know anything." (61)

Deshpande through the image of Jaya depicts the one who is unprotected and unshelled. She describes, "Distance from real life, scared of writing, scared of failing on God I had thought, I cannot take anymore. Even a worm has it can crawl into" (148). She compares herself to a worm that has its shelter, whereas she has not hers. This feeling of Jaya reminds of Virginia Woolf's fiction "*A Room of One's Own*", in which she presents her demand for a room for her creative work. The narrator believes that with money and a room she could have been a writer as living condition always affects one's creativity. Jaya also wishes to keep on writing. She breaks her silence of seventeen years in her writings, with which she expressed the thrust of craving identity of herself. She writes the responsibilities and social bondage in her view has been a failed writer and the universal voice is not heard in her works.

For her writing pieces, she is unanswerable to Mohan, which means that she does not have freedom and liberty both in her personal and her professional life. The creative and artistic zeal free her from her dubbed domestic roles. When she realises this, she makes her mind to be silent no more, she has the right to reveal her genuine feelings and emotions. So, she resolves to break her silence by putting down on paper that entire she has suppressed in her seventeen-year silence. Finally, she expounds:

> "The panic has gone. I am Mohan's wife I had thought, and cut off the bits of me that had refused to be Mohan's wife. Now I know that kind of fragmentation is not possible. The child hands in pocket, has been with me through the years." (191)

Shashi Deshpande effectively expounds the aim of individual happiness in marriage. From the beginning Jaya developed fear of speech for fear of reticulate from males Appa, her father, who always prevents her from doing any task of her taste. Her father and brother criticized whenever she got opportunities to rebuke. Due to all these she jumps into silence which becomes easier to her. Later she maintains the silence with Mohan also and the reason behind this was liberty and freedom shown in threads. The inability to find words loads Jaya to embark upon a long silent journey. Finally she holds silence, the utter silence "But the words remained unsaid. I know his mood was best met with silence" (78).

Her traditional upbringing makes her to sacrifice herself on the altar of marriage. Through the characters of Jaya, Asha, Mukta, Kusum, etc., Deshpande depicts the complexities of Indian women of the modern age. Marriage plays a pivotal role in the life of Indian women and it changes their entire life. The husbands rejoice in their life carrying no sign of being married. Jaya meditates why women plunge into the marital life and keeps burning silently. The reason that she finds to her is, "We're all frightened of the dark, frightened of being alone" (102). For women in the Indian society, it is both a personal weakness as well as a social fate.

Shashi Deshpande reveals the psychological distance between Jaya and Mohan. Before her marriage she is taught less without caring about her emotions and feelings. Vanita Mami told her that a husband is a "…sheltering tree. Without the tree you're dangerously unprotected and vulnerable. This… followed logically; and so you have to keep the tree alive and flourishing even if you have to water it with deceit and lies" (32). Ramu kaka reminded her that the happiness of her husband and home depends entirely on her. And her brother Ravi advises her "to be good to Mohan" (13). Mohan blames her to be careless to his family but she does not speak. She keeps on speculating in silence, "No question, no retorts, only silence" (144).

When a woman is free to live her life on her terms, our tradition redeems her. Before the old established orders in society, individual happiness is good for nothing. Another female character Mukta, neighbour of Jaya is a widow.

> "Mukta, to me, was that dancer, holding in her still, mute body all those ideas, emotions and feelings contained in the song. Sometimes, I'd often thought, the singer will stop singing, and then it will all flow out of her. Or did the song come to an end for her when Arun, her husband, fell out of the train and died?" (67).

She lives a life with merriment and this lifestyle irritates Jaya. And this stirs Jaya internally and externally. Jaya is jolted by Kusum, who plunges into a well to end all the problems and avoid monotony, depression, and melancholy. Jaya thinks about the reason for her suicide and finds the indifference of parents. Jaya's heart was badly shaken after hearing the news of Kusum's suicide. All these show how inhuman our patriarchal system has been.

Jaya was introduced to her neighbour Kamat who motivates her to think and act independently about her writing by appreciating it. This made Jaya to regain her self-confidence which had been lost. He made her speak frankly which she couldn't speak with Mohan. This made Jaya to realise her 'self'. Thus Kamat enabled her to break 'long silence'. This companionship of Kamat made Jaya to get her identity. Without the freedom and liberty there is no meaning of life and becomes worthless to live.

> "This man… it had been a revelation to me that two people a man and woman could talk this way. With this man I had not been a woman. I had just myself – Jaya. There had been the ease in our relationship, I had never known in any other. There had been nothing I could say not to him." (153)

By the end of the novel, Jaya's husband loses his confidence and position as an engineer. In the global society, her husband becomes the victim of corruption. During the 17 years of their marriage Mohan never asked Jaya's opinion on any matter. When an inquiry has been set against him, he asks Jaya to support the family through her carrier as a writer by holding her hands. But Jaya remained silent without knowing what to say. This is a kind of protest against her long silence, which makes her strong at the end of the novel.

Conclusion

Shashi Deshpande's "*That Long Silence*" is an expression of the silence of modern housewives. She realistically depicts the inner conflicts of Jaya and her quest for self or identity. As said by Hillary Rodham Clinton, "Human rights are women's rights, and women's rights are human rights. Let us not forget that among those rights are the right to speak freely – and the right to be heard". The protagonist Jaya remained silent for maintaining her tradition, but the quest for her individuality made her to break her silence. To establish social harmony, the harmony in the family needs to be established. There has to be an end to the discrimination on women based on gender. No gender is superior in this world. Gender equity, justice, and equality have a bearing on attaining gender development to have peace, harmony, and love in the family relations. Jaya's character portrays the narrator's split self; the writer and the housewife.

Works Cited

Beauvoir, Simon de. *The Second Sex.* Tran. Constance Board and Sheila Malovany Chevallier, Vintage, London, 2011 print.

Deshpande, Shashi. *That Long Silence.* New Delhi, Penguin Books, 1989 print.

http://www.enotes.com web

www.randomhouseindia.com web

CHAPTER 29

Feminist Concerns in the Novels of Shashi Deshpande

Chavan Sharad Uttam

Abstract

The novels of Shashi Deshpande represent the declining condition and complex experiences of her women characters. The focus is mainly on women belonging to a specific class and period, notably the nineteen seventies and eighties. The period saw changes at various levels and registered a transitional shift in social, political, mental, and economic spheres. It had a tremendous impact on the lives of middle-class women and spawned a slew of complex problems. The protagonists and the other women characters belong to the middle-class, where they encounter the usual domestic conflict, which contributes to forming the plot structures for these novels. In the guise of the central character and the middle-class domestic clash, the novelist reveals the problems, frustration, and disappointment experienced by contemporary women.

Keywords: The plight of women, subjugation, resistance, gender-discrimination, identity, patriarchal domination and middle-class women

Shashi Deshpande is the most prolific Indian woman novelist, with a plethora of works to her credit. She was born in Dharwad, Karnataka, in 1938. *Legacy* is the first collection of her short stories, which was published in 1978. Her first novel, *The Dark Holds No Terrors,* came out in 1980. *That Long Silence*, published in 1989, won the Sahitya Akademy Award and Nanjangud Thirumalamba award. She has published nine volumes of short stories, seven novels, two short crime novels and four children's books. Her novels were published both in India and abroad. The three of her novels have brought awards and a considerable reputation.

The novels mainly deal with the status of women in Indian society, revealing the conditions of highly educated women such as doctors, professors or journalists. These characters are capable of intellectual reasoning and interpreting the situation around them. Stifled and restrained by the surrounding conditions, the characters find it difficult to lead their lives amidst orthodox impositions. However, the rationalised and compromising approach to life enables them to overcome the situation. Simultaneously, conflicting situations allow them to carve out a path for creating identity and recognition.

Rooted in Indian culture and tradition, her protagonists do not endeavour any radical steps to uphold feminism. Despite profound emotional and intellectual awakening, the women protagonists hardly prioritise their individuality while enjoying their relations with other family members. Their highly individualistic nature does not endeavour to negate or undermine completely the social setup in which they live. Instead, they try to expose and catch up simultaneously with the system. It is this factor that discloses their well-bred intellectual and emotional abilities. They devote themselves to family relations as is customary in Indian culture. For them, maintaining family bonds is more significant than individualistic traits. Despite living within the enclosed circumstances, they preserve sufficient space and attempt to free off inhibitions. Within this system, they discover their worth and resist walking on the system's assigned path.

Although Shashi Deshpande's novels deal with women's struggles and status, she refuses to be labelled a feminist. Her way of sensitising the issues allows us to consider her as one of the leading Indian feminists. Despite her refusal, she deserves to be called a feminist. Each of her novels brings out unique experiences encountered by her female protagonists. The women characters, which bear the author's voice, help in reaching the desired object. Her candid and realistic involuntary portrayal of women's situations, sympathetic approach and profound understanding and focus on women's experiences allow us to consider her a prominent feminist.

Each of her novels depicts the diverse problems faced by various women characters. *The Dark Holds No Terrors* delineates the story of a professional triggered by gender discrimination, agonised and squeezed by the sadistic acts of her husband. The sadistic confrontation causes trauma, furthering profound introspection and evaluation of self. *Roots and Shadows* depicts the agony and suffocation experienced by the protagonist. *That Long Silence,* a prize-winning novel, describes the uneven struggles of a middle-class, educated housewife who tries to preserve her individuality and freedom. Compared to these novels, *The Binding Vine* gives a very dismal picture of marital life. It enacts the personal tragedy of Urmi, Kalpana and Mira. The work reveals how women are being cut off systematically and alienated from the male prerogative world. In *A Matter of Time,* she portrays male domination and humiliation encountered by the protagonist.

The novels like *Roots and Shadows, The Dark Holds No Terrors* and *That Long Silence* deal with a transformation brought about in the life of the protagonist through sorrows and sufferings. These catalysts trigger the protagonist to introspect and give her the ability to gloss over the surrounding situation. Ultimately, they lead her to the realisation of her status and significance in society. It is through this process, she emerges as a confident person towards the end. The novelist probes deeply and realistically into all the issues such as inequality, suppression, gender discrimination, and humiliation. Every incident from the novels reiterates sufferings as the inevitable part of a woman's life. The lives of women characters appear foreshadowed with sorrows and sufferings. However, they crave to be free and fulfilled amidst the unending chain of frustration and disappointment. Such a realistic portrayal contributes to arouse the reader's sympathies for the sufferings of women.

Roots and Shadows is her first novel that deals with the agony and trauma experienced by a woman in the Indian conservative system. It helps to expose absurd rituals and customs contributing to perpetuating male domination or male supremacy. The protagonist rejects her oppression and proclaims her freedom and individuality. The conflicts and the challenges faced by the protagonist help form a new identity.

The novel is about Indu, who is educated and sensitive. Born in a highly conservative family, she is individualistic and aspires for freedom. The orthodox family atmosphere and a dominating matriarch in the form of Akka create hindrances in her way of achieving freedom and self-fulfilment. However, as a rebel, she brushes aside all those obstacles that obstruct her way.

She defies the traditional role assigned to her by society. Her motive behind grabbing education and career is to resist her suppression. She becomes a journalist and starts writing for a woman's magazine. However, after some time, she feels muddled up in writing on women's problems and leaves the magazine to join another. She realises that her married life devoid of happiness and love has not materialised. She has merely surrendered to Jayant. She feels tired of living a life of deception and wants to tear down the façade of a happy married life.

The novel depicts the agony and suffocation of each woman character caught in the orthodox, male-dominated society. The protagonist Indu defies suppression through her acts and creates a space for individuality and freedom. She asserts herself through the sexual act she establishes with her cousin Naren. She does not succumb to the dominations imposed upon her by society.

That Long Silence portrays the struggle of an educated, middle-class married woman stuck in her obligations. It records the protagonist Jaya's hesitancy in fighting the oppressive system. Jaya has been subjected to tremendous dominance since she was a child and, when she confronts a similar situation after her marriage, she loses her grip and becomes defiant. She grows tired of playing the customary role that has been allocated to her. Finally, in her effort, she attains recognition and space.

Apart from Jaya, the story of Mohan's mother is another instance of suffering caused due to her husband's harsh and dominating nature. She symbolises the Indian wife who tolerates everything without any complaints. The presence of the male ego becomes a key factor in enslaving women and marital disharmony. The catastrophe in the Jaya-Mohan relationship is caused by the superior masculine mindset. Mohan takes pride in him as he provides bred-butter and security to the family. Consequently, he considers his right to control his wife or set parameters for her writing career.

The novel, *The Dark Holds No Terrors,* depicts the life of a highly educated woman who becomes the victim of gender discrimination and male domination. It is very tragic and reveals the pathetic condition of educated women in Indian society. The protagonist goes through a traumatic situation twice, in her childhood and after marriage. The traumas shatter her life entirely.

The protagonist suffers blatant discrimination due to her gender. She experiences domination from her childhood. Her orthodox family views her brother Dhruva, a boy, as a priority and Saru, a girl child, as an asset. Her brother's death exacerbates the situation, and she eventually becomes an unwanted child. The secondary treatment deeply affects the protagonist's emotional development. Saru develops an intense hatred and a sense of insecurity as a result of her childhood mistreatment and inattention. Because of this, she desires to be loved and cared for in the latter part of her life. She anticipated the fulfilment of her ambitions after meeting Manohar in the medical college, but this, too, proves to be a short-term mirage. Conjugal ties deteriorate into gloomy shadows.

The novel portrays a very bleaker picture of marital subjugation. Saru and Manohar's marriage exemplifies the evil side of patriarchal victimisation. Saru becomes the victim of male-superiority. She undergoes a lot of humiliation and neglect in childhood and marriage. To escape the drudgery of life, she dogs after success and emerges as a successful doctor; however, her success brings her husband's ego at stake and invites calamities. Her success in social and professional life makes her husband feel inferior. Her social and financial status foreshadows Manohar's career. The feeling of inferiority leads him to dominate his wife so rudely.

The novel uncovers gender-discriminating patriarchal mentality as the foundation of all evils in Indian society. Through the representation of discriminatory treatment suffered by Saru from her parents and husband, the novel reveals various factors of the unchanging Indian social system. It shows how stringent family rules subjugate determined and hardworking women. Despite continuous neglect and hardships, she achieves success. Unfortunately, whatever she obtains in the form of love, success and recognition prove fleeting, leaving her to severe disappointment.

The novel, *The Binding Vine*, narrates the tragic and pathetic tale of various women characters like Urmi, Kalpana and Mira. Urmi, the protagonist, describes the story of her mother-in-law, who was raped in her marriage, Shakutai, a deserted woman, and her elder daughter Kalpana, who was also raped. The protagonist feels oppressed while conforming to the patriarchal norms. She has been taught to be watchful to the rules and parameters of behaviour since she was a child by society. She feels helpless as a result of her subjugation.

The novel, *A Matter of Time* records the tragedies of women of three generations who belong to the same family. Sumi is the central character whose husband Gopal has deserted her after marriage. She becomes the victim of a broken marriage and suffers tremendous humiliation. However, Sumi possesses immense courage and stoicism, enabling her to counter grief and disappointment in her life. As a divorcee, she carries the stigma associated with the divorce while surviving in Indian society.

Shashi Deshpande, through this novel, tries to reveal the hardships encountered by a divorcee while re-habilitating in the family. A woman abandoned by her husband has no place in her husband's or her father's house. She is at a loss without any support. Because of the conservative patriarchal approach, Sumi suffers enormous humiliation in her life. Everybody looks down upon her without any fault. Deprived of a respectful place in her father's house, she must suffer a painful life without complaint. Despite this, Sumi faces the situation with a strong determination and tries to get on well with life.

The novel, *Small Remedies*, brings forth the deep-rooted social problem of gender discrimination. The instances from the novel indicate that women have to live a marginal life and cannot have an existence outside patriarchy. They have to be dependent and without any freedom for choice. The couple, Som and Madhu, experiences estrangement in their marriage due to the patriarchal mentality. The protagonist, Madhu, goes through an intense experience of gender discrimination in her life. She ponders over the privileges enjoyed by men in conventional society. Men, she thinks, have ample freedom and could live an unconventional life without any regard for family or other people.

The impact of gender discrimination, male dominance, a quest for identity and self-fulfilment, marital subjugation and victimisation, agony and suffocation within the domestic sphere, and career women are among the major concerns addressed in her novels. Each of her novels dexterously attempts to handle the issues. The concern and the depth of understanding of all these issues disclose her sensitivity towards these issues.

Work Cited

Singh, Anita. *A Voice after the Long Silence: Shashi Deshpande's Rootsand Shadows and That Long Silence. Shashi Deshpande: A Critical Spectrum.* ed. T.M.J. Indra Mohan, New Delhi: Atlantic publishers, 2004.

Iyengar, K. R. Shrinivasa. *Indian Writing in English.* New Delhi: Sterling Publishers, 2003.

"Interview: Shashi Deshpande Talks to Lakshi Holstorm" Wasafiri, no. 17, *Spring* 1993, p. 26

Chodorow, Nancy. *Feminism and Psychoanalytic Theory.* New Haven: Yale University Press, 1989.

Beauvoir, Simone. *The Second Sex*. Trans. Constance Borde and Sheila Molavony-Chevallier, New York: Vintage books, 2011.

Vimala Rama Rao. "Myth and Folkore in Shashi Deshpande," *The Fiction of Shashi Deshpande*. Ed. R.S. Pathak, New Delhi: Creative, 1998.

Swain, S. P. *"Shashi Deshpande's The Dark Holds No Terrors: Saru's Feminine Sensibility"*, Indian Women Novelists, ed. R.K. Dhavan, Set III, Vol. 4 New Delhi: Prestige Books, 1995.

Sandhu, Sarabjit. *The Novels of Shashi Deshpande* New Delhi: Prestige Books, 1991.

CHAPTER 30

The Theme of Subjugation in Kazuo Ishiguro's Select Novels

Maharudra Keshav Kapse

Abstract

Kazuo Ishiguro was born in Japan and brought up in Briton; he is a British novelist, screenwriter and lyricist. He has been a winner of numerous awards and honours, including the 2017 Nobel Prize for Literature, the Booker Prize, Order of British Empire, Chevalier de l'Ordre des Arts, et des Lettres, and Order of the Rising Sun etc. Ishiguro's female characters demonstrate highly complex behaviours in the novels. Certain characters face severe oppression; however, they stand firm, while others lose their minds. Feminism is termed broadly as an ideology of equal status for women in social, political, and economic spheres. Feminism classifies the problems faced by women due to gender bias in the fields of politics and sociology. The paper aims to study certain critical female characters of Ishiguro*'s novels like A Pale View of Hills, When We Were Orphans, The Remains of the Day,* and *Never Let Me Go.*

Keywords: Subjugation, Feminism, Feminity, Feminine Psyche

Introduction

Kazuo Ishiguro was born in Japan and brought up in Briton; he is a British novelist, screenwriter, and lyricist. Literature Kazuo Ishiguro is a British novelist. Ishiguro was born in 1954 in Nagasaki city in Japan on 8th November. His father started research at the National Institute of Oceanography; in 1960, Ishiguro and his mother travelled to England. He went to a boys' school in Surrey. He completed Creative Writing at the University of EastAnglia, where he met Angela Carter, who was an early mentor to him.

In 1983, shortly after publishing his first novel, Kazuo Ishiguro had designated *Granta* magazine declared him 'Best of Young British Writer'. He is widely acknowledged for his books such as *A Pale View of Hills, When We Were Orphans*, *The Remains of the Day and Never Let*

Me Go, The Buried Giant and *The Unconsoled.* Along with writing the novels, he has also written for the screen and lyrics.

Ishiguro's female characters demonstrate highly complex behaviors in the novels. Certain characters face severe oppression; however, they stand firm, while others lose their minds. These characters can be understood when they studied under feminism. Feminism classifies the problems faced by women due to gender bias in the fields of politics and sociology.It believes that equal status for women in social, political, and economic spheres brought all movements and struggles to better women's lives under the umbrella of feminism.

Feminism has changed prime perspectives in a broad range. It ranges from a variety of points like law and culture. Feminist people activists have raised their voices for women's cultural, sociopolitical, and economic rights. The paper aims to study certain critical female characters of Ishiguro in the novels, *A Pale View of Hills, Remains of the Day Never Let Me Go,* and *The When We Were Orphans.*

Interpretation of Women

It is noteworthy that many women characters in the novels of Ishiguro look like the typical 'Japanese women'. To start on with, in the book *A Pale View of Hills*, the significant Keiko, Etsuko, anda few minor characters such as Sachiko and the wife of Hanada is greatly dependent on others. Apart from the caseof Keiko, these supporting structures are the men in their life. Etsuko's marriage to Jiro, though not predominantlya sad one, was not satisfying either. The failure of marriage forced her to seek refuge in the affection shown by a British man and shortly marries him.

One more reason for this marriage is to provide a better life to Keiko, though it didn't work out. It had an opposite reaction on Keiko. She was isolated from her own family. Her insecurities made significant, leading to her suicide, which is another considerable trait in Japanese culture. In Japanese culture, suicide is always glorified with rituals and considered a means of regaining their honour. This belief flashed when the news report of Keiko's suicide news was published in the newspaper. Etsuko couldn't believe it and was shocked to know that the English people have generalised the Japanese as habitual to commit it.

More than one newspaper points out that Keiko is entirely a Japanese girl. The English people were rapid to put forward the Japanese race has an instinct for suicide. For this, there is no more explanation needed. Therefore, they reported that she was Japanese and that she had hung herself in her room.

Sachiko is like Etsuko in many ways as it does not come as a surprise, as they are both stereotypical Japanese women. Sachiko is depicted as a woman who desperately wanted a husband after the demise of her first one. The motive behind it is the same as Etsuko's, providing a better life for her daughter. Despite the repeated disloyalty from her American boyfriend Frank, she harbours hope that somehow, she will be able to go to the United States with him. Her loyalty to him is characteristic of Japanese women's dutiful behaviour to their spouses.

Hanada and his wife voting for different persons is an example of the general expectations from a woman in Japan. People often believe that women should not have any opinion of their own. Their ideas are supposed to reflect their husbands' views. If they choose to go against the decision of the husband, it is punished strictly with violence.

"Is that really true?" Ogata-San asked. He had not spoken since I had come back in with the tea. The other three stopped laughing, and the pale-faced man looked at Ogata-San with a surprised expression. "Well, no." He became suddenly formal and gave a small bow. "I didn't actually hit her." "No, no," said Ogata-San. "I meant your wife and yourself – you voted for separate parties?" Similar stereotype behaviour is identified in other women characters of other novels, such as Sarah Hemmings in *When We Were Orphans*, In *Never Let Me Go*, Miss. Kenton and Ruth show desperation when it comes to having a spouse or partner.

In *The Remains of the Day*, Sarah's desperation comes from her desire to be of some value in society. She hopes to achieve this through marrying some man of high reputation in the community. As an orphan, she believes that if she ever had parents, this would be one way of making them proud. She does not even think of any ways to achieve a reputation for herself.

> "If my parents were alive today,' she said, 'they'd be telling me it's high time I was married. And perhaps it is. But I won't do what I've seen so many girls do. I won't waste all my love, all my energy, all my intellect – modest as that is – on some useless man who devotes himself to golf or

to selling bonds in the City. When I marry, it will be to someone who'll contribute".

About Miss. Kenton, it can be seen that she is obviously in love with Stevens, Yet, she does not admit her love to him as she feels it is not appropriate for a woman to propose to a man. She waits for Stevens to say it first. When she finds that Stevens does not propose to her, immediately she moves on to find another man and marries him. Miss. Kenton is unhappy with her life with Stevens and decides to part with him, but when she discovers that her daughter is getting married and grandchildren are on the way, she chooses to stay with him. She says that she has learned to love him. It is a sign of submission and resignation.

The behaviour of Ruth is highly unpredictable and self-centred. Her love for Tommy is due to her need for a partnerand not her deep love for him. She even splits up on one occasion. But, later, when she finds that Tommy is attracted to Kathy also responds to the feelings. She decides to barge into their middle andtears them apart. In her last days, she corrects her mistakes. But, it could never make up for the lost time. "It should have been you two. I'm not pretending I didn't always see that. Of course, I did, as far back as I can remember. But I kept you apart. I'm not asking you to forgive me for that. That's not what I'm after just now. What I want is for you to put it right. Put right what I messed up for you."

The subjugation of Women

Some of the women characters in Ishiguro's novels face domination at the domestic and social levels. The examples of these are the mother of Christopher Banks in *When We Were Orphans,* Sachiko and the wife of Hanada in *A Pale View of Hills.* These women are real fighters in their lives, but they cannot break away from their fate all through.

The mother in *When We Were Orphans* faces the cruelest form of subjugation under the hands of her subjugator, Wang Ku, a drug lord. She has abducted his henchmen soon after her husband absconds her for his mistress. He is motivated by her act of causing his insult. Her action was not purposeful, but Wang Ku could not assimilate this insult from a woman. Therefore, he abducts her and makes her his concubine. He enjoys beating and insulting her in front of his visitors. She bears all this for the sake of her son. She finds the middle ground with Wang Ku on the condition that he provides for her son's education, sent away to live with an aunt afterher abduction. His mother insulted an opium warlord who arranged to be abducted and kept her as his courtesan. Several 22 years later, the warlord died, and she moved out to war-torn China. (Finney)

Sachiko's subjugation is self-inflicted as it was her option to stay with Frank, who was a drunkard. She works hard to make sufficient money to move to the United States. But, Frank misuses it all on alcohol. The way he deals with Mariko is also doubtful. Sachiko, in her desperation, does not kick out Frank and sees him as her way to a betterlife in the U.S. However, it is highly uncertain if frank would ever take Sachiko and Mariko to America. Despiteall this, she resides with frank and suffers the whole time. In a way, her oppression has its roots in longing for a better future for her child, and it is also the case of Banks' mother.

The oppression faced by Hanada's wife has quite a broad appeal as women worldwide seemto lose their views and decision-making rights to their husbands. In this case, even her right to vote was underattack. She asked to vote for the party favored by Hanada, and when she contrasted it, she got physical punishment. When other people hear this story, their surprise is not about him threatening to beather if she voted against his choice but about the fact that his wife voted for some other party than the one he favored.

Conclusion

To conclude, it can say that Kazuo Ishiguro has been somewhat doing well in portraying his women characters. Though most of these women display qualities and character behavior of the Japanese stereotype of women, they also possess the universal appeal, in the case of motherly natural feeling exhibited by them. They are mainly ready to bear for the sake of their children. Moreover, Ishiguro's understanding of the condition of women worldwide is noticeable in the treatment given out by these women in domestic and social spheres. He has pictured the anguish of women and their mental strength sometimes to bear sufferings and at other times to overcome them.

Work Cited

Ishiguro, Kazuo. *A Pale View of Hills*. London: Faber and Faber, 1982. Print.

.... *The Remains of the Day*. Boston: Faber and Faber, 1989. Print.

.... *When We Were Orphans*. London: Faber and Faber, 2000. Print.

……… *Never Let Me Go*. London: Faber and Faber, 2005. Print

Shaffer, Brian W. *Understanding Kazuo Ishiguro*. Columbia, S.C.: University of South Carolina P, 1998.Print.

"Figuring the Real: Ishiguro's *When We Were Orphans*" Finney, Brian CSULB.

CHAPTER 31

Tranquility of Women in Shashi Deshpande's *That Long Silence*

C. Leela and M. Premavathy

Abstract

In India, girls are supposed to be the alien's wealth and sent off to some stranger's house. There should not be a gender bias or discrimination in familial and social life. An identity of a woman is always screened with an anxiety, which is experienced the feel of vulnerable and insecure, because of the norms of patriarchal society. In *That Long Silence*, Shashi Deshpande discusses the mute supplication of Jaya not only to her husband Mohan but her continuous obeisance to her father then to her elder brother and finally the most to her husband. The protagonist Jaya undergoes submissive revolt against the constant psychological pressure of male superiority and social conventions. Shashi defies total subjugation of women before men absolving her responsibilities towards herself as a human being.

Keywords: Women status, self-realisation, submissive revolt and Silence.

> "The greatest hazard of all, losing one's self, can occur very quietly in the world, as if it were nothing at all. No other loss can occur so Quietly".- Soren Kierkegaard

Shashi Deshpande set forth her women characters in the light of their hopes, fears, aspiration and frustrations who are aware of their strengths and limitations, but find themselves thwarted by the opposition and pressure from a society conditioned overwhelmingly by the patriarchal mindset. Her fiction is mostly focused on the women's character who trapped upon a conflict between the modernity and tradition.

> "I don't like to call myself a feminist writer
> I say I am a feminist, but I don't right to propagate an ism".
> Shashi Deshpande 15:09 *(IST)*.

Deshpande raises the strong voice of disapproval in opposition to the male conquered Indian society and against man made regulations and conventions. The novel exemplifies the picture of women in the middle class family and depicts the story of Jaya, educated middle class girl, who finds herself restricted and constraint in her married life. Feminist thinkers like Simone De Beauvoir who understand man woman relationship in terms of fundamental antagonism:

> The category of the Other is as Primordial as consciousness itself. In the most primitive societies, in the most ancient mythologies, one finds the expression of a duality-of the Self and the Other.....Otherness is a fundamental category of human thought (De Beauvior: 1972)

It implies that human beings define themselves against each other demanding recognition from the other. It makes their relationship reciprocal that does not exist in man woman relationship. Man has always dictated terms and norms of action to woman as the other. Shashi Deshpande wants to break binary opposition and thinks that equal treatment should be given to all including marginalised.

Jaya the protagonist of *That Long Silence* who is an intelligent woman with graduation in English, a writer and a columnist had a bright career. Unfortunately, none of these attributes would provide her a respectable position in the eyes of her husband Mohan, who had socialisation in a typical traditional environment. He wanted his wife to be submissive like them as a homemaker. "I was born. My father died when I was fifteen. I got married to Mohan. I have two children and I did not let a third live."(Pg. 69).

Marriage becomes their destiny as Jaya thinks:

> ....As we grew into young women, we realised it was not love, but marriage that was the destiny waiting for us. and so, with young man, there was the excitement of thinking will this man be my husband? ....It had been our parents who had taken vague desires of ours and translated them into hard facts. It was like the game we had played as children on our buttons tinker, tailor, soldier, sailor.... (Pg. 19).

The relationship between them was a noiseless flow of judgment, lack of communication and opinions. Mohan was having the superior position were Jaya in inferior one. He had a clear idea of what he wanted to lead, the kind of home he would live in and she just went along with him without the importance or choices to do. They shared very delicate and balanced relationship. With confusion Jaya spokes:

> "A pair of bullocks yoked together.....that was how I saw the two of us the day we came here. It was an eerie sensation I had while climbing the stairs with him, as if there was for that one infinitesimal moment a pause in my being, and i, detached from myself, saw this...a pair of bullocks

> yoked together. Then the focus shifted and there were instead a man and a woman climbing the dingy stairs of a drab building in stairs of a drab building in the heart of Bombay".(Pg. 7).

Jaya's troubles in marriage stem from her husband's tolerance towards any deflection from her role of a subservient wife. She had no freedom to express or share her desires with Mohan. Her feelings of love and sex are suppressed as she says:

> In any case, whatever my feelings had been then, I had never spoken of them to him. In fact, we had never spoken of sex at all. It had been as if the experience was erased each time after it happened, it never existed in words. The only words between us had been his question, 'Did I hurt you?' and my answer, 'No' (Pg. 95)

Her father always encourages her by *saying* "'I named you Jaya' he said, 'Jaya means victory' (Pg 15). And after marriage, Jaya lives in the family life thinking about her family and her husband Mohan. On their wedding, Mohan renamed his wife Jaya as "Suhasini" as he wanted her to be 'Soft, smiling, placid, motherly woman' (Pg 16). Deshpande described Jaya's married life as,

> "A pair of bullock yoked together. It is more comfortable for them to move in the same direction. To go in different directions would be painful and what animals would voluntarily choose pain?" (Pg. 11-12).

When threatened with charges of corruption, he expects her to go into hiding with him; when she refuses to comply, he is greatly enraged and walks out of the house. If Jaya's behavior found to be odd towards him and his family, he tells, "My mother never spoke against my father, however badly he behaved to her" (83). Thus, he gradually pushes her into the traditional world and reveals his expectations from her. And he wants her to accept his words like Gandari (Myth character).

> "If Gandari who bandaged her eyes to become blind like her husband could be called an ideal wife, I had bandaged my eyes tightly. I didn't want to know anything." (Pg. 61)

Jaya is miserable as she followed her Vanitamami's advice that a husband is like a sheltering tree', which must be kept alive at any cost, for without it the family becomes unsheltered and vulnerable.

> ....A sheltering tree. Without the tree you're dangerously unprotected and vulnerable. This... followed logically; and so you have keep the tree alive and flourishing even if you have to water it with deceit and lies (Pg. 32)

She does so but finds herself and the children the more unsheltered and insecure. Jaya does not, will not and cannot admit, even to herself, her real feelings. She recollects the fable of the foolish crow and the wise sparrow which she had often heard as a child. She does not repeat the story to her children because of the fear that they might store it in their subconscious and eventually turn out to be like

> "that damnably, insufferably, priggish sparrow looking after their homes, their babies…. and to hell with the world. Stay at home, look after your babies, keep out at the way in which the seemingly harmless bedtime stories influence children at a tender age to believe that a woman's job at all times is to protect her family even if she has to resort to treachery or deceit. (Pg.71)

She (Jaya) once tells Kamat (her neighbor)

> "……..no women can be angry. Have you ever heard of an angry young woman? A woman can never be angry, she can only be neurotic, hysterical, frustrated. There's no room for anger in my life, no room for despair, either. There's only order and routine – today, I have to change the sheets; tomorrow, scrub the bathrooms; the day after, clean the fridge……." (Pg. 147-148)

It is said that the family is a cage where the wild self inextricably is fascinated and extraordinarily reared. The women have been usually considered as preferably warm, kind and submissive, who are to be set aside in subordination to the male members of the family. Manu Proclaims:

> "Day and night, women must be kept in subordination to the males of the family: in childhood to the father, in youth to her husband, in old age to her sons. Even though the husband be destitute of virtue and seeks pleasure elsewhere, he must be worshipped as God." (A Feminist Study)

Jaya became detached from everything and became fossilised about her career and her writing. It is noted that Mohan could not understand her emotions as a result she was torn from within and also he was not an empathetic listener which caused Jaya to feel unaccompanied and desperate. Shashi has effectively presented the plight of Indian women who grow suffer and die silently. Their silent sacrifice goes unnoticed in the society. Jaya's rebellious nature is not the solution to the problems of life rather it complicates the things around her. Deshpande explores the underlying pressures of being an Indian wife, mother, writer, and above all else, woman.

Work Cited

Deshpande, Shashi. *That Long Silence.* Haryana, Gurgaon: Penguin Books India Ltd, 1988.

Sharma Siddharth. *Shashi Deshpande's Novels: A Feminist Study*. New Delhi: Atlantic Publishers and Distributors, 2005.

Adele King, "Shashi Deshpande: Portraits of an Indian Woman," *The New Indian Novel in English: A Study of the 1980s,* ed. Viney Kirpal (New Delhi: Allied, 1990)

Beauvoir, Simone De. *The Second Sex*, trans. H.M. Parshely, Harmoundsworth: Penguin, 1972. Print.

Sarabjit Sandhu, "The Images of Woman in That Long Silence", *Indian Women Novelists* Set 1. Vol: V.K.Dhawan (Ed.) New Delhi: Prestige Books, 1991.p.139.

Sherry, Ruth. *Studying Women's Writing; In Introduction.* London: Edward Arnold, 1988.

CHAPTER 32

All Wo(men) are born free but everywhere... "*Split: A Life*" in Shackles

Atul Acharya

Abstract

An empirical scrutiny of the issues that pertains to the society Taslima Nasrin belongs to is reflected in this memoir. The splits stir her life and the lives of people of Bangladesh. The hold of patriarchy, the subjugation of women, the role of religion in defining the lives of people, the role of state, all seen within the memoir are analysed in this study. The paper talks about the various splits that the narrator is confronted with, and how she shows resistance in overpowering them. It discusses the impact of Babri-Masjid demolition on the life of the Hindus in Bangladesh and how her literary works create furore in the country's literary and political circles, post-demolition. The paper also studies the points of convergence between Taslima Nasrin and Salman Rushdie's lives and works (if any), and concludes how the splits in her life are instrumental in changing her life: for worse. She is banished from Bangladesh...forever.

Keywords: Patriarchy, Subjugation, Resistance, Psychological, Banishment

Introduction

From whatever oblique or right angles a reader looks at the life of the narrator, the split is invariably visible. The tornados of multifarious nature tried to violently pin her down but her placidity against all such odds is remarkably magnanimous. Her memoir (Dwikhanditho: the original Bengali version) is a sincere vivisection of her life that covers roughly a period from the time of Bangladeshi independence to the time when the "fatwaphilic maulanas" (462) waged an authoritative war against her. The original version of the book was initially banned by the Left Front in West Bengal and by the Bangladesh Government in 2003 for being seditious. Although the ban was vacated, the writer did not include the controversial sections in the subsequent Bengali editions and interestingly a page has been left blank in the memoir which states:

> Note: The book was originally banned in West Bengal because of accusations that certain sections might incite communal tension. Despite the injunction being later revoked by the Calcutta High Court persistent concerns over renewed communal tensions have forced the author to excise the section from further Bengali publications and leave a blank page in its stead. (53)

That's Taslima Nasrin at her literary best! A way to express her dissatisfaction and say more than meets the naked eye. The ban and later on the fatwa that was announced on her head didn't deter her steadfastness towards her resolve. Starting her career as a doctor (paternal bindings), to becoming a writer of verses (on her own volition) and subsequently to a one who was mannered into writing columns, and eventually fiction, Taslima Nasrin's journey has never been a rollercoaster ride. The magma of her raw emotions that was seething within erupts violently downhill through lava of words italicising her exasperation in this work. She unilaterally and univocally rakes up sensitive issues that have always been so pertinent and concerns every single soul of the nation.

The translated English version (by Maharghya Chakraborty) of the memoir: a 500 odd pages to me is autobiographical in nature, tone and character. It is also an onslaught on the country's sanctimoniousness in labelling itself as a democratic state. The dichotomy in words and actions of the state is glaringly palpable, which is emphatically uncloaked by Nasrin. The memoir, one among the previous seven part autobiography series, is a vent by her on the politics of the country, the religion, the imbalances in the society that foreground the chasms between rich and poor, between men and women and between the haves and have nots. The catharsis of disparate emotions finds place in her work with a dedicated sincerity. Her love relationships, broken marriages, trepidations, displeasures, outrage and betrayals: are all harmoniously synthesised to reveal the life of Taslima Nasrin in a country that banishes her, eventually. The article will talk about the Splits she discerns and visualises around her. The splits that are seen at home or at workplaces, splits that are seen on a political level, within the religion, the splits when it comes to gender equality, finally and more importantly the split that is within: on an emotional and psychological level. The memoir makes an overt reference to the analogy drawn between the narrator and Salman

Rushdie. The paper will address this reference and unearth whether there are any common grounds of convergence and any similarity and sanity in doing so.

Splits: Familial

The milieu of the narrative restricts itself mainly around the cities of Mymensingh, Dhaka and Calcutta (now Kolkata), where she moves around frequently. Born and brought up in a small town family at Mymensingh, subjugation starts from within the four walls of the house. Her father wanted the children to follow his footsteps and become successful doctors. "He was a doctor with an MBBS degree, why should his children remain stuck with the same? They should become FCPS doctors, even go abroad to get their FRCS and FRCP degrees" (19). That's a good example of patriarchy impacting the subjugation of a woman. It is perfectly fine for a father wishing his children to achieve big in life, somehow the wish of them becoming doctors seems to be something binding, without finding out what Taslima or her younger sister Yasmin wanted to be, as Taslima says, "Although I was a doctor, I was acutely aware that I was tired of the life it entailed; that I wanted to do something different". The writer writes very little about her father's relationship with the sons but a good space is given about how he shared a hot and cold relationship with her and also the younger daughter. Both are a constant target to father's abuses: physical and emotional, so much so that when one day Yasmin comes back home late, she is so badly physically assaulted by her father that she runs away. "Father had whipped Yasmin, his own daughter, like an animal. Not an inch of her body had been spared from the assault of the whip." (97) Father didn't care to find out who the boys were and Yasmin became an object of his abuse.

John Stuart Mill, one of the most famous English philosophers of the 19th century, feels that all such kinds of social norms working under the umbrella of patriarchy(like women staying late outside home or coming home late as in this memoir) are the main obstacles to human progress. This subjugation is faced by women at all levels and in multifarious forms like discrimination, assaults, indifference, negligence, denigration, ignorance etc. An act of all such age old barbarities on women is indeed a deterrent to women's progress. The binary oppositions created through patriarchy keeps the women at bay and under control. Any effort to assert and voice her claims against the power systems are met with sterner hands. Taslim too is beaten up by her father, twice. She too bears the brunt but whereas the voice of Yasmin remains muted, Taslima reacts vociferously to her father's reactions, and lives her life by her own choices. The constant tiff between both of them is penned down by her across the pages of this memoir. After her divorce with M, her next relationship with NM was not liked by her father.

Feminism as a movement is seen as advocating the equality of rights between men and women but we have seen that a woman living independently of her own is still something derided in the patriarchal world. Taslima moves to Dhaka and succeeds in renting a house (in Armanitola) with great difficulty. Mother accompanies her to the rented apartment but her voice over any of the domestic issues doesn't matter. She is a muted spectator of events. We see that Nasrin's independence is not happily accepted by her father and one day he storms into her compartment, only to pull her out of it, without giving any sound reasons. He feels she is misusing her freedom and needs to be taught a lesson. As Mary Woolstonecraft in her epic work *A Vindication of the Rights of Women* stresses "When chastisement is necessary, though they have offended the mother, the father must inflict the punishment; he must be the judge in all disputes…"[3], the divine responsibility of deciding good or bad, right or wrong, yes or no, rests on her father. Severely beaten up and bruised by her father, she picks up her battered determination, fixes it up and runs away from Abakash (parental house at Mymensingh), to be on her own, to live on her own, and to challenge the lopsided rules of the men's world.

Her marital bonds and amours do not turn out to be too fruitful. In this memoir, we find her in relationships with many men like H.A., N.M., H.S.S., M.H.I. (she never mentions the names but uses initials to hide their identity) but they hardly last long. She doesn't get a fair deal from any of them. Abeda Sultana in her article *Patriarchy and Women's Subordination: A Theoretical Analysis,* while talking about patriarchal structures in Bangladesh says that "Male domination and women's subordination are the basic tenets of Bangladeshi social structure"[8]. She talks about the systems of patriarchy: patrilineal descent and patrilocal residence and stresses that such patriarchy subjugates the status of women through multiple channels. A woman is discriminated against at home, is considered a burden, has a lack of educational opportunities, isn't provided freedom of mobility in the outside world, harassment at workplaces, no control over reproductive rights etc. "It is observed that all practices and structures support women's subordination in practice which undermine women's position in Bangladesh "(13).

As Abeda points out about the various patterns above, all are well reflected in Tasrin's relationships. She loves "R" (first husband) and "MM" (second one) selflessly. But the marriages do not last long. Her commitment is never under the scanner and even after divorce she stands by "R" when he is admitted to hospital, "R loved tuberoses and I bought some from a flower vendor near the main gate of the hospital" (177) and later when he is declared dead, "...I felt a vast emptiness in my chest, like a carcass with a gaping ribcage left half-eaten by vultures and abandoned in the dump. There was nothing inside me except desolation and emptiness". (185) Her sincerity towards him never remained under any kind of doubt, though "R" moved ahead in life after they got divorced.

Her bond with "MM" too doesn't turn out to be any better. As soon as they get married via court marriage, 'MM' shows his true colours. He asserts his dominance by asking her to stop writing columns to *Purbabhash*. She learns about his illicit relationship with a rich married woman. Physical abuses were hurled upon her and it became unbearable for her. "A series of slaps on my cheeks, a punch to my face that resulted in a bleeding eye, and soon he was choking me and I could not unclench his tightening fingers from my neck" (170-71). They finally part ways for good. Battering is a serious issue in Bangladesh. It is not just in Bastis that such violence is witnessed, but females of even middle class society are prone to such battering. Despite being an educated woman, and a doctor, who is so much into writing columns for newspapers, Taslima becomes a target of it. Women coming from a lower rung have little or no resources to counter such violence. But those like Taslima do have access but they are forced (themselves or due to societal bindings) to remain passive regarding such batterings. Reasons can be innumerable. Abandonment, rejection, isolations, seclusion, low on self-confidence, afraid of being abused more or being killed, no one to take stand for her or economic issues, all such reasons and many many more desist the woman to go on an offense and retaliate. As such, this matter has become kind of endemic in today's world, promoted by cultural conventions and gender traditions.

Splits: Non-Familial

Such violence, indifference or subjugation is not restricted to the four walls of the sweet home the women live in, it extends beyond that.

Women's experience is far more dismal across various environments: be it in society, on streets, in buses, at workplaces… almost everywhere. Taslima is no exception. As she joined her medical job, she found the chasms very vividly, where she was not listened to, her suggestions were turned down, simply "Suffice to say I lost the argument because Rehman had more authority than I did-he was a man" (8). On another occasion, DD (Boss and Deputy Director) does his best to complain against her and put her in a spot of bother, simply for the reason that, "He could not wait to teach me a lesson for turning down his amorous advances on a previous occasion" (127). The oppression, subjugation and constant, "... assault of these combined forces drove me to such a state that I seriously began contemplating suicide" (129). The combined forces are the one working at home (father) and outside (at the workplace).

As her passion for the verses grew, she involved herself into writing. The literary world didn't provide her any solace. Here too, she was thought of as an outsider, where men could only write… write better. The popularity and fame came to her, but with a price and with a question mark over her writing style, content and the issues that she picked up and reflected in her writings. Such kind of subjugation, as we have seen, is very personal, sometimes the woman becomes a target of a whole group and the attack is very systematic and clearly gender specific. Such kind of violence is: a kind of social phenomenon, very little of it is thought of as worthy to be talked about, and many cases go unnoticed. The sexist conjectures laid in the men's world play a dominant role in defining such violence. It is so ubiquitous that it knows no discriminations of caste, culture, race or religion. The popularity that Taslima gained did not go down well in the literary world. When the "Book Fair" started and she attended it, one day of the fair, there was a buzz around. Soon it came to the knowledge that a group (Taslima Nasrin Suppression Committee) held out a procession against her entry into the book fair and also a ban against selling of her books in the fair. Threats were issued against the selling of her books. She was aghast at the turn of events and was surprised to hear what the organiser of the book fair had to say, "Despite being a woman why do you try and write like a man? All this is because of that". (233) Writing like a man is a sin! And she is soon paid for indulging in such a daring enterprise. "The protestors had gathered whichever of my books they could get their hands on, collected them in a heap in the middle of the field and set the entire pile on fire" (234).

Now if we see, such acts have been an integral part of our history, where books of history, poetry, fiction, or philosophy and at times even libraries were burnt and proscribed and writers banished. Different reasons can be appended to such heinous acts: sometimes to attain power by kings, at other times to consolidate their authority and to destroy the roots of a religion of the opponents, during old times (who doesn't know about the fire that burnt the great library of Nalanda where nearly 9 million manuscripts were burnt, as the smoke lay hanging over the skies for months together, on the orders of Bakhtiyar Khilji in 1193), to restrict the mob in attaining awareness and knowledge and as seen in the 18th and the 19th centuries where the burning of the U.S. Library of Congress in 1812 to the burning of various libraries during World War-II by undemocratic regimes. Sexist undertones in works also result in creating furore as is seen with the writer of this memoir. The advent of digital deluge in the present era has also seen the banning of various online platforms that mobilise public opinion. So we see the banning or to the extreme: burning of books has always been part of our history.

Milton was tormented when his books were burnt:

> ...books are not absolutely dead things, but do contain a potency of life in them to be as active as that soul was whose progeny they are; nay, they do preserve as in a vial the purest efficacy and extraction of that living intellect that bred them. I know they are as lively, and as vigorously productive, as those fabulous dragon's teeth: and being shown up and down, may chance to spring up armed men. And yet, on the other hand, unless wariness be used, as good almost kill a man as kill a good book: who kills a man kills a reasonable creature, God's image; but he who destroys a good book, kills reason itself, kills the image of God, as it were, in the eye.[5]

The history of the world is wrought with such repugnant instances where books and its writers were subject to countless acts of violence. Renowned personalities like Nadine Gordimer, Gustave Flaubert, D.H. Lawrence, Vladimir Nabokov, Salman Rushdie and similar ones of the ilk have been confronted by stiff resistance and have seen their works banned or burnt and in some cases they were banished from their lands. All such acts lead to a situation where the whole history stands muted. The content of such books is considered as highly profane, anti-social, blasphemous, offensive and leading to the denigration of values. Taslima's writings were also thought of as against the norms of the society, sexist, anti-Islam, anti-patriarchial, and seen as a threat to the political powerhouses of the state which led to censorship and a fatwa against her name. (Both the parties: in power and in opposition didn't support her and found her writings blasphemous, obscene, and framed her as anti-national).

For the Ananda Puruskar of 1992 that was conferred upon her by *Anandabazar Patrika* for *Nirbachito Kolam*, she was hardly appreciated or congratulated by people known to him in literary circles and his family. Khoka (publisher of her works), didn't show much enthusiasm and there were many radical organisations that alleged her writings as Anti-Islamic. Another charge that was levelled against her was that she was working for RAW!

> "Ultimately, a legal case was lodged against the publishers of the book, and also against the publishers and editors of the journal I used to write for. My books were burnt in public yet again and books received warnings of dire consequences and severe violence if they continued to sell them" (276).

Bangladesh was divided into two. Whereas everyone seemed to be against her, there were some feminists, people in literary circles who supported her and for the advocacy of free speech, and came out writing articles in her support. But to no avail. The splits that we see in her relationships at home and outside, professionally or personally, were all visible and were bursting at the seams. Her feminism, her empathy and her love for verses and words: all was put under a microscope and dissected threadbare.

Splits: Subliminal

The splits at the emotional/ psychological level also dealt severe blows on her, and at times she is seen as a broken piece of glass never to be the same again. In the memoir, the inner dialectic conflict foregrounds her fears, doubts, suspicions, distrusts and insecurities. Her inner conscience is seen at loggerheads with the outside world and more often than not she ruminates over the chasms that aggravate such situations. At the outset, we find a very warm relationship she has with her mother, which is in variance to the bond she has with her father. This discordant relationship with her father, who is though well read, and is a doctor is very demanding on her psyche. Most of the time, he is over critical, indifferent and acutely judgemental over Taslima's relationships, demands and needs. The complexity of their relationship leads to splits in her personality, which is difficult to patch. She suffers much: emotionally and physically, and the scars are clearly visible. "So irritated was father with these anxieties that he did not hesitate to say the most uncouth things to me". (125). Although Taslima stands for the voice for the cause of women, as is seen in her works, she is seen as really weak when it comes to the oppression she has to face at home, as we see above. She is a tormented lot, and is psychologically and physically assaulted, to which she raises no voice, but takes an alternative route. Her relationship with her younger sister, which was quite intimate initially, was strained later on. "I had a broken marriage, I was a sinner and an amoral woman. How could a good housewife be associated with someone like me. So she studiously avoided associating with me, busy as she was with her in-laws and deeply concerned about their happiness. (127)". The internal struggle is reflective of the outer struggle of strained relationships she had with her near and dear ones. She keeps helping Yasmin at various points of time, helps get Yasmin's husband a job, and later on helps Yasmin to get a job, but the apertures never seem to be narrowing down. R's death also reveals her internal wrestlings. It jolted her badly and she found it difficult to come to terms with reality. "The love of my life, the man of my dreams, was gone. The man I had left but not left altogether, who I had got separated from but who I had never separated from me, was gone" (186). The inner turmoil and the desperateness is aptly summed up in these lines. The stream of consciousness still makes her feel ill deep within when she thinks about the treatment she was meted out by all.... family, near and dear ones, and by society. The pain looms large and she often vents it out, in public.

> It's been a quarter century in exile. What is my fault? That I wrote about humanism? That's it. To date, I receive *fatwas* and threats. I stand on shaky ground. How much more uncertainty and suffering must I endure? I can quite clearly see that no country in this world is mine. My language is my country. Whatever I had was taken away, but I hope no one will ever be able to take away my language.[9]

Splits at the Political and Religious Levels

All religious laws should be abolished. Women are still oppressed because of them: marriage, child custody and inheritance laws. There is no equality. I hope that, one day, Bangladesh will get a uniform civil code, based on equality. I don't think all women will become free and have access to their rights if we have uniform civil codes. But it will be a start. We have to fight misogyny and men also have to participate in this movement. It is not the women's duty alone to get equality for women; it is the men's duty too. Because it is our society, and both men and women need to make it better.[7]

Patriarchy, Taslima feels has seeped deep into politics and religion, too. It importunes women to mould themselves into the shapes framed as per the conveniences of the men's world. As such, women are chained to the stereotypes and live under the shadow of patriarchy. Taslima has tried to subvert the situation in her works. She lays bare the splits that operate through the locus of patriarchy by considering politics fit for men and religion deciding upon the fate of the women.

Chapter 4 of the memoir talks about Hussain Muhammad Ershad and his machinations of turning Bangladesh into a religious state. The whole chapter is a critique of the state's endeavour to declare Islam as a state religion. Taslim sees the futility of doing so. To her, "Do nations need a religion? It is the people who need it. The nation is not one individual; it is a guarantor of safety for people of all religious and ethnic identities. If the nation is not impartial… then is it surprising that its people will protest and create disruption? (42). She further opines, "Religion is like a cancer. Once it takes root it systematically corrodes the entire state apparatus and there is no way to arrest its growth; nor can it be cured." (51). The whole country stood against this "holy carrot" as she terms it in one of her poems, but the state declares Islam as the state religion. Ershad is pushed out of the country politics, subsequently, only to give way to the formation of a new government where the contest is between the Awami League and Bangladeshi Nationalist Party, and that leads to mud-slinging and indulging in dirty politics. With the coming in power of the BNP, the equation didn't change. The splits were as wide open as they were before. "In the end, one autocracy was replaced by yet another" (203) because "Neither did the government show any interest in removing the state religion from the constitution and reinstating the original secular ideals" (203). The immingling of state politics and religion created splits in the attitude that the public developed towards her writings. She was termed as a RAW agent after being felicitated with the *Ananda Puruskar.* Those who started and protesting against her termed *Ananda Bazar Patrika* as a Hindu fundamentalist mouthpiece and she was seen as anti-national and anti-Islam. "The ones against me were decidedly more in number, their pens sharper, more spirited and brimming with discontent. I also noticed that the tag 'popular', which was hitherto associated with my name, had been replaced by 'controversial'.... (280)

Babri Masjid demolition cast its shadows on the neighbouring country, too. The demolition had its impact in Bangladesh and the splits within the society were vividly seen. Bangladeshi Hindus were singled out, looted, mauled, killed, raped and were pushed out of the areas they had been living for years together. The state did nothing to stop this outrage against the minority Hindus.

> It seemed to me as if the Awami League was fine with the violence being rained upon Hindus to pave the way for future campaigns against the BNP. This issue could become a potential trump card for the opposition.... But in Bangladesh what usually happened was not a riot but a terror attack in which Muslim tortured Hindus. (322)

Whatever could have been the cause of this communal violence in India, it had catastrophic implications in Bangladesh. Taslima has pointed out many instances of the atrocities that were meted out to Hindu minorities. Deeply hurt and infuriated by the turn of events, Taslima came out with a book that changed her life forever. *Lajja*, a book written against the Babri Masjid demolition and the riots that followed in Bangladesh, talks about the minority Hindu family that was attacked by the Muslims. Instantly, the book gained notoriety. A fundamentalist group in Bangladesh named *Soldiers of Islam* issued a fatwa on her head by terming the book as blasphemous and unpatriotic. Taslima sought the help of the government, but instead of supporting and providing a safe haven for her, the Government of Bangladesh confiscated her passport and ordered her to stop writing and her book was banned by them.

If we try to see the role that religion and politics play in creating splits in the society, the picture gets clear. Certain fundamentalist groups in Bangladesh saw Taslima Nasrin as a threat to their hegemony, where they infer that religions lay down the rules for the women to follow, in the name of divine authority. Taslima's writing subverts all such divine interventions. She is a voice of the women, stands against any kind of oppression and denial of rights. Religious powers, as such, found all this disconcerting, and as such she became a target of all such hard core religious outfits. The state also found her writings improper and by using the handle of state written constitutional rules, forced her to write and supported the fatwa waged against her. Both the authorities got united with each other, thereby trying to mobilise public opinion against Taslima and creating vested splits. Banning of the book by the government is symbolic of the failure of the government in supporting the rights of minority Hindus in the country.

Her article in *The New York Times* evidently sums up the hands in gloves attitude of the state towards the controversy that led to the banning of the book, announcing a fatwa against her and the eventual banishment from her country. She wrote, "It is my conviction that politics cannot be based on religion if our women are to be free. Bangladesh must become a modern secular state; family laws based on Islamic principles should be replaced by a uniform code insuring the equal rights of women.[1] The splits are very clearly laid wide open.

Grounds of Convergence or Splits: Taslima Nasrin and Salman Rushdie

The parallels that have been drawn by many between Taslima Nasrin and Salman have some common grounds that force such congruence. We will see how fair it is to draw such kinship. While both being Muslims do not promote such comparison, the literary taste that led them into the world of words holds common ground for both of them. Both, at a very tender age, developed a taste of writing. With passage of time, both turned out to be celebrated writers. Now, what forces to draw out a similarity is the

1. Censorship of their works,
2. Fatwa that was announced on their heads
3. Banishment from the lands they belonged to.

Both the writers have raised serious issues that have been termed as controversial and blasphemous.

Rushdie is a wilful writer. Everything he writes is well planned. Moreover he was a student of History at King's college London. As such he has a good grasp over history. He very well knows the aporias in history and exploits them to his conveniences. Starting his career as a post-colonial writer with the publication of his renowned *Midnight's Children* he shot to fame. Soon he was termed as a blasphemous writer for his most controversial work *The Satanic Verses.* This work of his was declared to create sparks by many, including the legendary Khuswant Singh (he gave a big no to the publishers for the book to be sent to the print), who was given the manuscript of this work by the publishers. Despite the warnings, the publishers went ahead and the work was published. Although a text promotes multiple interpretations, Rushdie was very clever and aware of the interpretations the text would reflect on. From being a celebrity, he instantly turned out to be a sacrilegious writer. Ayatollah Khomeni, the spiritual head of Iran issued a fatwa against his name for writing profane about Islam and Prophet Muhammad (pbuh). This is what Ayatollah Khomeini had to say:

> In the name of Him, the Highest. There is only one God, to whom we shall all return. I inform all zealous Muslims of the world that the author of the book entitled *The Satanic Verses*--...--and all those involved in its publication who were aware of its content, are sentenced to death.
>
> I call on all zealous Muslims to execute them quickly, wherever they may be found, so that no one else will dare to insult the Muslim sanctities. God willing, whoever is killed on this path is a martyr.[6]

Whatever has been said and done, the fact remains that Rushdie was quite cognizant about the nature of his work, had done a lot of research and by using the smokescreen of migrancy, exile and magic realism, he camouflaged the controversial parts, very well. That's a mark of a genius writer, though the wizard of words had to pay dearer for it, and he was forced into hibernation for years together, once the fatwa was announced. The Satanic Verses was banned in India and elsewhere. The fatwa still hangs around his head like an albatross. And for this controversial work, he is now living a life of exile.

Taslima Nasrin had no such intentions of raking up disputations when she wrote her poems, articles in journals, autobiographies or her most celebrated work *Lajja*. The controversy lies in her living in a patriarchal world, where writing against social structures, religion, in disagreement to the intentions of the state, and venting out the state of women, is a serious felony. The fissures that were seen in the lives of Muslims-Hindus post Babri-Masjid demolition disturbed her so much that she released her emotions through words. If we try to look at her writing career, we notice that very early in her life, she felt the oppression at her home, outside, and the same meted out to the women in the society, that belong to all stratas of life, but live outside the margins. She wrote poems, articles in magazines, echoing all such divergence, subjugation and ill-treatment. Although she was a doctor by profession, she felt that her interest was much more into writing than in the medical profession. Designated as a Feminist writer, her writings ally with the formula of Art for life's sake and so the controversies which talk much about that is not good in the society. She crosses the boundaries of the male centric world, of the boundaries set by the fundamentalists and as such her works are the center of intense attraction, seriously questioned by many. She writes what she sees, what she feels and what she wants to change. Her intentions are not to rake up any controversy but to foreground controversial issues that create imbalances in the society. And when she becomes the target of mullahs or the so-called custodians of national integration based upon secularism, she readily accepts their remarks.

> Till date, of all the awards that I have won, it is this epithet, that of the 'whore' or the 'prostitute' that I cherish the most. I have earned this award because I have truly been successful in delivering a crippling blow to the filthy body of patriarchal power.[2]

Besides talking about the 3 points of convergence mentioned above between the two writers, we notice that the issues that both touch upon, the intentions with which they write, and the style they follow have very little semblance. The similarity starts and ends with the banning of their works, the fatwa that puts their life in peril and the banishment from their lands.

Conclusion

The very foundation that is supposed to support the pillars of the society seems to be tearing apart the life of the narrator as shown in the memoir. Termed as a feminist, she is a spokesperson of the oppressed voices of the women of her country. With the rise of politically motivated religious fundamentalism, the women are subjected to inequality and treated as sexual objects. Taslima is herself seen as a target of such persecution and she incorporates all such issues in her works. She shows how such inequality creates problems in the life of a woman and restrains her independence. She feels that the state tries to mute all such voices that talk against patriarchy, talk against religion and against freedom of expression. The banning of her works, the protests that were waged against her forced her into isolation and eventually to the banishment from her land: not only East but West Bengal too. Religion and Patriarchy, integral to our society, instead of liberating, strangulate such voices. Taslima says that whenever she tried to say anything against the both, she was challenged and forced to mute her feelings. Her life lay in split because of that. The Splits are penned down in her autobiography and she finds it very surprising that her freedom of expression is hijacked by the state and the mullahs. If she can't speak the truth of her life in autobiography, where else will she be? The patriarchy never sees a fault in the men, rather women are always thought of as the offenders. In one of her interviews, she remarks that the men in her life, who tried to dominate her and created splits, weren't held culpable. Rather, she was accused of a broken marriage and was termed as a whore. She announces that she will continue to portray the truth of the society, will speak for the women, and will endeavour for the freedom of expression, so that she lives a normal life, not a life in splits.

Works Cited

1. Archive.nytimes.com. 2021. *The New York Times: Book Review Search Article.* [online] Available at: <https://archive.nytimes.com/www.nytimes.com/books/97/05/11/ reviews/29339.html> [Accessed 10 June 2021].
2. Finger, T., 2021. *Taslima Nasrin and the Freedom to Write.* [online] Newslaundry. Available at: <https://www.newslaundry.com/2016/10/25/taslima-nasrin-and-the-freedom-to-write> [Accessed 08 June 2021].
3. Library.um.edu.mo. 2021. [online] Available at: <https://library.um.edu.mo/ebooks/b33216423.pdf> [Accessed 07 June 2021].
4. Nasrin, Taslim. (2018). *Split A Life.* Penguin Random House India.
5. Oll.liberty fund.org. 2021. *John Milton opposed censorship for many reasons but one thought sticks in the mind, that "he who destroys a good book, kills reason itself" (1644) | Online Library of Liberty.* [online] Available at: <https://oll.libertyfund.org/quote/john-milton-opposed-censorship-for-many-reasons-but-one-thought-sticks-in-the-mind-that-he-who-destroys-a-good-book-kills-reason-itself-1644> [Accessed 16 June 2021].
6. Pipes, Daniel. The Rushdie Affair: The Novel, the Ayatollah, and the West. New York: Carol, 1990. 27.
7. Readersdigest.in. 2021. *Taslima Nasrin On A Rebellious Childhood, Facing Death And Being A Woman In Islamic Bangladesh.* [online] Available at: <https://www.readersdigest.in/features/story-storytelling-event-readers-digest-taslima-nasrin-124570> [Accessed 05 June 2021].
8. Sultana, Abeda. "Patriarchy and Women's Subordination: A Theoretical Analysis." *Arts Faculty Journal,* www.banglajol.info/index.php/AFJ/article/view/12929.
9. ThePrint. 2021. *25 yrs ago, today I lost my home Bangladesh. Language is my only country now: Taslima Nasreen.* [online] Available at: <https://theprint.in/opinion/25-yrs-ago-today-i-lost-my-home-bangladesh-language-is-my-only-country-now-taslima-nasreen/273997/> [Accessed 06 June 2021].

CHAPTER 33

A Lonely Muted Voice from the Veiled World: Salma – The Tamil Poet

T. A. Shamsun Sarika and Deepakumari S.

Abstract

Salma is the lonely surviving voice of Tamil Muslim women writers in India. Her literary creations reflect on the native regional marginality unveiling the secluded space of Tamil Muslim community. Her poems are strong expressions of the acute cultural sensibilities of the Indian Islamic world. She has created a powerful lasting impression in Indian regional representations by voicing the 'culture of silence' that prevailed for centuries in this veiled world, despite the censorious objections leveled against her. She is one of the pioneers in heralding a new approach to Indian feminism unlike the Western idea offering a different dimension of thought on 'body politics'. Her writings are forceful commentary on Tamil Muslim community for she never compromises on her regional identity depicting a socio-cultural study on the deep-rooted beliefs and customs prevalent in the community. Her expressions conferred a voice to the silenced women's consciousness, calling for a 'cultural revivalism'. Her solitary representation of freedom from the domestic restraints of a male-dominated Muslim community shows her indomitable fearless spirit. Her works, both fiction and non-fiction, addressing extremely sensitive issues, explodes as a silent resistance against the patriarchal impositions on Tamil Muslim women. It serves as an authentic record of the Tamil Muslim women lives because Salma herself belongs to its inner quarters and her own life could be credited for how a twentieth century Muslim wife comes to pen the first-hand experiences of her community to the world.

Keywords: Culture of silence, Body politics, Cultural revivalism, Silent resistance.

Salma, Tamil poet, novelist, short story writer and social activist, the lonely voice of Tamil Islamic feminist expression creates an identity and makes a representation of Tamil Muslim culture through her writings. Salma's literary contributions include three volumes of poetry, *Oru Maalaiyum Innoru Maalaiyum* (An Evening, Another

Evening) (2000), *Pacchai Devadai* (Green Angel) (2003), and *Thaanumanaval* (Self-Made) (2021), novels *Irandaam Jaamangalin Kadhai* (The Hour Past Midnight) (2004) and *Manaamiyankal* (Women, Dreaming) (2016) with a short story collection titled *Caapam* (The Curse) (2012), including a travelogue *Kanavu Vazhi Payanam* (Journey through Dreams) (2014). She writes under the pseudonym Salma, her original name being Rajathi alias Rokkeyya. Her novel *Irandaam Jaamangalin Kadhai* was translated into English, German, Malayalam and Marathi and Lakshmi Holmstrom's English translation of her novel *The Hour Past Midnight* was shortlisted for the Crossword Book Prize, and Man Asia Booker Prize. She has been the recipient of several awards like Mahakavi Kanhaiyalal Sethia Award (2019) and honours and a documentary film *SALMA* by Internationally – acclaimed, award winning director Kim Loginotto screened at Sundance (2013) received as many as fourteen international awards in various international film festivals. Apart from her literary career, she had also been the elected President of the Ponnampatti Panchayat from 2001-2006, and was also the Chairman of the Social Welfare Board of Tamil Nadu. Currently she's an active politician, social activist and media spokesperson.

Debarred from school education and restrained to stay at home by her family, from the age of thirteen, her very act of writing became a form of resistance against the established patriarchal ideologies. Even in the face of personal crisis, she remained firm in her determination to pursue writing, resolute in creating her own space for identity and addressing issues of unspoken taboos. Kim Longinotto, in *Salma: Filming a Poet in her Village* rightly remarks, "She refused to conform. She refused to be silenced. Against all odds, Salma found a way to survive and be heard", thereby making a representation through her writings. Regarding Salma's exposure to literature, it was confined only to the Tamil language and the limited access she had to world literature was through the scant availability of Tamil translations of foreign works.

Salma's representational world is claustrophobic, confined, limited and restricted in its exposures. Her two volumes of poetry – *Oru Maalaiyum Innoru Maalaiyum* (2000) (One Evening Another Evening) and *Pacchai Devadai* (2003) (Green Angel) portray the vulnerability and female longings in sensitive words shocking the Tamil Muslim community that remained completely veiled to the outer world. Her choice of words threatened the modesty of Indian women and labelled as obscene and vulgar. In the poem, "Padimam" from the collection, *Pachai Devadai*, translated as "Image" by Kalyan Raman in which she draws on the image of a dead cockroach as a comparison to her own self-deprived of identity and freedom:

> Stepped on in the dark,
> the cockroach was crushed
> To pulp. All night,
> An army of ants have
> Marauded its flesh,
> Leaving behind the carcass to show me
> The novel sight of myself
> With wings that can no longer rise in flight
> And stick legs – no longer of use

The last lines are evoking imagery of her veiled self, her subjectivity and her lifeless soul left discarded and ignored. The fragile flightless wings and the sticky legs refer to her inability and precarious existence within the purdah world. Her mutual relationship with loneliness finds voice in one of her poems titled "Yarumilladha Idaththil" from the collection, *Oru Malaiyum Innoru Malaiyum* translated as "The Deserted Place" by N. Kalyan Raman:

> Only when I was totally forsaken did it commence:
> This enduring bond of mine with loneliness
> Someday, the language wrought
> By this loneliness of mine

The lines are impressive for their exploration of loneliness. She juxtaposes this state of loneliness with the metaphors of transcending beyond the physical spaces to convey a series of connotation like seclusion, lonesomeness inclusive of privacy and solitude, into which she engages to discover her real identity. As Lakshmi Holmstorm puts it in her introduction to "*Wild Girls, Wicked Words*", "She needs a thanimai (loneliness) in order to find her thanmai – selfhood."

> This loneliness of mine
> Might even meld
> Into the sky's azure,
> Acquire its own hue
>
> My life is ebbing away
> Beyond the reach of my will
> With a loneliness that shall never end,
> I am living here still

Salma seeks to resist the conventionally accepted roles assigned to woman and ventures to validate their desire and sexuality, as she claims in her interview to Kalyan Raman (one of the translators of her poems to English) that, "A women's subjective feelings are structured in relation to her body", where her poems are bold expressions of female subjectivity and female desires, the latter being unexpressed, confined in its natal state in the Tamil Muslim community. Radha Chakravarty in her introduction to *Bodymaps* states the multiple ways in which the women writers have dealt with the female body both as a site for oppression as well as resistance:

> The body in these stories functions as a constitutive rather than merely thematic element in representations of gendered identities. It connects the traditional "female" areas of experience such as marriage, motherhood, family dynamics, women's education and work, with broader issues of class, caste, sexuality, political citizenship, cultural practices, religion and social responsibility (xxii).

Thus in "The Contract", she openly confesses on her unhappy marriage and the lack of support from the family which compelled her to write under a pseudonym:

> My sister hisses at me in anger
> What my mother whispers tactfully:
> That all failures
> On the conjugal bed
> Are mine alone
>
> The first words I hear
> Every night in the bedroom:
> 'What's it tonight?'
> These are, most often,
> The final words too
>
> You, too,
> Might have complaints
> My stand, though,
> Has been made clear
> By Time and History

According to Salma, belief in the codified patriarchal moralities suppresses women's body and her desires controlling her psyche and thoughts. The oppression of woman must be perceived as interrelated to a larger exploitative structure initiated by patriarchy but she goes to ironically express the power of the subjugated female body. This poem was received with heavy criticism from the orthodox Indian community as these expressions (particularly the word vagina and the sexual implications) challenged the prescribed virtues of modesty and the limitations of being a Muslim woman:

> To receive
> A little of your love,
> Muddy though it might be
>
> To fulfill
> My duties
> As the mother of your child
>
> To have you bring Sanitary towels and contraceptives
> From the outside world;
> And to seek more such petty favours
>
> To order you around a bit,
> If I could
>
> To affirm a little
> Of my authority
>
> My vagina opens,
> Knowing all that it should

Her books are controversial because she uses strong sexual language. As Salma says, "...apart from giving a raw deal to women in every way, the community also seeks to silence voices of protest. There are no villains. .. We have only men stunted by a brutally patriarchal tradition, and women who have been rendered myopic by social institutions" (Prema Nandakumar). It indirectly also addresses the repressed sexual desires seeking avenues for sexual pleasure and fulfillment, thereby threatening and subverting the patriarchal establishment.

The expression of the female desire in these poems becomes an explicit threat not only to the orthodox Indian society but also to the veiled Indian Muslim community. Talking about her translation of Salma's writings, Lakshmi Holmstorm says that the voice "is heavier, more burdened, speaking under the weight of the entrenched structures of patriarchy. Repeatedly in these poems, we sense a speaker having to argue with the world before she can be allowed to argue with herself". In "Irandaam Jaamangalin Kadhai" from the collection *Oru Malaiyum Innoru Malaiyum* translated by Lakshmi Holstrom as "A Midnight Tale", Salma talks about nature's betrayal to woman alone by making a reference to the transformation of a woman's body after childbirth that leaves behind permanent scars.

The poem foregrounds female subjectivity, the many layered female psyche finding the appropriate expression in Salma's verse:

You search, dissatisfied,
Through the familiar nudity of our nights,
For my beauty's unblemished past

My bloated body
And belly creased by stretch marks
Are truly repulsive, you tell me
Also that
My body will never change –
Not now, not ever

My voice, long buried
In a trough of silence,
Mutters to itself:

My voice, long buried
In a trough of silence,
Mutters to itself:

The pitfalls of female subjectivity are precisely vented out in this poem. She writes, from "my once unblemished beauty" and after childbirth "a thickened body and a belly crisscrossed with birthmarks;" in contrast to a man's "though, is unchanging you say, today, hereafter and forevermore". Nature gives man the advantage of an unchanging body perpetually giving no clue of his marital status to the outside world. Her startling frankness was something that the Tamil Muslim world had never before encountered and her open comments on female desires were strictly forbidden. Salma's language adapts and molds the inner conflicts and turmoil of the female psyche:

After my pregnancy and childbirth,
Yes, it's true,
Your body is
Not at all like mine,
With its fanfare
And its flagrancy

In the years past,
You might have had children
By strange women, in unfamiliar lands
No traces left on you, of course –
You can be proud of that

What can I do?

These stretch marks are
The same as my decline:
Not so easy to repair or mend
This body is not paper you can cut and graft

Nature's betrayal of me
Has been far more terrible than yours
It was you, after all, who commenced
The first stage of my downfall

This world, says Salma, is not a private one, but shared by millions of women in similar life situations, "Neither my pain nor my feelings are solely that of an individual; they belong to all such women." (Subramaniam). Thus, she creates an identity and space for all silenced voices through her writing as a passive act but powerful resistance against the traditional patriarchal Tamil Muslim society. Salma's world was a restricted one where her access to the external world was deprived to girls after attaining puberty and there was no question of challenging the same. Salma hints at the "profound and painful gap between the highest potentials women intuit in lives actually turn out on a day-to-day basis" (Mob-Affu 3). These Muslim women writers have boldly ventured to establish the visibility of the Muslim women by recuperating the problem of their invisibility and silence.

In these representations, the female body serves as the source of artistic experimentation and her works are startling invasion into this veiled world of the Muslim women – the female domain highlighting the subject of suppressed female desire. Each community has its own defined prerogatives, and they allege their responsibility to uphold certain moral values irrespective of the social reform movements. One such concern has always been the issue controlling sexuality and to evade subjects of sexual desire. There are two variants in understanding this suppressed female desire from an Islamic perspective from the other communities – the practice of polygamy and the exclusive woman's space. Polygamy is a distinct feature of Islam where men were allowed to have maximum of four wives at the same time. Even in the Indian context, Muslim men practiced polygamy. Any Muslim household is partitioned into two spaces namely the '*mardhana*' (men's quarters) and the '*zenana*' (women's quarters), where '*zenana*' is a symbol both of isolation and privacy. This woman's private space in the Muslim household influences the lives of the women folks bearing a silent witness to all changes happening around them. It indirectly intensifies hidden desires ultimately challenging the so-called traditional religious moralities, "Women's mobility was restricted to the women's quarters or the zenanas. The segregated spheres also emphasised the separate worlds of men and women who lived together and yet apart in the same house" (Chanda 29).

The community of women is deprived of an individual identity and access to the outer world due the prohibition of public emergence as practiced in a Muslim household, "It was not only that women had no place outside the home, but even within, subservience and abject dependence were a lot" (Chanda 20). There is an induced religious restriction on Muslim women that they are forced to adhere and inculcate. In the Muslim household, apart from observing 'purdah', there also existed regulations and intricate code of seclusion, which indirectly controlled women's lives determining even to the extent of who were allowed entry into this space as well as who they could meet and talk to. Ultimately, this practice was upheld in the pretext of protecting feminine modesty and code of conduct, whereby the patriarchy claimed to differentiate 'homely girls' against 'courtesans'. Eunice de Souza in her introduction to *Purdah* explains that segregation and veiling of women might have been for several reasons:

> A wide variety of reasons for purdah exists: religious injunction, notions for female behaviour, group solidarity and defensiveness about identity, the control of sexual impulses in men and women, status, family honour and respectability and, where women have property rights, the fear that misalliances would lead to the depletion of property (xi xii).

Salma's representations are enquiry into this less-exposed space of Muslim women focusing chiefly on the woman-to-woman relationship unveiled by a well-versed insider. This accounts for the authenticity of the experience which makes her writings as an act of passive resistance. The body-politics articulated chiefly through her poems received derogatory comments not only from the public sphere but also from the literary world as the notion of female desire is interrelated with the concept of morality. She was condemned for her outspokenness about sexuality, female longings and abused for being obscene and shameless and apparently the very act of writing becomes a transgression. The subjectivity and oppression represented through her writings challenge the patriarchy (power) in turn creating an identity that had never existed before where it obviously becomes an act of resistance and representation. It is only in recent times that feminists "have attempted to develop new approaches to the study of the body, in order to transcend the often dualist and conflicting relationship between the natural biological body and the socially constructed body" (Reed 16). This representation of female desire at times transgresses beyond inhibitions and challenges the well-framed sacraments of religion and culture.

Seclusion, in one form or the other exists in the Muslim community, which constructs the gender disparity. This seclusion is a code of conduct emphasised as per Islamic laws and it becomes a challenge for the Muslim women to break or trespass these defined boundaries to create an identity or write their experience. It must be understood that while reading the Muslim women writings, the following factors must be considered: the fact of seclusion and the 'exclusive women's space' – zenana. 'Space' renders a crucial understanding to literary experience, and 'exclusive women's space' as practiced in the Muslim households defines their experience, unique and as the 'Other'. The pivotal point in understanding Indian Muslim feminism is the exclusive woman's space, the 'female domain', inside which their experiences remain unheard of and discarded, veiled and protected by the Islamic patriarchal structure. Defying the impression of an ideal woman in an ornamental style, Salma's poems are live images of a Muslim woman earnestly striving for deliverance. The absence of another Tamil Muslim woman writer to be named after Salma is a standing testimony to the prevailing rigid conditions within the community.

Works Cited

Salma. "A Deserted Place." *Poetry International Web*, translated by N. Kalyan Raman, 2006, \www.poetryinternationalweb.net /pi/site/poem/item/ 8141/auto/0/A-DESERTED-PLACE.

.... "Four Poems." *The Caravan: A Journal of Politics and Culture*, Translated by Lakshmi Holmstrom, 01 Mar. 2012, www.caravanmagazine.in/poetry/four-poems-3.

.... "Image". *Poetry International Web*, translated by Kalyan Raman, 2006, www.poetryinternationalweb.net/pi/site/poem/item/8139/auto/0/IMAG E.

.... "Two Poems by Rajathi Salma." *Development in Action*, translated by Kalyan Raman, 5 Dec. 2013, www.developmentinaction.org/rajathi-salma-poems/.

Chakravarty, Radha. "Bodymaps: An Introduction." *Bodymaps: Stories by South Asian Women*, edited by Radha Chakravarty, Zubaan, 2007, pp. xi-xxx.

Chanda, Geetanjali Singh. *Indian Women in the House of Fiction.* Zubaan, 2008.

Holland, Sara. "Salma – The Winehouse Mag." WMM, 4 May 2013, www.wmm.com/filmcatalog /pages/c845.shtml.

Holmstorm, Lakshmi, editor. *Wild Girls, Wicked Words.* Translated by Lakshmi Holmstorm, Bangalore, Sangam House, 2012.

Longinotto, Kim. "Hot Docs Expanded Review: Salma – The Winehouse Mag." *The Winehouse Mag*, www.thewinehousemag.com/hot-docs-expanded-review – salma.

Nandakumar, Prema. "Tragedy of Women." *The Hindu*, 3 Oct. 2006, www.thehindu.com/todays-paper/tp-features/tp-bookreview/tragedy-of-women/article3209267.ece.

The Contributors

1. **Dr. Arvind M. Nawale**, Associate Professor and Head, Dept. of English, Shivaji Mahavidyalaya, Udgir (Maharashtra).
2. **Prof. Itishri Sarangi,** Associate Professor, School of Humanities, Kalinga Institute of Industrial Technology, Deemed to be University, Odisha.
3. **Dr. Koshy A.V.,** Visiting Professor, English Department, School of Engineering and Technology, Jain University, Bengaluru, Former Faculty, Department of English, Jazan University, Saudi.
4. **Debdatta Mallik,** teacher, South Point School, Kolkatta, WB.
5. **Dr. Sukanya Saha,** Assistant Professor, Department of English and Foreign Languages, SRM Institute of Science and Technology, SRM Nagar, Potheri, Kattankulathur, Chengalpattu District, TN.
6. **Dr. Hitesh D Raviya**, Professor and Head, Department of English, Faculty of Arts, the Maharaja Sayajirao University of Baroda, Vadodara, Gujrat.
7. **Ms. Rohini Sharma**, PhD Research Scholar, Department of English, Faculty of Arts, The Maharaja Sayajirao University of Baroda, Vadodara, Gujrat.
8. **Ms. Saroj Bala**, Research Scholar, Department of Humanities, Delhi Technological University, Delhi.
9. **Dr. Rajiv Ranjan Dwivedi**, Associate Professor, Department of Humanities Delhi Technological University, Delhi.
10. **D. Ashwini**, PhD Research Scholar, Periyar University PG Extension Centre, Dharmapuri, Tamil Nadu.
11. **Dr. P. Kiruthika**, Assistant Professor, Department of English, Periyar University Extension Centre, Dharmapuri, Tamil Nadu.
12. **Dr. Manju Kumari**. K, Head & Assistant Professor, Department of English, Nirmala College for Women, Coimbatore, Tamilnadu, India.

13. **Dr. Rajiv Kumar Singh**, Assistant Director (OL), DCPW, Ministry of Home Affairs, Govt of India, New Delhi.
14. **J. Priyanka**, Ph.D. Research Scholar in English, Kanchimamunivar Government Institute for Postgraduate Studies and Research, Puducherry.
15. **Dr. R. Rajavelu**, Head & Associate Professor of English, Kanchimamunivar Government Institute for Postgraduate Studies and Research, Puducherry.
16. **Dr. R. Gandhi Subramanian**, Reader in English (Retired), Government Arts College (Autonomous), Coimbatore, Tamilnadu.
17. **Ratna Prabha Kalyan**, Ph.D. Research Scholar, P.G. Dept. of English & Research Centre, Magadh University, Bodh-Gaya, Bihar.
18. **Dr. Ritu Priyadharshini.**V, Assistant Professor Department of English, Sri Krishna College of Engineering and Technology, Coimbatore, Tamilnadu, India.
19. **Nayana George,** Doctoral research scholar, CHRIST (Deemed to be University), Bengaluru.
20. **Saranya Devi. P**, Assistant Professor, Department of English, Kongu Engineering College, Perundurai, India.
21. **Dr. Keerthi G**, Assistant Professor and Head, Department of English, Government Arts and Science College, Komarapalayam, India.
22. **Dr. Bharati Sukalal Khairnar**, Associate Professor &Head, Department of English, M.P.H. Mahila Mahavidyalaya, Malegaon Camp, Dist. Nashik (MS).
23. **Dr. Satarupa Sengupta**, Assistant Professor, Department of English, Techno India University West Bengal.
24. **Sagar Vyas**, PhD scholar, Department of English, Hemchandracharya North Gujarat University, Patan (Gujarat).
25. **Suparna Roy**, Independent Researcher, Kolkata, West Bengal.
26. **Namitha Nandan**, Research Scholar, Christ Deemed to be University, Bengaluru.
27. **Ekta Laddha**, Research Scholar, Department of English, Gujarat University, Ahmedabad, Gujarat.

28. **Dr. Pulin Bhatt**, Professor of English, City C. U. Shah Commerce College, Gujarat University, Ahmedabad.
29. **Dr. Nisha Bhagwat Gosavi**, Assistant Professor, Department of English, S. M. Joshi College, Hadapsar, Pune.
30. **Jancy,** B.A English, Nazareth Margoschis College, Pillaiyanmanai
31. **Dr. M. Beulah Hemalatha,** Assistant Professor of English, Nazareth Margoschis College, Pillaiyanmanai.
32. **Dr. Geeta V. Waghmare**, Assistant Professor of English, Jaikranti Senior College, Latur. (MS).
33. **Megha Soni**, Research Scholar, Department of English, Jiwaji University, Gwalior (Madhya Pradesh).
34. **Dr. S. Sandhya,** Guest Lecturer, PG & Research Department of English, Arignar Anna Government Arts College for Women, Walajapet, TN.
35. **R. Devendiran**, Ph.D Research Scholar, Thiruvalluvar University,Vellore, TN &
36. **Prof. B. Kathiresan**, Professor and Head, Dept. of English, Thiruvalluvar University, Vellore.TN.
37. **Krishna Priya J.,** Sri Sarada Mahavidyalayam Arts and Science College for Women, Ulundurpet, Tamil Nadu.
38. **Dr. Chavan Sharad Uttam**, Assistant professor in English, MGV's Arts and Commerce College, Yeola, Dist. Nashik (MS).
39. **Maharudra Keshav Kapse**, Lecturer in English, Bharati Vidyapeeth's Jawaharlal Nehru Institute of Technology, Pune (MS).
40. **C. Leela**, Research scholar, Department of English, Government Arts & Science College (Women), Orathanadu (TN).
41. **Dr Atul Acharya**, Assistant Professor of English, Faculty of Languages, Government College, Matour (HP).
42. **Dr. T. A. Shamsun Sarika**, Assistant Professor, Dept. of English, Anna Adarsh College for Women. Chennai (TN).
43. **Deepakumari S.**, Assistant Professor, Dept. of English, Amrita School of Engineering, Amrita Vishwa Vidyapeetham, Bengaluru, (KS).

Index